FINANCIALLY LITERATE YOUTH

FLY

THE HANDBOOK

F.LY

THE HANDBOOK

For life's important financial decisions and milestones, from high school and beyond

JAI
HOBBS
and
MARLIES
HOBBS

Cover illustration and design by Angelo Vlachoulis
Cover design © F.L.Y Pty Ltd
Internal illustrations by Tess Wethereld
Author photographs by Paul Furse
Internal typesetting by Midland Typesetters, Australia, adapted from a design by Tess Wethereld
Editor: Cassandra Charlesworth

NATIONAL LIBRARY OF AUSTRALIA

A catalogue record for this book is available from the National Library of Australia

ISBN 978 0 6459524 0 7

We dedicate this handbook to every person who has faced adversity, moved through it and used the hard-earned wisdom for their ultimate success and happiness, as well as that of others. The right mindset and taking the higher ground is not always easy, but it's definitely worth it. Your actions inspire those around you, including future generations – and for that we salute you.

CONTENTS

INTRODUCTION

> **The future promise of any nation can be directly measured by the prospects of its youth.**
> John F. Kennedy

WHY FLY?

In 2018, Australia's annual HILDA[1] survey revealed a frightening trend: fewer than 25 per cent of young people aged 17–24 could accurately answer five questions on financial literacy.

It comes at a time when household debt is rising, the employment landscape is changing, housing affordability is in crisis, and our youth step into the workforce with a greater education debt than ever before. The economic impacts resulting from the recent coronavirus pandemic highlight more than ever the importance of financial literacy and informed, empowered decision-making.

The generation currently leaving school will set out in the knowledge that the household debt-to-income ratio currently stands at 190 per cent[2].

They will exit the doors of tertiary education with a debt that is almost twice[3] that of the generation before them.

They will enter a property market where housing affordability is currently in decline[4] and first home buyers bear the brunt of escalating prices[5].

Those aged 15–24 seeking employment will face an unemployment rate almost three times[6] the national average.

In short, Australia's future will start their adult lives with their wings clipped and their financial destination unknown. They will do so fully aware of the challenges ahead.

In 2019, Deloitte[7] found slightly more than half of Millennials globally think their personal financial situations will worsen or stay the same in the year ahead. They believe financial burdens will exceed any raises or moves to better paying jobs.

This is what Australia's young people face and feel, and it is time to break the trend.

Armed with financial knowledge and literacy, young people can set themselves up for stability and success despite the challenges that might greet them. They can embark on the journey into adulthood equipped to make financial decisions that will better position them throughout the course of their life.

This handbook is designed to empower our young people to do just that.

FLY: Financially Literate Youth is a factual and inspirational guide to encourage and motivate young people to take control of their financial future and protect themselves from making unnecessary and costly mistakes.

It is designed to arm readers with the information they need in one convenient and credible resource, allowing them to make informed decisions and spread their wings as they embrace life after school.

FLY has been created in the knowledge that financial literacy empowers young people to leave the nest safely and securely and make better financial decisions. Ultimately, it gives them more freedom, confidence and choice to live life on their terms with the knowledge, the strength and the resources they need to fly.

A QUICK GUIDE TO FLY

This handbook is designed to give you the knowledge and confidence to fly (out of the nest, and safely) into life after school.

Keep it handy, cherish it like a best mate, and refer to the relevant parts as they become relevant in your life. Use it to help make informed financial decisions and avoid making costly mistakes that may set you back from achieving your goals.

Note: Emergency financial relief and stimulus grants have not been covered in *FLY* due to their short-term nature.

If you need more information, always ask for help or advice from credible sources until you completely understand the options and consequences of your decision.

Why? Because *"Flying starts from the ground. The more grounded you are, the higher you fly."* – J. R. Rim

Figure 1 – An overview of FLY

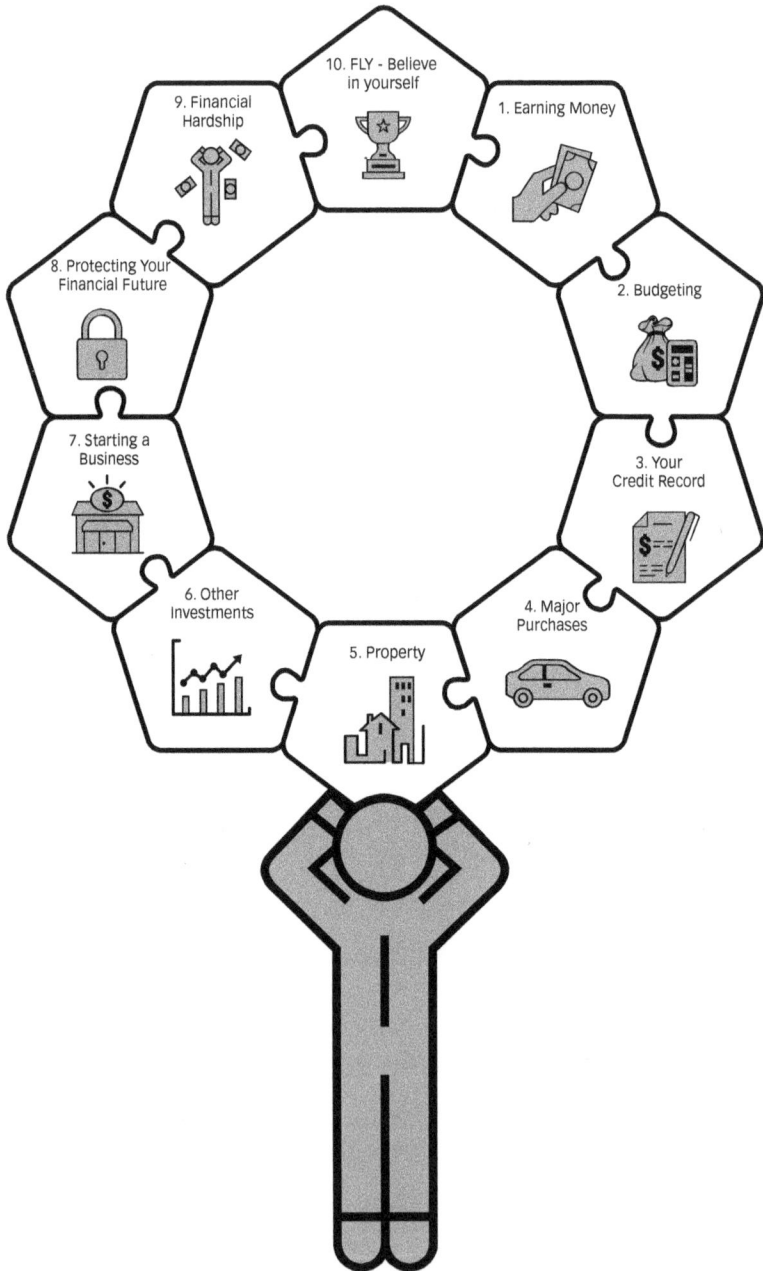

- 10. FLY - Believe in yourself
- 9. Financial Hardship
- 1. Earning Money
- 8. Protecting Your Financial Future
- 2. Budgeting
- 7. Starting a Business
- 3. Your Credit Record
- 6. Other Investments
- 4. Major Purchases
- 5. Property

EARNING MONEY

Whether it's a casual job after school, weekend work in a café or your first full-time position in your dream career, earning money comes with both freedom and responsibility.

For many people, the first job you have in your teens is the first real interaction with financial institutions like banks. It's also your first real experience of budgeting, saving for and buying the items you want, and the first time you have to consider responsibilities like expenses, tax and superannuation.

To really enjoy the fruits of your labour, aka the money you're earning, it's important to set yourself up properly at the outset.

Pennies that should drop in Chapter 1 . . .

In the pages ahead we'll cover all the basics, including the nuts and bolts of monetary admin and employment, taking a deep dive into areas like:

- Bank account types
- How to set up and access a bank account, and what to look for
- Interest, including the different types of interest and how they can work for and against you
- Credit – how it works, what it is and the unexpected types of credit you might unwittingly incur
- Employment – outlining the different types and the rights and implications that go with each
- The responsibilities that come with employment, such as tax returns
- The entitlements you should receive as part of employment, including superannuation and holiday pay.

By the end of Chapter 1 you should have a fairly firm grasp on the the foundations of finance and employment, which will help you navigate banking, the workforce and getting paid a little more clearly.

So, as you set off into the workforce, here's what you need to know . . .

> **The way to get started is to quit talking and begin doing.**
> Walt Disney

Figure 2 – Important considerations of earning money

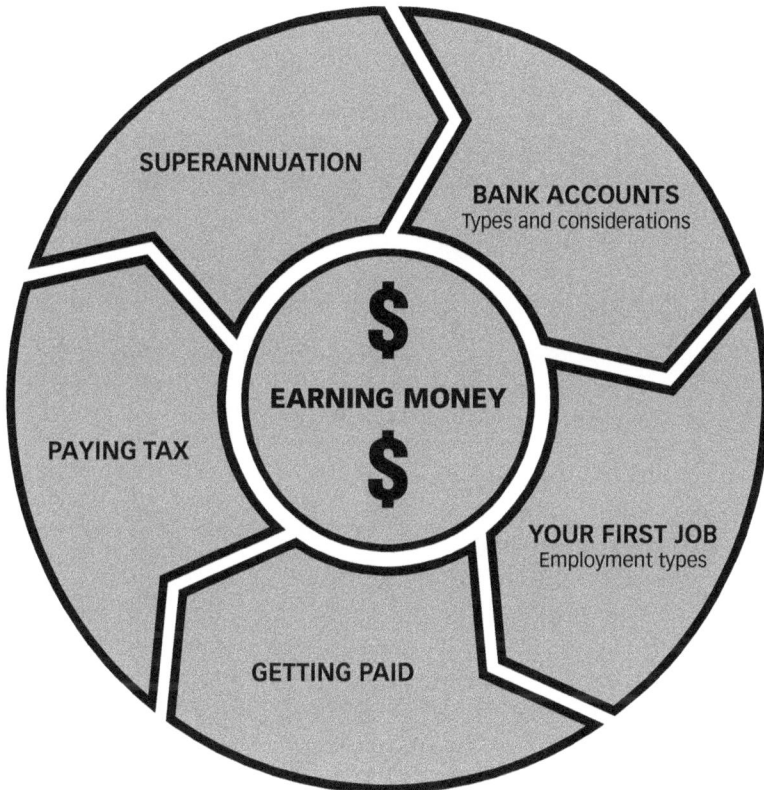

Figure 2 – Important considerations of earning money

SUPERANNUATION

BANK ACCOUNTS
Types and considerations

$

EARNING MONEY

$

PAYING TAX

YOUR FIRST JOB
Employment types

GETTING PAID

BANK ACCOUNTS: SET-UP, ACCESS AND STRUCTURE

If you're making money, you need somewhere to safely secure it and, with the right bank account, that money might even do a little work for you by earning interest on the savings you have.

Most banks offer a variety of account types to accommodate your saving and spending habits, but they all come with slightly different terms, conditions and rewards. They also come with different fees and access.

A LITTLE ABOUT FEES AND INTEREST

To put it simply, when you have a bank account, the bank might charge you fees to look after it.

Depending on the account type you have, they also might charge you fees if you access that account too often, or if you overdraw it (i.e. you happen to spend more money than is actually in the account).

On the other hand, the bank also offers you interest on the savings you have in that account. This interest rate varies depending on the type of account, the going interest rate at the time and the way you use your account. But it could mean your money is earning a little while it's sitting in the bank.

We'll go a little deeper into interest at the end of this chapter, but in the interim, let's talk about account types.

BANK ACCOUNT TYPES

There are different bank account types for different purposes, and this is worth considering when you first look at opening an account. Some are designed for convenience; others help you reach your savings goals.

Transaction accounts – Transaction accounts are designed for you to access your money whenever you want, how often you want.

That means they tend to have low or no monthly fees, and the likelihood is you can deposit or withdraw what you want at any time. The downside is they tend not to attract much interest. So while you can access them freely, they won't make much money for you.

Savings accounts – Savings accounts are designed to help you save money. That means the bank will offer you higher interest on the money you have in the account.

These accounts also tend to have conditions applied to them. So, you might have to make a deposit into that account by a set time each month, and you might be discouraged from making withdrawals. For example, if you make a withdrawal, you might not receive the benefit of the full interest.

Term deposits – Term deposits are designed to lock your money away for a set period while earning you higher interest.

The period you nominate to lock your money away for can vary from 30 days to 12 months and even five years.

These accounts also tend to come with minimum required deposits to get started. To be eligible to open a term deposit you might have to already have minimum savings of $5,000 or more, and you will also need to be at least 18.

With a term deposit, you're basically agreeing you will not touch that cash for the period you elect. If you need to access any of that money, you have to provide the bank with advance notice of a withdrawal (usually 31 days), and the interest you are then paid will be reduced.

So which account for what purpose? Well, let's look at Jake, Richie and Brie, who are all looking to open a bank account, but with slightly different outcomes in mind.

Jake's transaction account

Jake is opening a bank account for pure convenience. This is where his wages will go, and he'll be accessing the account regularly for day-to-day expenses. He has no immediate savings plans.

Jake opts for a simple transaction account. It has no monthly account-keeping fees, no minimum deposit requirements and allows him to make withdrawals whenever he wants for free at all his bank's ATMs. It also has no fees on transactions made in Australia.

On the flipside, if Jake happens to accumulate money in that account, it's not going to earn him very much interest. The convenience of his transaction account means his interest rate is just 0.1 per cent.

Richie's savings account

Richie is keen to buy a car in two years so he's looking to channel as much money into a bank account as possible in the hope that it will earn some interest. He's prepared not to touch that account unless he has to, and he's intent on depositing money into it monthly.

Richie does his homework and elects to go with a savings account offering an interest rate of 1.5 per cent. This includes a bonus that he receives for not making any withdrawals, and for depositing money by the end of each month.

Richie opens the account with $500, doesn't make any withdrawals and contributes $200 to it each month for two years.

At the end of two years, Richie has $5,385 in his account, and $85 of that is interest.

If Richie had opened a transaction account with 0.01 per cent interest, had not touched it and still made the same deposits, he would only have enjoyed interest of $6.

Brie's term deposit

Brie was given $5,000 on her 18th birthday. As she has a job that pays for her everyday expenses, she wants to set this money aside with a view to letting it grow.

Brie opts to invest it into a two-year term deposit with an annual interest rate of 1.15 per cent. At the end of the two years, Brie's initial $5,000 has resulted in interest of $115.

WHAT TO LOOK FOR IN AN ACCOUNT

Each bank offers detailed information about the types of accounts they offer and the conditions that apply, and you can generally find this online on your bank's website.

With the increased competition and emergence of online banks, account and transaction fees are also starting to become a thing of the past. If you search hard enough you should be able to find an institution that provides you with a suitable account with no or very low fees.

When selecting the right account for you, it's important to consider how often you'll use the account and the type of transactions you'll be making.

Then look at key information, including:

- Monthly account fees
- Transaction fees and frequency limits
- Overdrawn fees
- Minimum deposit conditions and amounts
- Interest rates
- Overdrawn interest rates. (Aside from any fee, you might also be charged interest on the amount of money you have outstanding and owe the bank.)

You can learn more about choosing a bank account at MoneySmart here:

- moneysmart.gov.au/banking
- moneysmart.gov.au/banking/transaction-accounts-and-debit-cards
- moneysmart.gov.au/banking/savings-accounts.

ACCOUNT ACCESS

There are different ways to access your bank account depending on what type of account you have selected.

Savings and transaction accounts generally come with debit cards and four- to six-digit Personal Identification Number (PIN). Debit cards allow you to deposit and withdraw money at an ATM and pay for items using EFTPOS.

Some cards also offer a contactless feature, which allows you to tap your card without entering a PIN to make a payment of up to $100[8].

In addition to debit cards, there are also a host of new ways to access your money, including digital payment options like Apple Pay, Samsung Pay and Google Pay.

Basically, this allows you to pay for items using your smartphone or wearable device, like an Apple Watch. At present not all banks allow you to connect your account to this feature, but it is becoming increasingly popular.

If your bank does offer Apple Pay, Samsung Pay or Google Pay, then you can set up the service on your smartphone or wearable device, connect it to the relevant account and you can then make contactless payments when shopping.

If you do use mobile payments like Apple Pay, ensure you protect your phone using unlocking codes or fingerprint/facial recognition access. Often the payment will also need to be further authorised using facial recognition, Touch ID or iris scanning.

Meanwhile, you can also visit the bank branch in person or use online banking to access your accounts.

Online banking allows you to log into your bank account via app or internet, see the balance and make transfers to other people or pay bills. Your bank will provide you with a user number, and you select a password to use this feature.

SECURITY

It's very important that you protect the security of both your bank card and PIN. Once you've selected the four to six-digit PIN, commit that number to memory.

Don't write it down. (Instead, you might want to consider using a password savings apps such as 1Password, Lastpass, etc.) Don't tell anyone what your PIN is, and when you're entering your PIN at an ATM or store, cover your hand so the number you enter cannot be seen.

Should your bank card be lost or stolen, and someone knows your PIN, they can access your bank account.

Meanwhile, contactless cards with this symbol 📶 allow people to use their card to make payments up to a certain amount (usually $100) without the need to even enter a PIN. That means someone can potentially use your bank card simply by tapping it. If you're concerned about this feature, many banks allow you to disable it in the 'usage controls' section of their app, or via online banking.

If you do happen to lose your bank card, get in touch with your bank immediately. These days most banks allow you to cancel or put a hold on your card through their mobile banking apps or by phone.

> ## *Cath's stolen debit card*
>
> Cath was shopping at the supermarket when her purse was taken from her trolley, but she didn't realise until she reached the register 25 minutes later. In the interim, the thieves had completed a number of transactions under $100, totalling $325. They had done this using contactless payments.
>
> Cath quickly phoned her bank on their stolen card hotline. The bank immediately stopped her bank card to ensure no further money could be taken.
>
> Later, after Cath proved the transactions were fraudulent, the bank kindly reimbursed the $325 in lost funds.

OPENING AN ACCOUNT

To open any bank account you need to meet minimum identity requirements to prove you are who you say you are.

For young people opening a bank account, eligible identity documents include a birth certificate or current passport, while a secondary document could be a Medicare card.

If you're younger than 14, a parent or guardian might need to attend the bank with you, and they might also be required to present identification.

CREDIT AND LOANS

Of course banks aren't just about saving. They are also the largest providers of credit in Australia through things like personal loans, credit cards and mortgages. But before you consider opening any type of credit account, you really need to know how they work and the implications involved.

Basically, credit is a loan and it comes at a cost. When a bank offers you credit, they expect regular repayments plus a little extra for the privilege of loaning you money. This is called interest, and we'll take a deep dive into it shortly.

Banks aren't the only people who might offer you credit either. Credit pops up in all manner of places, including:

- Store cards
- Interest-free offers
- Mobile phone plans (where you pay for the handset in instalments)
- Payday loans
- Buy now, pay later services, like Afterpay and Zip Pay.

In addition to personal loans, credit cards and mortgages, each of these is considered a loan where you are being offered credit.

Depending on the type of loan, the credit provider will charge a different level of interest. For example, a personal loan might command 13.56 per cent[9] interest per annum, a credit card might incur 19.74 per cent[10] per annum for purchases and 21.74 per cent for cash advances (when you withdraw cash), while a home loan might have an interest rate of 3.74 per cent[11] per annum.

Again, this is the figure they use to charge you for the privilege of borrowing money from them. When you use credit to buy something, it inevitably means you pay above and beyond what that product or item is actually worth at that time.

Every time you apply for or are given credit, it also goes on something called your credit report (we'll talk a lot about this in Chapter 3), but when you accept credit, you sign up for a legally binding financial obligation, and if you don't manage it carefully, it can quickly get out of hand.

In some cases, there will be no avoiding credit, like when you go to buy a home, but in all instances only borrow what you can afford, and don't enter into credit lightly.

If you do choose to utilise credit, including credit cards, there are strategies for using them effectively.

So, a quick recap: what do you need to consider about credit?

- Be aware that credit comes in many forms, including buy now, pay later services and store cards.
- Things like credit cards can encourage you to spend money you don't have.
- Always consider the interest rate on the credit you are offered.
- Seek the right credit for the right occasion – buying a $5,000 car using a credit card will cost you a lot more than buying it with a personal loan due to the different interest rates attached. (Either option will still cost you more than saving!)
- Try to borrow as little as possible – saving may take time, but it will cost you a whole lot less.
- Know that your credit inquiries and current loans are listed on your credit report (as is any poor repayment history).
- If you do have a credit card, be smart about its use. (We'll give you some tips on that right now.)

SMART TIPS FOR CREDIT CARD USE

As we mentioned, Australia has a pretty hefty credit card debt, but there are ways to use them effectively.

MoneySmart[12] offers the following advice:

- Find a card that suits your spending habits and the way you'll pay it off.
- Look for a low interest rate and features you'll use – make sure any rewards or extras are worth it.
- Stay on top of your spending – only spend what you can afford to pay back.

- Pay your bill on time every month – pay in full, or as much as you can.
- Check your statement and tell your credit provider if there's a charge you didn't make.
- If you're struggling with debt, avoid using your credit card to make ends meet. Find help to get debt under control.

You can learn more about credit cards here: moneysmart.gov.au/credit-cards.

Canstar also has a fabulous insight into credit cards and minimum repayments here: canstar.com.au/credit-cards/credit-cards-and-minimum-repayments.

If you have a credit card and you're struggling, help is available here: moneysmart.gov.au/managing-debt/get-debt-under-control.

MoneySmart also has some further great resources about loans, credit and debt, which you can access under the dropdown menu on their homepage here: moneysmart.gov.au.

Meanwhile, we'll be circling back to a number of these topics in detail in later sections of this handbook.

Catrina's credit card

Shortly after opening a bank account, 18-year-old Catrina is offered a credit card attached to that account with a credit limit of $2,000 and an interest rate of 17 per cent. She happily embraces the opportunity and enjoys an epic spending spree that maxes out the card. At that moment she is $2,000 in debt to the credit provider.

Later that month she receives her credit card statement. On it there are two amounts: The minimum monthly repayment she needs to make and the closing balance (the total sum she needs to pay to eliminate the full debt right now).

Catrina's minimum repayment is $41. So she goes ahead and pays that amount and continues to each month. At that rate Catrina's credit card will take her 16 years and nine months to pay off. During that time, Catrina will be charged $3,067 in interest, meaning in total she will pay back her credit card provider $5,067.

What could Catrina have done differently? Well, for a start, she could have resisted the urge to spend money that wasn't hers. But even if she did, she could have slashed the amount of interest charged by making payments of more than the minimum amount.

For example, if Catrina had paid $98 a month instead of $41, she would have paid her card off in two years and been charged just $340[13] in interest.

Better yet, if Catrina had paid the full closing balance by the due date, she would have incurred no further interest at all.

LET'S TALK INTEREST

OK, listen up, we are about to take a deep dive into interest and how it works.

Why? Because interest affects you financially throughout life when it comes to both your savings and your loans. It's also a key term that banks and lenders often refer to.

When it comes to savings, your bank will often offer you interest on the amount in your account. When it comes to loans, they will charge you interest on the amount you owe them.

This interest is generally calculated based on two key criteria – the going rate at the time (what everyone is charging or offering), and in the case of loans, how risky you might be to lenders.

So what do we mean by the "going rate"? Well, that's where interest rates come in, and you might have heard a fair bit of discussion about them in the media at the start of each month.

THE CASH RATE

In Australia, banks usually base their interest rates on something called the cash rate, which is set by the Reserve Bank of Australia (RBA). This cash rate is examined by the RBA every month (except January) to see how the economy's performing.

If the economy is slow, for example there is low employment, the property market has stalled and people aren't spending much, the RBA may lower the cash rate to make borrowing more affordable. This is designed to stimulate the economy and encourage spending. A low cash rate means people will generally pay less interest on the money they owe.

If the property market is going gangbusters, employment is solid and people are borrowing more than they should, the RBA might raise the cash rate to make borrowing more expensive. People will then pay more interest on the money they owe.

At the time of writing this handbook the cash rate is 0.10 per cent, which is the lowest it has ever been. In years gone by it has been as high as 17.5 per cent.

We're going to cover interest rates again in the section on property, but for now it's important to understand that the cash rate can affect the amount of interest you receive on your savings and what you have to pay on your loans.

It's also important to note that while the cash rate influences the interest rates that a bank sets, the two are not the same figure.

The banks will often alter their rates to reflect a rise or fall of the cash rate, but they don't necessarily have to. Meanwhile, financial institutions are businesses, so when they lend you money they tend to charge a higher interest rate than what they would offer you on your savings.

HOW INTEREST IS CALCULATED

Interest can be calculated in two different ways: simple interest and compound interest.

So, let's get to it, starting with simple interest.

Simple interest

Simple interest is calculated on what's called a principal sum, which is the amount of money you owe a lender or the sum of money you have in savings in your account.

It is based on a simple formula: principal (p) x rate (r) x time (t) = interest amount.

So, say you borrow $500 from mum and dad for a term of nine months at an interest rate of 3 per cent per month, the formula would look like this:

principal ($500) x rate (0.03) x time (9 months) = interest of $135.

Therefore, you would pay your parents $135 for the privilege of borrowing $500 for nine months.

In the finance world, simple interest is commonly applied to loans including home loans, personal loans and car loans. Accounts like term deposit accounts also usually earn simple interest.

Compound interest

Compound interest works slightly differently to simple interest, and used effectively, it can really boost your savings. Instead of just being applied to the principal amount, compound interest also earns money on the interest you accrue monthly.

Yes, we know that sounds pretty complicated. So let's explain a little further with an example.

Dan deposits $2,000 into a bank account with an interest rate of 2 per cent. Each month, he earns interest on the principal amount ($2,000) and also on the interest that amount accrues.

Year 1: $2,000 x 2% = $40 interest (total in bank $2,040)
Year 2: $2,040 x 2% = $40.80 interest (total in bank $2,080.80)
Year 3: $2,080.80 x 2% = $41.62 interest (total in bank $2,122.42)
Year 4: $2,122.42 X 2% = $42.44 interest (total in bank $2,164.87)
Year 5: $2,164.87 x 2% = $43.30 interest (total in bank $2,208.17)

Over five years, compounding interest sees Dan earn a total of $208.17 on his principal sum, all because he didn't touch it.

Meanwhile, compounding interest can really start to accumulate in the long term, especially if you look at it over decades rather than years, as MoneySmart[14] illustrates in the following example:

If you put $10,000 into a savings account with 3 per cent interest compounded monthly:

- After five years, you'd have $11,616. You'd earn $1,616 in interest.
- After 10 years, you'd have $13,494. You'd earn $3,494 in interest.
- After 20 years, you'd have $18,208. You'd earn $8,208 in interest.

As you can see, compound interest works beautifully when you're saving, but on the flipside, if you owe money and the interest is compounding, things can start to quickly add up.

MoneySmart has a great compound interest calculator available to help you see just how much you can beef up your savings using compound interest, here: moneysmart.gov.au/budgeting/compound-interest-calculator.

Alternatively, they also have a good explainer including the compound interest formula, here: moneysmart.gov.au/saving/compound-interest.

YOUR FIRST JOB

For many Australians their first real experience with employment comes while they are still at school in the form of a casual or part-time job. This initial foray into the workplace allows you to earn money, gain skills and offers an insight into employment conditions.

It's interesting to note there is no minimum working age that applies across Australia. Instead, each state and territory has different conditions that apply to workers younger than 15, such as a maximum amount of hours they can work each week or day.

If you're wondering which conditions apply to you, Fair Work Australia[15] (www.fairwork.gov.au) is your best first port of call. They also note you can check with the following authorities for the age when you are eligible to start a job:

- ACT Government Community Services on 13 22 81
- NSW Office of Industrial Relations on 13 16 28
- NT Government on (08) 8944 9274
- QLD Government on 13 74 68
- Safe Work SA on 1300 365 255
- Work Safe TAS on 1300 366 322 (within Tasmania) or (03) 6166 4600 (from interstate)
- Business Victoria on 13 22 15
- WA Wageline on 1300 655 266 (within Western Australia) or (08) 6251 2100 (from interstate).

Meanwhile, if you have a paid role when you are younger than 15, your parents or guardian might also have to give written permission.

And, if you wish to work during school times, Fair Work Australia[16] explains that generally you must be of the minimum school leaving age or have completed the minimum year of schooling, and each state and territory has their own rules about when you can leave school.

If you're looking for further information on starting your first job, Fair Work Australia has a wealth of excellent resources, including preparing for your first day, pay rates and more.

You can find them at: fairwork.gov.au/find-help-for/young-workers-and-students.

Alternatively, ASIC's MoneySmart also has a detailed section on first jobs, here: moneysmart.gov.au/student-life-and-money/getting-a-job.

EMPLOYMENT TYPES

When it comes to employment, there are a number of ways your employer can classify and pay you as part of their team.

It's important you understand the difference between each type of employment because it not only affects your pay rate but also your entitlements, including superannuation, annual leave, holiday pay and sick days.

In Australia, the most common employment types are:

FULL-TIME EMPLOYMENT

If you are a full-time employee, you work for your employer on a permanent basis. That means you can expect to work and be paid for a minimum of 38 hours per week.

You can also expect to be paid on a regular basis (weekly or fortnightly), you will be required to pay income tax and there are minimum employment standards both you and your employer must meet.

These might include the requirement that you have approximately four weeks of paid holiday leave each year and should you fall sick, there are a set number of sick days each year which you are also entitled to be paid for.

Jenna the journalist

Jenna is a young journalist who is employed at a country newspaper in Far North Queensland.

Her industry body, which is the Media Entertainment and Arts Alliance, has negotiated the following conditions[17] on her behalf:

She can expect to receive a minimum $941.10 per week as her wage ($24.77 per hour). If she's lucky she might be paid more, but by law she cannot be paid less.

In addition, she will be paid extra for overtime when she works beyond 38 hours, and will also receive additional pay for working public holidays. Each year she receives two weeks paid sick leave and four weeks paid annual leave.

How much you are paid, how long your holiday entitlements are and how many paid sick days you receive are based on what's called an 'award'. The award is the specific conditions your industry body has negotiated on your behalf.

Awards vary from industry to industry and they change over time, but if you're looking to learn more about them, Fair Work Australia[18] has links to industry awards, here: fairwork.gov.au/awards-and-agreements/awards/list-of-awards.

Meanwhile, the more experience you have in an industry, the greater pay, responsibilities and entitlements you are likely to have.

PART-TIME EMPLOYMENT

A part-time employee works less than 38 hours per week, but still their hours are guaranteed. Those hours tend to be regular and the employer must offer the same entitlements as they would to a full-time employee but on a 'pro-rata' basis.

In other words, if you are in part-time employment, you still receive holiday pay and sick leave, but the amount is reduced proportionately based on the number of hours you actually work.

For example, if Jenna worked part-time, she would still receive $24.77[19] per hour, and her wage would still be paid regularly. But because she works 20 rather than 38 hours each week, she would instead receive approximately 52 per cent of the full-time employment annual holiday and sick leave entitlements.

CASUAL EMPLOYMENT

For many young workers their first job is casual. This means the hours you work each week may vary, and they are not guaranteed. As a casual employee you are also not entitled to sick leave or holiday pay. Therefore, if you're sick or not available, you won't get paid. On the flipside, your hourly rate is often higher, in recognition of the instability and lack of entitlements.

So, if Jenna is employed casually as a journalist, under the current award rates, she would be paid $30.96[20] per hour in casual employment, rather than the full or part-time rate of $24.77 per hour.

George (still in high school, working part-time in the fast food industry)

On Sunday each week, George's employer puts up the staff roster. George has indicated that because he's studying and in Year 12, he can only work Friday afternoons and nights, Saturday days and nights, and Sunday days.

Under the hospitality award[21] (at the time this handbook was written), George's rates are:

- $24.36 for normal hours
- $24.36 per hour plus $2.27 per hour or part of an hour (Monday to Friday 7pm to midnight)
- $29.24 on Saturdays
- $34.11 on Sundays.

This week is busy and George is rostered to work:

- Friday: 5pm to 11pm (6 hours)
- Saturday: 7am to 3pm (8 hours).

Therefore, George can expect to receive $48.72 for the first two hours worked on Friday, plus $106.52 for the hours after 7pm, then $234 for Saturday, meaning his gross wage (before tax and deductions are taken out) for the week will be $489.24. Next week is quieter and more staff are available, so George is rostered to work:

- Sunday: 12pm to 5pm (5 hours).

George's wage for the week will be $170.55 gross.

If George is unwell and cannot go to work his hours will be allocated to someone else and he will not be paid.

If the restaurant is quiet and George is sent home early, he will not be paid for the hours he was rostered to work but was not needed. While there are no guaranteed hours of work for casual employment, you should check your employment agreement or award as many employers stick to a minimum of two or three hours per shift for casual staff.

Most first jobs tend to be casual and they're often in industries like hospitality or retail. That means each week your employer is likely to include you on a staff roster that indicates when you are required to work based on the availability you have indicated.

FIXED-TERM EMPLOYMENT

Fixed-term employees are employed for a set period. That might be two months, six months or even three years, but their employment usually has a set end period rather than just being ongoing.

Fixed-term employees can be full-time or part-time and have the same entitlements, but it works on a pro-rata basis. So if a fixed-term employee has a six-month full-time contract, they will receive two weeks paid leave rather than the four they would be entitled to if they worked the entire year.

INDEPENDENT CONTRACTOR

An independent contractor tends to be an external person who is brought in to complete set tasks. As such, they usually come with their own fixed rates of pay and they aren't considered an employee.

Instead, an independent contractor has their own business and an Australian business number (ABN). They set their own rates and usually quote on a job prior to being employed to complete it.

For example, a plumber might be an independent contractor. They are called into a home or workplace when something goes wrong to fix a problem at a price they determine.

Independent contractors are responsible for filing their own paperwork with the Australian Taxation Office (ATO), setting aside their own holiday pay and paying their own superannuation.

If Jenna was working as a freelance journalist who was called in by a newspaper to complete occasional tasks, this is the role she might fall under. She would be paid per job, probably work for other organisations as well, and then invoice each organisation for the work she had done for them.

Basically, she runs her own writing business and needs to set aside enough money to pay her own tax, her own superannuation and also cover any time off she requires for holidays.

To help determine whether you should be regarded as an employee or a contractor you need to review the entire working arrangement.

The Australian Taxation Office has created a helpful 'Employee or Contractor Decision Tool', here: ato.gov.au/business/employee-or-contractor/how-to-work-it-out--employee-or-contractor.

GETTING PAID

When you work full-time, part-time or casually, your employer must provide you a payslip either in hard copy or electronically every time you get paid. This payslip should indicate how much you have earned gross. This is the amount you were paid before tax and any other withholdings.

It should also indicate what period or what hours you have been paid for, any tax that has been deducted, any superannuation that has been allocated to your super fund and any other withholdings, including the repayment of your tertiary study debt (HECS-HELP).

Your payslip should also clearly note your net pay (the take-home amount after all deductions have been taken out). This is the dollar amount that will be paid directly to you or into your bank account after all other items (tax, super, HECS) have been taken out.

It's really important you check your payslips to make sure you have been paid the right amount for the time you have worked and the correct tax, super, etc. has been taken out.

For more information about pay rates and minimum wages, visit: fairwork. gov.au/pay/minimum-wages.

If you are a sole contractor, you submit an invoice to the organisation you have worked for, which must include important information like your ABN, address, the invoice number, the employer's address and your bank account details along with your payment terms.

When they pay that invoice, the information should either be clearly seen on your bank transaction details, or they may issue a remittance advice to indicate the account has been paid.

Heads up – we'll be talking a lot more about getting paid when you're in business a little bit later.

PAYING TAX: THRESHOLDS AND RETURNS

Employment brings with it the obligation to pay tax, and one of the first things you'll need when entering the workforce is a tax file number (TFN).

You can apply for your tax file number in person at Australia Post or at the Department of Human Services (Centrelink), or alternatively you can apply by post.

Identification documents will be required, and if applying at Australia Post, you will need to attend a short interview.

Your tax file number stays with you for life. It's the number that you will need to provide every employer throughout your career, and it will also be required when you complete your annual tax return.

For further information and downloadable forms, visit 'Australian residents – TFN application': ato.gov.au/individuals/tax-file-number/apply-for-a-tfn/ australian-residents---tfn-application.

TAX THRESHOLDS

In Australia, all workers earning above a certain amount are required to pay tax on the money they earn, and this goes up in increments (thresholds) the more you are paid.

In other words, the more money you earn, the more tax you are required to pay. This figure is calculated as a percentage of each dollar you earn above each tax threshold.

In Australia, the current tax thresholds are:

Taxable Income	Tax on this income
0 – $18,200	Nil
$18,201 – $45,000	19c for each $1 over $18,200
$45,001 – $120,000	$5,092 plus 32.5c for each $1 over $45,000
$120,001 – $180,000	$29,467 plus 37c for each $1 over $120,000
$180,001 and over	$51,667 plus 45c for each $1 over $180,000

Source: ATO[22] Individual Income Rates 2020–21 (ato.gov.au/Rates/Individual-income-tax-rates)

Julia, apprentice chef

If Julia becomes an apprentice chef, earning $36,000 between July 1 one year and June 30 the following year, she will be classed within the second tax threshold.

$18,201 of the money she earns will be exempt from tax; however, she will pay 19c tax on every dollar she earns above that.

That means Julia will be required to pay tax on $17,999 and will therefore pay $3,419.81 in tax that year.

In most cases your employer is responsible for deducting tax on your behalf during each pay period, based on your annual salary.

However, if you are self-employed, you will need to account for this tax yourself and set it aside.

TAX RETURNS

If you have had tax taken out of your income, you will need to file a tax return within a set period after the end of the financial year.

For individuals filing their own return, the ATO[23] notes the deadline is October 31. If you're using an accountant or registered agent you have a little bit longer, but you still need to contact that agent before the October 31 date.

The best way to understand whether you have had tax withheld is to check your payslips as you receive them. At the end of the financial year you can also refer to your employment summary via either your tax accountant or, if your employer is using Single Touch Payroll (STP), via ATO online services on your MyGov (my.gov.au) account.

For more information about accessing your payment summary or income statement, visit: ato.gov.au/Individuals/Working/Working-as-an-employee/Accessing-your-payment-summary.

Your payment summary outlines the amount you have been paid in wages, the amount deducted for tax and the amount contributed to your superannuation.

This information is then used to prepare your tax return, where you can also claim deductions for some items you have purchased specifically for your work. Deductions are legitimate work-related expenses that reduce your assessable income on which your income tax is calculated. Eligible deductions vary from profession to profession and can sometimes even change over the years.

The best way to understand what you are able to deduct from your tax is to visit the ATO website: ato.gov.au/individuals/income-and-deductions/deductions-you-can-claim, or speak directly to your accountant.

Throughout the year, you will need to keep receipts of any work-related purchases that you intend to claim as deductions and then provide them if required when you lodge your return.

While you can file your own tax return, an accountant can be a prudent investment. They may cost a few dollars, but a good, reputable accountant will minimise your tax usually well in excess of the fee they charge.

In Australia, all individual tax returns that are not being filed through a tax agent need to be submitted by October 31 following the end of the previous financial year. In other words, you need to submit a tax return for the financial year 2024–2025 by the end of October 2025.

If you use a tax agent, that deadline is slightly later. However, if you leave it too long to file your tax return you could be fined by the ATO.

> ## *Success is the sum of small efforts, repeated day in day out.*
> Robert Collier

SUPERANNUATION

Superannuation is like a compulsory savings account that is set up for when you retire. It's a way for the government to ensure people have money to live on once they stop working in their older age.

Under Australian law, if you are paid more than $450 per month or are over 18 and work more than 30 hours a week, employers must set aside a certain portion of your salary to go towards this fund.

In most cases, this figure is currently 9.5 per cent of your annual salary. You can also add extra to that fund if you like, and the government may also contribute.

The fund that you invest this money into then pools your money with other people's superannuation and they look to invest it and grow it over time.

Over the years that you pay super, it steadily begins to add up.

For example, Matt has a job earning $45,000 a year. That means his employer must deposit $4,275 of his wages into his superannuation account that year. It usually happens as an amount taken out of his weekly pay cheque. As Matt's salary grows, so does his superannuation contribution. So Matt's super contribution might look like this over five years:

	Matt's wage	Matt's super contribution	Matt's super fund balance (without interest)
Year 1	$45,000	$4,272	$4,272
Year 2	$47,500	$4,512.50	$8,784.50
Year 3	$50,000	$4,750	$13,534.50
Year 4	$51,000	$4,845	$18,379.50
Year 5	$52,000	$4,940	$23,319.50

You can just imagine how much that adds up over approximately 40 years in the workforce.

Meanwhile, Matt's superannuation should also be accruing interest. That's because the job of a super fund is to make extra money on the funds deposited into it. Their role is to find good investments to direct your money towards in the aim of getting more back in return.

Different super funds have different types of investments, but most include things like shares and property. (Put simply, a "share" is a percentage of ownership in a company or a financial asset. If you invest in shares, you are a "shareholder".) They also have different rates of return, depending on the year and the fund you are invested in. In the interim, Matt can also opt to contribute extra money into this account. He may then receive extra money from the government or additional tax incentives for doing so.

To calculate your predicted super or set yourself a target, use ASIC's MoneySmart super calculator: moneysmart.gov.au/tools-and-resources/calculators-and-apps/superannuation-calculator.

In Australia, you can access your superannuation when you reach 65 or when you reach 'preservation age'. Once you reach 65 you can even access your super if you're still working.

Preservation age is a minimum age set by law that your superannuation must be 'preserved' or held until. It varies depending on when you were born, and MoneySmart has a guide to the different preservation ages here: moneysmart.gov.au/how-super-works/getting-your-super.

The Federal Government can change the preservation age if it feels the need, meaning by the time you go to retire, the preservation age might be 65, or even higher.

If you've reached preservation age but haven't permanently retired, you can access part of your super via a transition to retirement pension, which MoneySmart explains here: moneysmart.gov.au/retirement-income/ transition-to-retirement.

Regardless of when you choose to retire, superannuation is an important part of preparing for your future, and in many but not all cases you have the right to select the superannuation fund where you want your money to go.

You can learn more about the importance of superannuation here: moneysmart.gov.au/how-super-works.

SELECTING A SUPER FUND

It might be your retirement money, but believe it or not, the subject of selecting a superannuation fund is slightly contentious.

In most cases, Australian workers have the right to select the superannuation fund that best suits them.

You can make this judgement based on the investments that fund prefers, the fees charged by the fund, the rate of return (the average percentage of interest they provide on the money invested with them) or simple convenience.

Some super comparison websites include:

- finder.com.au/super-funds
- canstar.com.au/superannuation
- chantwest.com.au/fund-ratings/super
- morningstar.com.au/Tools/NewFundScreener
- ratecity.com.au/superannuation
- selectingsuper.com.au
- superratings.com.au.

Once you decide, you can then nominate that fund as the place you would like your super to go. You can only change that fund once a year with your employer.

There are major benefits to nominating your own fund. When you select your own superannuation fund you can generally keep it as your fund for life. That means there is no doubling up on fees and account handling, and the money keeps accumulating in one place.

A word to the wise, when it comes to selecting a fund, look into the fees they charge and their history of returns.

All funds are required to make their fees and returns available to prospective customers, so compare funds to ensure you are getting a good return and are not overpaying on fees. What may seem like a small difference now, when compounded over 30–40 years, will make a huge difference to your super balance.

If you're not sure which superannuation fund to nominate, your employer can choose one for you. But either way, if you are over 18 and work over 30 hours per week, or if you earn more than $450 a month, your employer must pay you super.

In some cases the industry you work in may have a specific agreement as part of your salary negotiations that means your employer can only pay your super into a set fund.

In this instance, a specific superannuation fund may have been nominated as part of your enterprise bargaining agreement (or award).

In other words, the union that represents your type of workforce has set a super fund as part of your salary and work entitlements. This cannot be changed – not by you, not by your employer. If this happens to apply to your sector, you can always roll the funds that are in the superannuation fund into another one later in your career.

Which brings us to the importance of keeping your super together . . .

TRACKING YOUR SUPER AND KEEPING IT TOGETHER

Over the years and through various jobs, you might acquire more than one super fund. It's really important that you keep track of where your superannuation is. Remember, this is the money you have earned for your future. It's yours, and you worked hard for it.

You should make sure you advise your superannuation fund/s whenever you change addresses. Alternatively, if you've lost track of where your super is, you can find it using the ATO online services through MyGov.

For more information, visit: ato.gov.au/Individuals/Super/Growing-your-super/Keeping-track-of-your-super.

Once you've found your super and accounted for it, you can also then roll it into one fund if you choose.

MOVING YOUR SUPER INTO ONE FUND

Each super fund you have will likely charge fees, which can take little pieces out of your nest egg. If you have more than one super fund, and particularly if you have a few, these charges can soon add up, making it a great idea to roll all your super into one fund.

That said, if you're considering "rolling over" your super, there are a few things you need to consider . . .

- Exit fees – Some funds charge an exit fee when you close your account and move your money. You should check how much this is.

- Insurance – In addition to superannuation, some funds have insurance policies attached to them. You should check whether your fund has insurance with it, and see whether you lose any benefits when you exit.
- Contact all funds – In order to move your money, you need to provide authorisation and identification. Contact the fund to obtain the forms you require, fill them out and have your money moved to the fund you prefer. It's important to note that if you have changed names since you opened your original fund (for example, you got married), you will also need to provide proof of that name change.

In time, once you acquire considerable super, financial and legal knowledge, you may wish to consider managing your own super in the form of a self-managed super fund (SMSF).

There are various things to consider when it comes to self-managed super, which are beyond the scope of this handbook, but for more information you can visit: moneysmart.gov.au/superannuation-and-retirement/self-managed-super-fund-smsf.

The book *Join the Rich Club: How to enrich your life and the lives of others* by Peter Switzer is also an excellent resource regarding the considerations and pros and cons of SMSFs.

2

BUDGETING: COVERING YOUR EXPENSES

When you get your first job, you may imagine that accumulating cash is easy. You earn $450 a week, you put it in your bank, you spend a little on the things you want. It seems relatively simple.

But, of course, it isn't quite as cut and dried as that.

Pennies that should drop in Chapter 2 . . .

At this point we're going to turn our attention to managing money, including how to budget, how to save and how to make your money work for you. We'll also look at funding tertiary education, in the knowledge this is one of the big first expenses most people incur, and it comes at a time when many are leaving home.

The chapter ahead includes:

- An insight into basic budgeting and cashflow
- The 50/30/20 rule as a guide to necessary expenditure, discretionary spending and saving
- A quick look at how much of your income should go where
- Budgeting tools, resources and savings tips
- Paying for tertiary education, including government assistance, like HECS-HELP.

By the end of Chapter 2, you should feel pretty comfortable with budgeting, saving and funding your immediate future.

> *Don't be afraid to fail.*
> *Be afraid not to try.*
> Michael Jordan

EXPENSES

With maturity comes commitments, and among them there will be expenses. These are the non-negotiable items that you are required to pay for as part of everyday life.

Everyday expenses might include:

- Rent/boarding/accommodation
- Monthly mobile phone/internet plans
- Electricity bills/water charges
- Books for study
- Transport costs (public transport costs, car registration, petrol, car maintenance, etc.)
- Food/groceries/personal care items
- Uniforms and clothing, etc.

Throughout life, most people have predictable expenses and occasional ones that they cannot budget for, such as a car that breaks down or perhaps unexpected dental costs. But by budgeting for the expenses you know you have, you can also set aside money for the unknown and save towards the things you really want.

The bottom line is this: budgeting is a really important part of managing your finances throughout the course of your life.

Often budgeting is made to sound complex, but it's actually really simple. It's the straightforward tally of exactly what comes into your bank account (income) and what money needs to go out (expenses).

Anything left over once you have deducted expenses from income is your surplus cash that you can put towards the non-essentials you want (going out, buying new clothes), set aside for the unknown, or alternatively channel into savings and investing for your future.

From the outset, it's critical you only incur the expenses you can afford. When you fail to budget and pay for necessary expenses, especially accommodation and utilities (phone/electricity/loans) you can start to damage your credit rating, and that's a hard stigma to shake.

BASIC BUDGETING (A LIFE SKILL)

Use a notebook, use a spreadsheet, or refer to your bank account – for most people income versus expenses is pretty plain to see. But the best way to effectively budget is to list every expense you are likely to incur across a year and then break it down into weekly amounts.

So, your income-to-expenses ratio might look something like this:

Income:

- $450 per week from a part-time job in hospitality.

Expenses:

- Accommodation – $125 per week
- Mobile phone – $40 per month = $10 per week (approx.)
- Electricity – $200 per quarter = $200/12 weeks = $17 per week (approx.)
- Text books – $400 per annum = $400/52 weeks = $8 per week (approx.)
- Fuel – $10 per week
- Car registration – $737.10 per annum = $737.10/52 = $14.20 per week (approx.)
- Comprehensive car insurance – $1,837[24] per annum = $1837/52 = $35.30 per week (approx.)
- Food/groceries – $50 per week
- Clothing – $40 per month = $10 per week (approx.).

Weekly income = $450
Minus weekly expenses = $279.50
Funds after expenses = ($450-$279.50) = $170.50

Therefore your income minus expenses is $170.50 per week. This final figure is the money that you can call your own.

The best thing about breaking down your expenses into weekly increments is that it accounts for the major financial hits you are likely to take across a year (like car registration, electricity and text books) and considers them manageable weekly amounts that you set aside.

Any 'surplus' that you have left over after weekly expenses can go to savings or be used to buy the things you want (rather than need) and fund non-essentials, like going out.

As life goes on, both your income and expenses are likely to increase. If you take out a car loan for a new vehicle, this becomes a weekly expense that's added to the list. Insurance is another expense that needs to be factored in to protect the things you have. If you have a credit card, that becomes another one, and of course, if you have a mortgage, that is a major weekly expense you need to budget for as well.

No matter what your income is, keeping track of your expenses is a critical life skill. So how much of your income should ideally be going where when it comes to budgeting and expenses? Let's have a look at some percentages that can help you understand how you're tracking in terms of incomings, outgoings, essential expenses and savings.

THE 50/30/20 RULE

First made popular by US Senator Elizabeth Warren, the 50/30/20[25] rule is a simple way to look at budgeting and ensure you have enough money to handle necessary expenses, while still setting aside savings for emergencies. Using this principle, you look at your take-home pay (after tax) then ensure no more than 50 per cent of your income goes to needs (essential for survival), 30 per cent is set aside for wants (not essential for survival), and a further 20 per cent is put aside for savings.

Needs – 50 per cent

Needs are the necessary financial commitments you are required to meet each week or month to live and survive. They are the items that we listed above, including accommodation costs (mortgage and/or rent), electricity, credit card repayments, transport, food, clothing, medicine, etc.

These should account for no more than 50 per cent of your take-home income throughout life, no matter what you earn.

Wants – 30 per cent

Wants are your variable expenses. They are items like entertainment, dining out, home decor, gifts, designer clothing, sport, travel, etc.

Savings – 20 per cent

This is the money you set aside for a rainy day or to help achieve major life goals, like buying a car or house, travel, etc.

The great thing about the 50/30/20 rule is that it offers a fair bit of wiggle room, but the most important thing is to keep your necessary expenses (needs) at or below 50 per cent. Bear in mind the bulk of your needs will also be taken up with housing, so let's have a closer look to help you understand how much you should dedicate to accommodation.

Figure 3 – The 50/30/20 budgeting rule

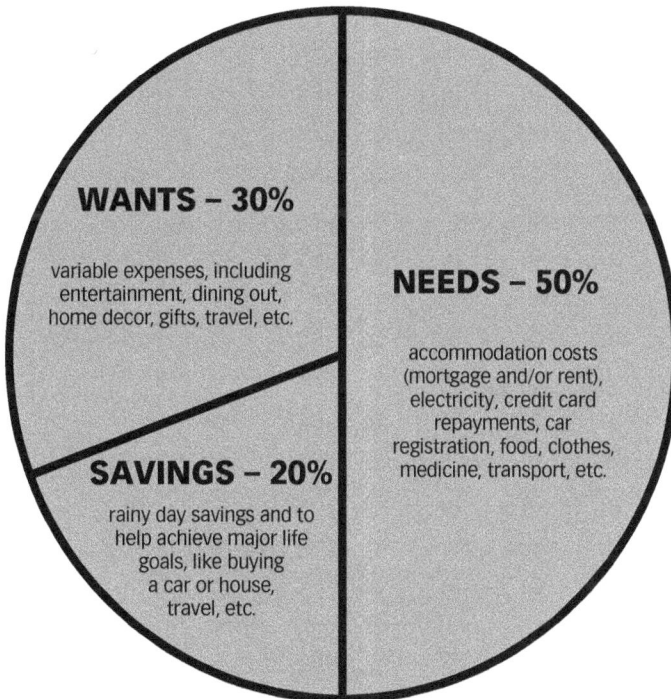

WANTS – 30%
variable expenses, including entertainment, dining out, home decor, gifts, travel, etc.

NEEDS – 50%
accommodation costs (mortgage and/or rent), electricity, credit card repayments, car registration, food, clothes, medicine, transport, etc.

SAVINGS – 20%
rainy day savings and to help achieve major life goals, like buying a car or house, travel, etc.

Housing costs

Throughout life, housing will often be one of your biggest monthly or weekly expenses, regardless of whether you rent or own the property where you live. So how much should you be spending on accommodation?

Well, ideally as little as possible, but in reality absolutely no more than **30 per cent** of your take-home income.

If you own your home, that 30 per cent doesn't just encompass the mortgage either – it includes rates and required insurance.

OK, let's go back to the 50/30/20 rule and see how you'd fare using the income/expenses scenario we outlined above, based on that $450 per week part-time job in hospitality.

Income (after tax)

$450 per week

Needs

Share house accommodation – $75 per week = 16.6 per cent (well under the 30 per cent threshold – nice work!)

Food – $50 per week

Mobile phone – $10 per week

Electricity – $10 per week

Transport – $40 per week

Insurances – $10 per week

Clothes – $10 per week

Needs total – $205
Percentage total – 45.5 per cent (under the 50 per cent threshold – that's good!)

Wants

Gifts – $8 per week

Sport – $10 per week

Dining out/fast food – $50 per week

Home decor – $40 per month = $10 per week

Current wants total – $78
Current percentage total – 17.3 per cent

But let's add in some entertainment, because you don't seem to be getting out much, and quite frankly you deserve to!

Entertainment (movies, concerts, travel, etc.) = $50 per week

New wants total – $128
New wants percentage – 28.4 per cent (under the 30 per cent threshold – that's good)

Savings

New savings total – $120.50
Savings percentage – 27 per cent (well over the ideal 20 per cent ideal, meaning you're in a solid financial position to save)

BUDGETING RESOURCES

If you're looking to really get on top of your expenses and work out where exactly your money goes, there are a wealth of amazing resources to assist, ranging from apps and spreadsheets to digital spending trackers.

In fact, your bank probably even has a savings or money tracker available as part of your online banking that can help you drill down into what you're spending where.

But if you want to go old school and easy, here's an excellent budget template courtesy of MoneySmart[26] to get you started.

Budget planner

		View :	Annually	
Income	$	Frequency		$0
Your take-home pay		Weekly		$0
Your partner's take-home pay		Weekly		$0
Bonuses / overtime		Annually		$0
Income from savings and investments		Monthly		$0
Centrelink benefits		Fortnightly		$0
Family benefit payments		Fortnightly		$0
Child support received		Monthly		$0
Other		Monthly		$0
Home & utilities	$	Frequency		$0
Mortgage & rent		Monthly		$0
Body corporate fees		Quarterly		$0
Council rates		Quarterly		$0
Furniture & appliances		Annually		$0
Renovations & maintenance		Annually		$0
Electricity		Quarterly		$0
Gas		Quarterly		$0
Water		Quarterly		$0
Internet		Monthly		$0
Pay TV		Monthly		$0
Home phone		Monthly		$0
Mobile		Monthly		$0
Other		Fortnightly		$0
Insurance & financial	$	Frequency		$0
Car insurance		Monthly		$0
Home & contents insurance		Monthly		$0
Personal & life insurance		Monthly		$0
Health insurance		Monthly		$0
Car loan		Monthly		$0
Credit card interest		Monthly		$0
Other loans		Monthly		$0
Paying off debt		Monthly		$0
Savings		Monthly		$0
Investments & super contributions		Monthly		$0
Charity donations		Monthly		$0
Other		Monthly		$0
Groceries	$	Frequency		$0
Supermarket		Weekly		$0
Butcher		Weekly		$0
Fruit & veg market		Weekly		$0
Fish shop		Weekly		$0
Deli & bakery		Weekly		$0
Pet food		Weekly		$0
Other		Monthly		$0
Personal & medical	$	Frequency		$0
Cosmetics & toiletries		Monthly		$0
Hair & beauty		Monthly		$0
Medicines & pharmacy		Monthly		$0
Glasses & eye care		Monthly		$0
Dental		Monthly		$0
Doctors & medical		Monthly		$0
Hobbies		Monthly		$0
Clothing & shoes		Monthly		$0
Jewellery & accessories		Monthly		$0
Computers & gadgets		Monthly		$0
Sports & gym		Monthly		$0
Education		Monthly		$0
Pet care & vet		Monthly		$0
Other		Monthly		$0

Entertainment & eating-out	$	Frequency	$0
Coffee & tea		Weekly	$0
Lunches bought		Weekly	$0
Take-away & snacks		Weekly	$0
Cigarettes		Weekly	$0
Drinks & alcohol		Weekly	$0
Bars & clubs		Monthly	$0
Restaurants		Monthly	$0
Books		Monthly	$0
Newspapers & magazines		Monthly	$0
Movies & music		Monthly	$0
Holidays		Annually	$0
Celebrations & gifts		Monthly	$0
Other		Monthly	$0
Transport & auto	**$**	**Frequency**	**$0**
Bus & train & ferry		Weekly	$0
Petrol		Weekly	$0
Road tolls & parking		Weekly	$0
Rego & licence		Annually	$0
Repairs & maintenance		Annually	$0
Fines		Monthly	$0
Airfares		Annually	$0
Other		Monthly	$0
Children	**$**	**Frequency**	**$0**
Baby products		Monthly	$0
Toys		Monthly	$0
Babysitting		Monthly	$0
Childcare		Monthly	$0
Sports & activities		Monthly	$0
School fees		Monthly	$0
Excursions		Monthly	$0
School uniforms		Monthly	$0
Other school needs		Monthly	$0
Child support payment		Monthly	$0
Other		Monthly	$0

Summary $0

Congratulations! Your budget is in surplus.

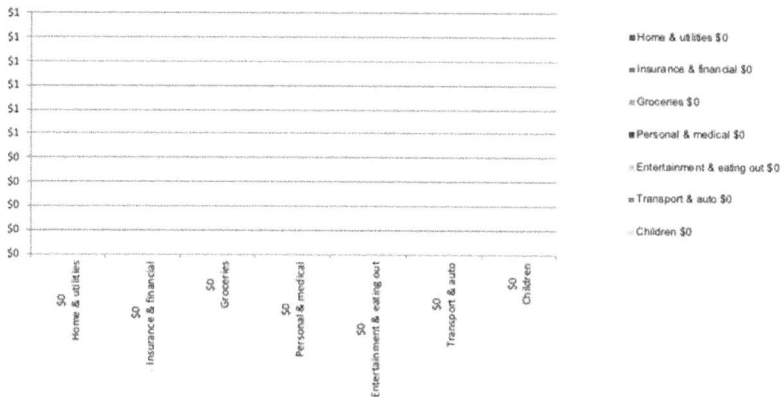

Legend:
- Home & utilities $0
- Insurance & financial $0
- Groceries $0
- Personal & medical $0
- Entertainment & eating out $0
- Transport & auto $0
- Children $0

Meanwhile, these resources are also great:

- MoneySmart budget tracker excel spreadsheet: moneysmart.gov. au/budgeting/budget-planner
- MoneySmart Simple Money Manager: moneysmart.gov.au/ budgeting/simple-money-manager
- MoneySmart how to do a budget: moneysmart.gov.au/budgeting/ how-to-do-a-budget

Alternatively, you can download a wide range of budget apps. A list of some to get you started is available, here: mozo.com.au/fintech/the-seven-budget-and-savings-apps-every-aussie-needs.

LIVING WITHIN YOUR MEANS

When you accurately budget and account for your expenses in life you are better equipped to live within your means, and that becomes increasingly important as you progress through life and begin to acquire and manage debt.

In fact, good budgeting could help you eliminate small debts and reduce the larger ones that crop up through life. Budgeting can enable you to manage your credit card effectively, pay off loans faster and reduce your mortgage years earlier than your peers.

It can allow you to have the things you want in life now and in the future – whether that's a car, a house, a family, travel or early retirement.

You don't necessarily need a high-paying job to achieve these goals either, but you do need to be educated, to be disciplined and to have a plan.

The fact is, it's never too soon to start budgeting and setting the financial goals that you want to achieve, but too often people do not properly consider their financial future.

In 2019, the ABC[27] noted Australia has the second highest household debt levels in the world (second only to Switzerland). Our debt levels are driven by an appetite for spending that goes far beyond our means.

As of October 2019, Finder[28] reported there were 14,754,488 credit cards in Australia, resulting in a national debt accruing interest of $29 billion.

The average available balance on those cards was $3211, and the average amount outstanding was $2007.

That means for every credit card in Australia, people were $2007 in debt. And that's just one area where we continue to rack up expenses for items using credit.

In the ABC's Australia Talks survey[29] of almost 55,000 people, they found 90 per cent of respondents rated household debt as a problem for the nation.

On an individual level, they noted 37 per cent were struggling to pay off their own debts, with almost half of Millennials reporting that debt is a problem for them personally.

This debt is causing significant stress to people, but importantly it's also keeping them in the workforce longer, and for many it's avoidable.

While debt is a national issue, the truth is you don't have to be part of the statistics. By tracking your expenses, budgeting and saving, you equip yourself to live within your means, only incurring debt when you absolutely need to for the things that matter most.

So how do you do that?

SAVING: SETTING GOALS AND SAVING TOOLS FOR SUCCESS

Life isn't just about getting by and paying for necessities. Working gives you the chance to have the things you really want, like travel, a house, a car. But often buying these big-ticket items requires setting goals and saving. So let's take a look at some of the top tips and tools for setting goals and saving.

Let's start by reiterating, the first priority is to live within your means! It can be tempting, especially in today's society, to reward yourself with fancy or luxury items before you can actually afford them.

Paying interest to purchase a depreciating asset such as a car, fancy clothes, a holiday or furniture will cost you more in the long run. For example, a $30,000 car over a five-year loan at an interest rate of 10 per cent will result in a total cost of more than $38,000.

Budgeting and saving while living within your means is painful at first, but will set you up for success and save you thousands of dollars in the long haul.

A few basic saving tips:

- Track your income and expenses so you know exactly what is coming in versus what is going out. Use a budgeting tool, such as MoneySmart's budget planner: moneysmart.gov.au/budgeting/budget-planner.

- Review your budget every 3–6 months to ensure that it remains accurate and up-to-date.

- As recommended by the author Scott Pape in *The Barefoot Investor*[30], you may choose to set up multiple bank accounts and automatically transfer income into those accounts.

  A good setup may see you have one account for your expenses (so these are always covered), one for savings/goals (an interest-earning account that you avoid accessing) and one for spending and unexpected expenses (which inevitably pop up from time to time).

- When trying to save, look at your budget and decide where you can cut back on spending. Good places to start are to shop around for the best deals by service providers and set a budget for non-essentials, such as personal expenses and entertainment, then try hard to stick to it.

- Setting a savings plan towards a particular goal (a holiday, house deposit, etc.) will help motivate you to stay on track.

  In your savings plan, include how much you need to save and the date by which you want to achieve your goal, then break the amount down into weekly and monthly targets, which are easier to track.

MoneySmart has a great savings goal calculator that shows you how long it will take to reach your goal and the steps you need to put in place: moneysmart.gov.au/saving/savings-goals-calculator.

- If you get off course with your savings, acknowledge where you went wrong, how you can improve and avoid that happening again in the future, and then get back on track. It's never too late!

- When you've got surplus cash, consider your options to help grow your money – open a high-interest savings account, consider investing the money in things like shares, property or a business (discussed later in this handbook), or make an additional contribution to your super and benefit from the magic of compound interest.

For more helpful tips and information on simple ways to save money, you can also visit: moneysmart.gov.au/saving/simple-ways-to-save-money.

Savings snapshot

Lucy and Linda's travel adventure

Lucy and Linda are about to embark on a travel adventure to the UK and Europe. The pair have been planning it for years.

In the year prior, Lucy sets herself the goal to save $100 a week for spending money when she's overseas. She realistically looks at her income and expenses, and determines she has $150 she could potentially set aside each week after all outgoing expenses. If she eliminates her daily takeaway coffee, that figure could actually be $170.

Lucy knows she's going to want to still buy the occasional non-essential item in the meantime, so despite potentially saving more, she settles on a savings goal of $100 each week. She sets up a savings account and direct debits $100 into it each week automatically.

At the end of the 52-week period, Lucy has $5,200 in a bank account, plus interest of $40[31]. In the interim she has allowed herself to spend up to $70 each week on non-essential items.

Lucy happily goes overseas with $5,240 in her account and spends money she saved. She returns home with no ongoing debt.

Linda on the other hand thinks a credit card might be a better idea. She'll just pay it back when she gets home, she reflects.

Linda applies for a $5,200 credit card that has an interest rate of 13.99 per cent and accesses it throughout her time overseas. She's having a blast so takes it right up to its credit limit. By the time she returns home, she has a debt of $5,200.

Linda now has to pay that card off. She makes only the minimum monthly repayment of $156. At this rate, Linda will take three years and seven months to pay off her credit card, incurring interest of $1,422.27.

In total, Linda's trip costs her $6,622.27, and instead of just a year of saving, she has to pay it off for more than three years.

So what if Linda channelled $100 a week into that card, in a similar way to how Lucy saved prior to departing?

Well, in that case, it would still take Linda 14 months to pay off the debt, and Linda would have paid $433.33 in interest, meaning it cost her $5,634.27.

But of course the plot thickens ...

The trouble is, once you have a credit card, you tend to use it. The likelihood for Linda is that although she might channel money back into the card, she's probably going to be tempted to use it for further expenses here and there.

That means Linda's initial travel credit card could potentially take far longer than 14 months or even three years to pay off. In the process she has an ongoing debt that affects her chances of saving for other important goals.

It also affects the amount of money Linda will be able to borrow in the future. (We'll explain more on this later.)

The bottom line? Saving is far more effective than spending credit that you have to repay. Saving, no matter your income, is also entirely feasible with a little planning.

PAYING FOR TERTIARY STUDY

If you choose to go on and study beyond high school at TAFE or university, it's considered an investment in your career future. As such, the government offers higher education and vocational education loans to help fund tertiary education, but it's important you understand how these impact your financial future.

When it comes to tertiary study, it's broken into two broad bands:

- Higher education (aka university)
- Vocational education (aka TAFE).

It's also interesting to note, the higher education loan scheme in Australia is pretty unique. Available since 1989, higher education loans are designed to ensure all Australian citizens can affordably access the education they deserve.

So, what are the options?

THE PRICE OF HIGHER EDUCATION

In Australia, higher education costs a lot of money, with a three-year university degree likely to set you back more than $32,000[32]. In reality, these costs can vary depending on the type of degree you decide on, the majors your elect, the length of the course and the university you go to.

Very few people can afford to foot the bill for university upfront, but they can do so if they wish. Otherwise, they are more likely to opt for a government-backed loan. This scheme was previously known as the Higher Education Contribution Scheme (HECS). These days it's known as the Higher Education Loan Program (HECS-HELP).

DEGREE FEE STRUCTURES

When you are offered a place at university, you will either be admitted into a Commonwealth supported place (CSP) or a full-fee-paying position.

COMMONWEALTH SUPPORTED PLACES

Commonwealth supported places see the government subsidise part of your study directly. These positions are available for undergraduate degrees and some post-graduate degrees at public universities and some private universities. A Commonwealth supported place means the course will be cheaper than a full-fee-paying course as the government pays part of your fees directly to the university.

As a student, you then foot the remainder of the study bill – including accommodation costs – yourself but you can also access a government-backed loan to cover some of these costs through the Higher Education Loan Program (HECS-HELP).

FULL-FEE PAYING

If you attend a private university or are embarking on postgraduate study, the likelihood is you will be offered a full-fee-paying position.

This means all costs of study are borne by the student, however you are still generally eligible to pay for this using a FEE-HELP loan.

THE HIGHER EDUCATION LOAN PROGRAM

The Higher Education Loan Program comprises four different loan types:

HECS-HELP – This is by far the most common type of loan. Most undergraduates are eligible for it, and the SBS[33] recently noted 90 per cent of those who are eligible take it up. This loan type is available to all students who are in Commonwealth supported places.

While it covers tuition fees, it does not cover accommodation, study tools like computers and laptops, or textbooks.

FEE-HELP – This loan is available to students studying at eligible institutions where a Commonwealth supported place is not available.

Again, it does not cover accommodation, laptops, computers or textbook costs.

FEE-HELP also has a lifetime loan limit (a maximum amount you can ever borrow as an individual). For most study that limit is currently $104,440 (as at 2019[34]). If you study medicine, dentistry or veterinary science, the FEE-HELP limit is $150,000.

SA-HELP – This is a loan that you can take out in addition to your HECS-HELP or FEE-HELP loan. It covers your student services amenities fee (usually around $300 per annum). This is a fee charged by your uni to provide things like child care, food services, financial and career advice.

OS-HELP – If you have been offered a Commonwealth supported place and wish to study for some of that degree overseas, you may be eligible for OS-HELP. You cannot get this loan if your actual degree or qualification will be awarded at an overseas institution, only if some of your study takes place there.

This loan is paid directly to you by your provider and can go towards things like airfares, accommodation and travel.

You can access two OS-HELP loans in your lifetime, and they cannot be accessed within the same six-month period.

VOCATIONAL EDUCATION AND TRAINING (VET) STUDENT LOANS

If you're looking to study for a diploma at TAFE, the government offers Vocational Education and Training (VET) student loans to assist with the costs of tuition.

These loans are available to eligible students completing higher level (diploma and above) VET courses, when they study with approved course providers like TAFEs.

If you're looking for more information about loans available for higher education, *The Good Universities Guide* has comprehensive resources available, which you can find at:

- gooduniversitiesguide.com.au/study-information/funding-your-education
- gooduniversitiesguide.com.au/study-information/funding-your-education/degree-costs-and-loans
- gooduniversitiesguide.com.au/study-information/funding-your-education/vet-costs-and-loans
- gooduniversitiesguide.com.au/study-information/funding-your-education/scholarships-and-financial-assistance.

PAYING BACK YOUR STUDENT LOANS

Whether you have a HELP-FEE loan or a VET student loan, the deal is you will be required to pay this money back once you start working and earn above a certain amount. And the more you earn, the more you repay.

The repayments are calculated as part of your annual tax return but are generally taken out of your salary in addition to general tax, so you need to tell your employer if you have a HELP debt or VET student loan.

In 2019/20, the threshold for when people need to start repaying their student loan is $45,881. That means that when you earn above that amount each year, you have to repay a percentage of your loan.

This repayment kicks in at one per cent for those earning $45,881 – $52,973 and increases in increments up to 10 per cent based on your wage bracket.

2019–2020 repayment threshold	Repayment % rate
Below $45,881	Nil
$45,881 – $52,973	1.0%
$52,974 – $56,151	2.0%
$56,152 – $59,521	2.5%
$59,522 – $63,092	3.0%
$63,093 – $66,877	3.5%

2019–2020 repayment threshold	Repayment % rate
$66,878 – $70,890	4.0%
$70,891 – $75,144	4.5%
$75,145 – $79,652	5.0%
$79,653 – $84,432	5.5%
$84,433 – $89,498	6.0%
$89,499 – $94,868	6.5%
$94,869 – $100,560	7.0%
$100,561 – $106,593	7.5%
$106,594 – $112,989	8.0%
$112,990 – $119,769	8.5%
$119,770 – $126,955	9.0%
$126,956 – $134,572	9.5%
$134,573 and above	10.0%

Source: studyassist.gov.au/paying-back-your-loan/loan-repayment 2019

Louise's law degree

Louise studied law at university. She could not afford to pay for her tuition upfront, and her parents were not in a position to assist either.

After completing her degree, Louise started a job with a wage of $50,000 a year and had a $32,000 HELP debt.

Therefore, in the 2019/20 financial year, Louise was required to make a compulsory repayment of $500. If she worked the full financial year, that equated to just under $10 per week.

It's important to understand that the government has the power to change these thresholds, and although they do not incur interest, they are indexed to reflect rises in the consumer price index.

VOLUNTARY PAYMENTS

In addition to making compulsory payments, you can also voluntarily contribute to your debt to pay it off faster.

Voluntary payments can be made directly by you in lump sums or small amounts, or also through something called salary packaging (salary sacrificing). This is where you arrange with your employer to pay off extra money on your HELP debt each time you are paid your wage.

Either way, voluntary repayments may not reduce the compulsory payments you have to make, but they can help you get rid of that HELP debt faster.

The ABC has an awesome guide to paying back your higher education debts, here: abc.net.au/life/paying-back-your-help-hecs-student-debt-explainer/10982072. (Just bear in mind at the time it was written the repayment threshold was significantly higher.)

YOUTH ALLOWANCE

In addition to receiving help paying for your study, you may also be eligible to receive payments from the government to cover some of your living expenses, depending on your family's financial circumstances and your employment.

Known as Youth Allowance[35], this is a fortnightly government payment that you receive through Centrelink, which is available to those who are:

- 18 to 24 and studying full-time
- 16 to 24 and doing a full-time Australian apprenticeship
- 16 to 17 and independent or needing to live away from home to study
- 16 to 17, studying full-time and have completed Year 12 or equivalent.

Depending on your circumstances, the maximum current allowance[36] that those studying or in an apprenticeship can receive is:

- $299.80 for those who are between 18 and 24, single, have no children and live at their parent's home
- $455.20 for those who are between 18 and 24, need to live away from home, are single and have no children.

The payment is income and assets tested, meaning the government will need you to fill in a form indicating how much you earn and what type of assets you have (property, shares, etc.).

This will determine if you are eligible for Youth Allowance and how much you can be paid. If you're a dependent (you still live at home), your parents' financial position will need to be assessed.

When you receive Youth Allowance, you also have an obligation to tell Centrelink if your circumstances change, for example, or you earn some or more money, or if your study load alters.

It's important you keep Centrelink abreast of any changes, as you will be left with a debt if they pay you too much.

You can learn more about your eligibility for Youth Allowance as a student or apprentice at: humanservices.gov.au. Scroll down and click on the 'Students and Trainees' link. Look under Payments – Youth Allowance.

> ## It is never too late to be what you might have been.
> George Eliot

3

YOUR CREDIT RECORD

The moment you start applying for loans and credit cards, this information is compiled into something called your credit record.

This information is the tool that all lenders use to see whether you are reliable at repaying debt and whether you are a 'safe bet' to lend money to.

You'd be surprised at what can potentially pop up on your credit record. It's also an asset that you should consistently work hard to protect.

Pennies that should drop in Chapter 3 . . .

We cannot stress enough how important your credit record is, which is why it's got a whole chapter all to itself.

In this chapter, we'll cover:

- What a credit record is
- What a credit rating is
- How they're used by lenders and why they're important
- How to avoid common mistakes that negatively affect your record and rating
- Less obvious things to watch out for that may impact your record and rating
- Ways to make your credit record healthier.

By the end of Chapter 3, we're aiming to see you armed with all the tools you need to ensure a squeaky clean credit record that allows you to achieve what you want in life.

Righto, let's dive in and start with the basics.

> *Exceptional people convert life's setbacks into future successes.*
> Carol S. Dweck

WHAT IS A CREDIT RECORD?

A credit record is a dossier that contains information about all the loans you've ever had, when you repaid them, how reliable you were at repaying and whether you've ever been bankrupt (declared by law as unable to pay your debts).

It's a really important record that affects your ability to borrow from banks and lending institutions throughout life, and keeping it in tip-top shape is critical.

YOUR CREDIT REPORT INCLUDES THE FOLLOWING INFORMATION:

Personal details – Your name, date of birth, current and past addresses, employment and driver's licence number.

Credit applications – Any credit that you have applied for (successfully or unsuccessfully) as well as any loans that you have been a guarantor on.

Credit cards – Information about the current credit cards you have, including the amount outstanding and the total balance.

Credit liability information – Information of each credit product you have held in the past two years, including the type of credit product (car loan, personal loan, home loan, store credit card) the credit limit on the product and opening and/or closing dates of the account. The identity of the credit provider is also included.

Your repayment history (this one's important) – Your credit report contains detailed information about when your credit payments were due, and whether or not you made the payments in full by the due date. It also includes the dates you made any missed payments. Missed payments are classified as repayments that were not made within 14 days of the due date. This information relates to all credit products held in the last two years.

Defaults and other credit infringements – These could be utility bills (like your phone bill or electricity bill) or other loan payments that are 60 days or more overdue and where debt collection activity has started.

Joint applicant – A joint applicant's name will appear if you applied for the credit with another person and both your names appear on the credit card contract.

Debt agreements – Any bankruptcies, court judgements, debt agreements or personal insolvency agreements in your name.

Commercial credit applications – Any commercial or business loans you have applied for since March 2014.

Report requests – A list of which credit providers have requested copies of your credit report.

You can see an example of what a credit report looks like at this address: moneysmart.gov.au/media/499937/credit-report-sample.pdf.

WHY IS IT IMPORTANT?

Your credit report creates a complete picture of what sort of debts you have had in the past, what you currently have outstanding and how reliable you are at repaying them.

It's basically a written history of how good you are at managing your financial obligations to others, including banks and utility providers.

Lending institutions then use this information to assess whether they're willing to take a risk on you by lending you money.

That means it's vital to keep your credit report looking good. It's also important to note there are small things that can come back to bite you later in your report, such as late or missed payments on your phone bill.

DEFAULTS

One of the key things lenders check your credit report for is a default. This is when you fail to make a repayment on a debt when you should, and it includes failure to pay electricity bills, phone bills, credit card minimum amounts and more.

The organisation you owe money to must tell you they intend to list a default on your credit rating, and they can do so verbally or in writing.

The Office of Australian Information Commissioner (OAIC)[37] explains a credit provider may only report a default if:

- The default amount is $150 or more
- You're a 'confirmed missing debtor' or 'clearout', which means your creditor can't contact you, or
- 60 days or more have passed since the due date for payment, and
- The creditor has asked you to pay the debt either in person (for example by phone call) or in writing (sending a written notice to your last known address).

Defaults remain on your credit report for five years. If you're considered a confirmed missing debtor or clearout, that period is seven years.

Meanwhile, if you make repayments on the overdue amount, that will also appear on your report. Once a default is listed on your credit report it remains there for five years from the listing date, even if you pay the debt in full. Once paid in full it is updated to 'paid' but not removed until five years from the initial listing.

If a default is put on your credit file in error then fight hard to have it removed. The company who put the default on your credit file is the only party that can request to have it removed. In the event this happens, contact the company who listed the default to have them remove it.

Why is this so important? The bottom line is it doesn't look good on your lending history and a bank or lending institution may knock you back in the future when you go to apply for a loan.

More information about what's included on your credit report can be found here: oaic.gov.au/privacy/credit-reporting/repayment-history-and-defaults.

You can find out more about obtaining a copy of your report here: oaic.gov.au/privacy/credit-reporting/access-your-credit-report.

SHOPPING AROUND

It's important to remember that every time you apply for credit, it is listed on your report, and for lenders this can paint a telling picture about a borrower's attitude to debt.

If they see you have made a number of credit applications with a lot of different providers in a short time, they're likely to take a dim view of lending to you further as it may indicate you're in financial distress.

REJECTIONS

If you are denied credit by a lending institution, it's imperative you understand why before applying for credit again or elsewhere.

As all credit inquiries are listed on your report along with information about whether an account is open or closed, a series of rejections will affect your ability to obtain a loan.

HOW YOU CAN ACCESS YOUR CREDIT REPORT

Before you apply for any loan, it's a good idea to know exactly what a lender or credit provider will see on your credit report.

This gives you the chance to remedy any problematic behaviour or fix any mistakes, because believe it or not, mistakes do occur.

By law, you are entitled to receive one free copy of your credit report each year, and there are three major agencies in Australia that look after credit reporting:

- Equifax.com.au
  PO Box 966, North Sydney, NSW 2059
  Ph: 13 83 32

- CheckYourCredit.com.au (Illion, formerly Dun and Bradstreet)
  PO Box 7405, St Kilda Rd, Melbourne, VIC 3004
  Ph: 1300 734 806

- Experian Credit Report
GPO Box 1969, North Sydney, NSW 2060
Ph: 1300 783 684

You may have a report with more than one agency, so if you're looking to really understand what is known about your history, you should check with all three of the above.

When you access your report, ensure the information about you is correct, that all credit and account closures have been taken into account, and that the inquiries and listings on the report were actually made by you.

In addition to giving you an insight into how good you look to lenders, checking your report regularly also protects you against fraud.

You can also learn more about obtaining a copy of your report here: oaic.gov.au/privacy/credit-reporting/access-your-credit-report.

QUICK RECAP – WHAT LOOKS BAD ON YOUR CREDIT REPORT

- **Submitting multiple applications (aka shopping around)** – A number of credit applications with a series of lenders in a short period of time
- **Poor repayment history** – Failure to pay bills and loan repayments on time
- **Defaults** – Repayments that are overdue by 60 days or more and have a value above $150
- **Rejections** – One rejection might be easy to explain, but a series of rejections or continuing to apply for credit after you have been rejected is a red flag for lenders.

Figure 4 – What your credit report includes

EQUIFAX

Equifax Apply

Report for:		Data level:	Comprehensive
		Date generated:	12 Jan 2017 - 15:30
Age of file:		Transaction ID:	
Permission type:	Consumer report + Commercial report	Charge Back No.:	

Table of Contents

Summary	Insolvencies & court actions
Identity details	Accounts & repayments
Credit enquiries	Business relationships

Summary

Scores

Comprehensive Score

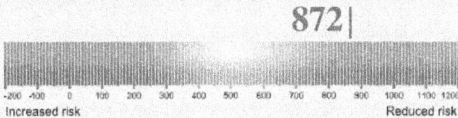

872|

| -200 | -100 | 0 | 100 | 200 | 300 | 400 | 500 | 600 | 700 | 800 | 900 | 1000 | 1100 | 1200 |

Increased risk — Reduced risk

<1 % chance of adverse recorded at Equifax in the next 12 months

Score key contributing factors

✓✓ **Lack of Consumer Adverse Information**
Having no consumer adverse information can have an impact on risk.

✓ **Account Repayment History**
Repayment history information can have an impact on risk.

✓ **Current Consumer Credit Application Information**
The type and amount of credit being applied for can have an impact on risk.

✗ **Historical Consumer Credit Application Information**
The type and frequency of historical credit applications can be an indicator of risk.

Score (Negative data only): 773   **VedaScore 1.1:** 692

About the score
Bureau scores use available Equifax bureau data to calculate a risk estimate. The primary purpose of this score is to predict the likelihood of a future adverse event being recorded on the individual's Equifax bureau records in the next 12 months.

Disclaimer
The score is a statistical rank ordering tool only and as such should always be used in conjunction with your organisation's credit policies and procedures and other relevant information you may have about the individual, company or business. The score should not be and is not intended to be the sole basis for making a decision about whether or not to deal with a particular individual, company or business.

Headlines

Adverse on file	No	Worst RHI status last 24m	0
Credit enquiries	8	Insolvencies & Actions	0
Accounts	1	Business relationships	0
Defaults	0	Disq. directorships	0
Total limit	$45,000		

Credit enquiries & defaults   No. of enquiries: 8   No. of defaults: 0

	Consumer			Commercial	
Time since last enquiry	0 month			7 months	
	Number	Total		Number	Total
Enquiries in the last 3 months	1	$10,000		0	-
Enquiries in the last 5 years	6	$378,100		2	$200
Defaults	0	-		0	-

Personal insolvencies & court actions   No. of actions: 0

Personal insolvency	0
Default judgement	0
Other court actions	0

YOUR CREDIT RATING

While a credit report is a written history, your credit rating is a numerical figure that represents how creditworthy you currently are.

This figure takes into account the information on your credit report and compiles it into a figure so banks can quickly determine how good you look on paper.

What it looks like

Also known as a credit score, a credit rating is a figure calculated by a credit reporting agency based on information available on your credit report.

Some reporting agencies use a figure between 0 and 1,000, while others calculate up to 1,200, but in all cases it works on a five-point scale, and your position on this scale helps lenders determine how risky it is to offer you a loan.

The five-point scale

The five-point scale ranges from below average to excellent:

- **Excellent** – You are highly unlikely to have any adverse events harming your credit score in the next 12 months
- **Very good** – You are unlikely to have an adverse event in the next 12 months
- **Good** – You are less likely to experience an adverse event on your credit report in the next year
- **Average** – You are likely to experience an adverse event in the next year
- **Below average** – You are more likely to have an adverse event being listed on your credit report in the next year.

What's taken into account

Your credit score takes a whole host of factors into account, including the amount of credit you have borrowed, the types of credit facilities you have used (banks, store cards, etc.), the number of credit applications you have made, any unpaid or overdue loans, and debt agreements or personal insolvency agreements relating to bankruptcy.

In addition, a suite of changes also came into effect in 2018, with banks required to add further information.

This new information includes the types of credit products you have had over the past two years, your usual payment amount and whether you made repayments by the due date.

Accessing your score

You can access your credit rating for free from the reporting agencies listed previously, and it's a good idea that you do, particularly if you're considering applying for a loan in the near future.

Credit ratings can vary from one company to another depending on the information the credit reporting agency has about you, so it's also worth considering accessing the score from more than one company.

It's dynamic

Your credit rating is dynamic, meaning it changes over time, and is affected by factors like:

- Applying for a new loan or credit card
- A listing on your credit report expiring
- A change to your credit limit on an existing loan or credit account
- New information from a creditor
- Closing a loan or credit card account
- Late repayments.

HOW DO YOU MAKE YOUR CREDIT REPORT AND RATING LOOK GOOD?

If your credit report and rating is in need of a little TLC, look to your general financial habits. Simple acts that can improve your rating include:

- Making repayments on time
- Paying your credit card off in full each month
- Reducing the limit on your cards
- Limiting the number of credit inquiries you make.

WHAT TO AVOID WHEN IT COMES TO YOUR CREDIT RECORD AND RATING

In addition to embracing the good financial habits listed above, there are a couple of key things you should also keep in mind to help create a good-looking credit report and rating.

Pay your rent on time – If you are renting accommodation make sure you pay on time. Rental defaults of 60 days or more can be listed on your credit report. We'll also come back to rental history later, because these days a good rental history can also help when it comes time to apply for a mortgage

Watch your phone bill – The latest iPhone and a big-data phone plan might be really appealing, but when you sign up for a plan be sure you can pay it now and in the future. Phone bill defaults also appear on your credit rating, while big monthly repayments can limit the amount you can borrow. And just a quick word to the wise, phone and internet providers are one of the most common defaults seen on credit reports!

Credit cards – Credit cards can quickly become a financial liability, and often lenders look not only at the amount you have outstanding and your repayment habits, but also the credit limit you have on that card.

The credit limit is the total amount that you could access if you wanted to. They check this to understand what your debts would be in the worst-case scenario that you 'max your card out'.

The key takeaway is, if you must have a credit card, limit it to one card only, be sure you repay the minimum amount required by the due date each month, and where possible try to repay the entire amount outstanding each month.

Also seek to have a small credit limit on that card, even if a credit card provider offers you more.

INTEREST-FREE PRODUCT OFFERS

These days a lot of stores will offer interest-free purchases. Furniture stores and electronics retailers commonly offer interest-free deals, but a lot of other places do to.

The principle behind this offer is that you pay nothing for the product when you 'buy it', then you pay it off in installments with no interest over a set period. This period is usually six months, 12 months or two years.

On the surface this might sound amazing, but it actually comes with some serious catches that could get you into a whole lot of trouble in a host of different ways.

When you buy an interest-free product, the product is actually 'purchased' by a credit provider. Often this provider also issues you with a credit card too.

Each month you are required to make a minimum payment, but often that payment is not enough to actually fully pay the product off in the interest-free period.

At the end of the interest-free period you then have an amount outstanding that incurs interest, and it's likely to be a lot higher than the interest rate a bank credit card or loan would have.

For example, some come with an interest rate of 22.74 per cent compared to a bank credit card rate of 13.99 per cent.

If you have made additional non-interest free purchases on the card, they will incur interest too, and cash advances might be even higher.

Meanwhile, this interest-free credit is counted on your credit report, and the upper limit of your card is also factored in.

People often find they make an interest-free purchase that takes years to pay off, and in the interim they pay far more than what it would have cost them to buy the product outright.

The key takeaway here is that if you opt for an interest-free product, you must understand the risks.

If you're paying in instalments, calculate the amount you need to pay each month (beyond their minimum repayments) so you can completely pay off the product before the interest-free period expires. Do everything in your power to pay the full product off before this date.

Be aware that with some products there are terms and conditions that mean you cannot make additional repayments above and beyond the minimum amount. That means at the end of the interest-free period you will definitely be left with a balance that incurs interest. Set money aside to pay off this balance as quickly as possible.

Also, be aware the purchase and associated card are considered credit, and they will be listed on your credit report. You should also seek to minimise any limit on the associated card so it does not affect your borrowing power.

Resist the urge to make additional purchases using this card. The interest rates can quickly make any purchase very, very expensive.

More information about interest-free offers is available here: moneysmart. gov.au/other-ways-to-borrow/interest-free-deals.

BUY NOW, PAY LATER – AFTERPAY, OPENPAY, ZIPMONEY AND ZIPPAY

In recent times, a range of new payment options have become increasingly popular in the retail sphere. Known as 'buy now, pay later', they include products like Afterpay, zippay, zipMoney, and Openpay.

Available for purchases both small and large, these options allow shoppers to buy an item that they may not be able to afford upfront, but again, it's important to understand, they can affect your credit report.

When you opt to use these services, some may check your credit report, and should you fail to make a required repayment, they will disclose this to the relevant credit reporting agencies.

At present, these payment methods are under review by regulators, but as a general rule, if you can't afford a product outright, save until you can rather than relying on credit.

Remember, it's the small things that add up to create the complete financial picture of your credit report, and buy now, pay later might illustrate that your shopping habits are impulsive rather than based on a clear savings plan and living within your means.

Meanwhile, the monthly, weekly or fortnightly repayments these require are another expense that will be added to your general expenditure, and if you're considering applying for a loan such as a mortgage, buy now, pay later repayments are considered a liability that can drastically affect your borrowing capacity.

More information about credit reports and scores is available here: moneysmart.gov.au/managing-debt/credit-scores-and-credit-reports.

4

MAJOR PURCHASES

It could be a car, the latest and greatest mountain bike, a top-of-the-line laptop or a travel adventure around the world, but every now and then there will be some major expenses that you will need to cover as part of the exciting journey of life.

It's how you cover them and also how you protect these investments that could potentially set you up for financial success or stress.

Pennies that should drop in Chapter 4 . . .

This chapter is all about helping you make major purchases while understanding the costs involved. It's designed to give you an educated choice when it comes to funding big-ticket items like cars and mobile phones.

We're going to look at:

- Cars and the options to fund them
- Ongoing expenses associated with cars (spoiler alert, there are a few)
- The value of car insurance and the different types of coverage
- Mobile phones, including how to buy them and additional costs involved.

By the end of Chapter 4, you should have a clear perspective of how big-ticket items can be paid for and what extra costs you might incur. You'll also be given options to help you decide which method might work best for you.

So let's start with buying a car, because that's likely to be one of the largest early purchases you will make. When it comes to money, it's got all the ingredients that come with important financial decision-making.

> **There are no shortcuts to any place worth going.**
> Beverly Sills

BUYING A CAR

Getting your licence and buying your first vehicle is almost a rite of passage. It's as much a symbol of embracing adulthood as it is an important step in the journey of life, but as you take that step there are important financial decisions that need to be made.

Some people might be lucky enough to have their parents or relatives purchase their first car for them, but for many, buying a car will be something they save for, contribute to or fund through a loan.

So, let's start at the beginning.

WHAT TYPE OF CAR?

One of the first decisions you'll need to make is whether you opt for a new car or a used one, and for most people that comes down purely to budget.

Even the most affordable new cars cost tens of thousands of dollars, while used cars can be far more budget friendly. If you're in a position to be deciding between the two, it's worth weighing up the following . . .

NEW CARS

Yep, there's nothing like leaving the showroom in a brand-new, shiny car, but bear in mind the moment you drive out of that parking lot, your car is already decreasing in value. CommBank[38] notes new cars can depreciate by up to 20 per cent by the time you leave the dealership.

That said, there are some serious advantages to owning a new vehicle. They often come with security, like after-sales service and warranties, which can cut your ongoing costs.

They're also likely to be far less prone to mechanical problems, making them more reliable in the immediate term.

It also pays to do your homework, even when purchasing a new vehicle. Look for a brand and model with a good reputation, and be aware of ongoing costs, like registration and insurance. These can vary depending on things like the number of cylinders the engine has, and whether the car might be prone to theft.

Some great sites for information about vehicles, their reliability, performance and safety features include:

- The Australian New Car Assessment Program (ANCAP) – ancap.com.au
- Choice (consumer advocates) – www.choice.com.au/transport/cars
- NRMA – h.racq.com.au/Living/Articles/Australias-Best-Cars-2019-revealed
- RedBook – redbook.com.au
- Carsales – carsales.com.au.

CommBank also suggests asking the following questions of the dealer:

- What are the standard features?
- What are the on-road costs?
- How long is the warranty and is there capped price on servicing?
- Are there any promotional deals on?

USED CARS

The reality is, the car that most young drivers first purchase is likely to be a used model, and if you're buying a used car there are a few things you should know.

When you buy a used car, you are not privy to that vehicle's complete history. You won't necessarily know how it's been driven, who has driven it or how well it's been maintained, but you can do a little detective work to help you get a bit of an idea.

Whether you're looking to buy from a used car dealer or by private sale, always ask the following questions:

- How many owners has the vehicle had?
- Is the service history and log book available?
- Has the car ever been in an accident?
- How many kilometres has it done? (You can also check this on the speedo.)

- Can I take it for a test drive? (The answer to this question should be yes, and when you do, have someone experienced with you who might be able to identify potential problems.)
- Can I get it mechanically inspected?
- Is the car debt-free? (This is important, and we'll come back to it in just a tick.)

After asking these questions, you can also complete some checks to verify the information provided.

These include:

- Having the car mechanically inspected by a trusted mechanic or your state's motoring authority (NRMA, RACQ, RACV, etc.)
- Conducting a Personal Property Securities Register check (also known as a REVs check) to ensure the vehicle does not have debt attached to it – You can do that here: ppsr.gov.au
- Conducting a full check to ensure the car has not previously been written off, water-affected or stolen – You can do that here: revscheck.com.au.

OK, so back to that bit about asking whether a car is debt-free. This is important. If the car you purchase has a debt outstanding on it, you (the new owner) become liable for that debt and all outstanding repayments. Ultimately you could be at risk of losing the car if you cannot make these repayments.

A dealer has a legal responsibility to tell you if a car has finance outstanding, but a private seller may not be so accommodating. That's why you need to check either ppsr.gov.au or revs.com.au to be totally sure.

In the interim, Choice also has a great guide for buying a used car, here: choice.com.au/transport/cars/used/buying-guides/cars.

SAVINGS OR LOAN?

One of the biggest questions you need to consider when buying your first car is how exactly will you fund the purchase, and there are a few options available: savings, secured personal loan, car finance.

So, let's take a quick tour through the pros and cons of each.

SAVINGS

In a perfect world, buying your car outright using your own savings is the ideal scenario. It allows you to take full ownership of the vehicle without the ongoing expense of repayments and interest.

But unless you've come into some money, it will require you to save hard to achieve your goal, and you will likely need thousands of dollars to buy a car that's roadworthy and safe.

That said, saving for a car is totally feasible, especially if you have a part-time job or have been putting a little cash aside for a long time.

Our top tips?

1. Start early – Begin saving for your car long before you get your licence. This allows you to build cash over time. Imagine if you'd started saving at 15 for the car you buy at 17, putting aside just $50 a week. That's going to give you a savings of about $5,200 to put towards your car. Start at 14 and you'll have a budget of $7,800.

2. Work backwards – Set a budget for yourself for a car purchase and work backwards. $10,000 might be a good milestone to aim for, as this is going to give you a decent amount of choice when it comes to fairly new second-hand vehicles.

    Now you've got a benchmark, use calculators like the MoneySmart goals calculator to see what you need to save each week. It's available here: moneysmart.gov.au/tools-and-resources/calculators-and-apps/savings-goals-calculator

3. Add lump sums – Wherever possible add in lump sums, like birthday or Christmas money. That could see those $5,200 savings you started at 15 nudging closer to $6,000, or even higher.

4. Don't forget high interest accounts – If you let your money work for you in a high interest account or term deposit, it's going to start to build up. Say for example you put $5,000 in a term deposit for 24 months. At current average rates, you'll earn about $200 in interest[39]. (Sure, it's not a huge amount, but all you had to do was not touch it.)

5. Forgo other expenses – If you plan to save for a car, try forgoing some of those other expenses, like that top-of-the-range mobile phone. (Yeah, it's pretty snazzy at the time, but can an iPhone drive you to the beach?)

CAR LOANS AND FINANCE

The other way to purchase a car is through a personal loan with the bank or via finance offered by a finance broker or car dealership. And if you're keen for a new car or more expensive used model, these are probably the options you'll be looking at. So, what's the difference and what's the risk? (Yes, there is risk.)

PERSONAL LOANS

When it comes to personal loans there are two major types: secured and unsecured – so what exactly is the difference?

Secured loans

A secured loan is available from a lender, like a bank or credit union. It's generally used for newer cars and is called secured because the lender uses the car as security for the money you borrow.

Basically that means they can take your car and sell it to recoup their money should you be unable to make repayments. As they have the car as security, a secured car loan is usually a cheaper option than an unsecured personal loan.

The thing to remember here is that often any new car will be worth far less than you paid for it the moment you drive it away from the dealership. So even if the lender sells your car, chances are you will still be left with a sum to pay back.

Unsecured loans

An unsecured loan is a type of personal loan that's not tied to any particular item. That means this is also the type of loan you might acquire to finance a holiday, or perhaps to consolidate some debt. Unsecured loans are often the type of loan suggested for used cars.

Unsecured loans tend to command higher interest rates on repayments because the lending institution is taking a greater risk. (After all, it's not secured against something they can sell, should you be unable to pay.)

But they do offer greater flexibility and the option of borrowing more than the price of the car for extras or add-ons.

DEALER FINANCE

If you purchase your car from a dealership, they might offer you dealer finance. In this case, they connect you with a financing institution to cover the cost of your loan.

While convenient, dealer finance may not be the most affordable option. The interest rates might be higher and the loan term might be less flexible – you might have to repay it in a shorter amount of time. So it could pay to shop around in advance, and contact a reputable finance broker or your bank to see if they might have a better option.

VEHICLE LEASING

This one often tends to apply to businesses and professionals more than it does first-time car buyers, but we'll touch on it anyway just in case it crops up in the future.

Vehicle leasing allows you to rent your car for a set amount of money each week for a set term. That means you don't actually own it. At the end of the term, you give the car back and it's sold as a used vehicle.

THINGS TO CONSIDER

Loan terms – Personal loans, such as car loans, have a term (time period) attached to them, which might be anywhere between one and seven years. You need to repay the full loan within that time.

Some loans have an option for what's known as a balloon payment (also referred to as a residual payment). If you opt for this, you still make your regular payments and then pay a lump sum amount at the end of the finance term.

Balloon payments can seem attractive, as they reduce your regular repayments, however, with the lump sum payment plus interest due at the end of the loan, the total cost of the loan may be higher.

If you miss repayments or don't make even repayments, you might also be left with a lump sum that needs to be paid off.

Fixed rate versus variable – Loans can be fixed or variable. A fixed-rate loan has an interest rate that is set, while the interest rate of a variable one goes up and down in line with the market.

Fixed rates offer the benefit of knowing what your repayments will be. Variable rate loans mean the interest rate you pay over the course of the loan could fluctuate. That's good news if interest rates drop, but not so great if they rise.

We talk extensively about interest rates in the property section, so if you're looking to explore it further read on.

Your credit rating – Personal loans and dealer finance will be listed on your credit rating. Therefore, having a car loan will affect your ability to borrow further, for example if you want to buy a house. It's also critical you meet the repayments on time to keep your credit report looking good.

MoneySmart[40] has a suite of great tools available when it comes to buying a car. You can kick off at this address: moneysmart.gov.au/borrowing-and-credit/car-loans, but be sure to check out the fact sheets, buying tips and saving guides listed at the bottom of the page.

ON-ROAD COSTS

When you first buy a vehicle there are some initial costs to factor in. For example, you need to transfer the car into your name, and you may also need to renew the registration for it.

Most state motor registries charge a transfer fee and motor vehicle duty for this process. Basically the transfer fee is a small charge that covers the paperwork involved, while the motor vehicle duty is a levy on the value of the vehicle. It's usually a percentage of the vehicle's total value (as in the price you paid for it).

Many dealerships cover these costs as part of the vehicle purchase, but it pays to check, because some may not. Meanwhile, if you have bought a vehicle privately, there are fees you will need to pay, and often there's a time frame that this transfer must be completed within.

ONGOING COSTS

Regardless of whether you buy a new car or used one, there will be ongoing costs and you need to budget for these accordingly. Ongoing costs include:

Car maintenance, servicing and repairs

You will need tyres every couple of years, your vehicle should be regularly serviced, and in some states your car will need a safety check prior to registration. Meanwhile, expect the unexpected – cars can and do breakdown due to both minor and serious problems, and the cost of repairs could quickly add up. Have cash set aside for those unexpected costs.

Fuel

Unless you have an electric vehicle, fuel is an inevitable cost associated with running a car. Fuel prices fluctuate based on market conditions, while the amount you consume depends on the type of car you drive, the way you drive it and how often and how far you have to travel.

Fuel costs should be factored into your weekly budget.

Registration

Every car on Australia's roads needs to be registered, and this is likely to be one of your more significant ongoing vehicle costs.

Vehicle registration in Australia is handled through each state and territory's individual motor registry, and often they have either six-month or 12-month registration periods available. The total registration includes a series of fees, taxes and levies.

The cost of registration can also vary depending on the type of car you have or its weight. For example, in NSW the heavier the vehicle is, the more it costs to register, while in Queensland four-cylinder cars are often cheaper to register than six-cylinders or V8s.

As part of your registration, you will also be required to take out compulsory third party insurance (CTP).

This insurance is a non-negotiable and is designed to cover you should someone be injured or die in a car accident that you are responsible for. In some states you can pick your own insurer as part of the registration process. In others, the government automatically allocates you one.

To give you a quick idea of annual registration costs, in NSW it would cost $368[41] to renew the registration on a medium-sized vehicle, in addition to approximately $560 for CTP (total cost $928). In Queensland, it would cost $385.90[42] to renew the registration on a four-cylinder privately used vehicle, while CTP costs $359.20 (total cost $745.10).

Insurance

The likelihood is you will want to insure your car to protect you should an accident happen. We're about to take a deep dive into insurance, but suffice to say, it is another ongoing expense, and if you're under 25 it can be significant.

INSURING YOUR ASSET

As your mode of transport and an important possession, your car is a valuable asset. It's also a potential liability. For example, what happens if you are involved in a car accident and found responsible for injuring another person or damaging their property?

That's where car insurance is essential, and failing to have it simply isn't a risk worth taking. Car insurance is available in a series of different protection levels, so let's have a look at each.

Figure 5 – Types of car insurance

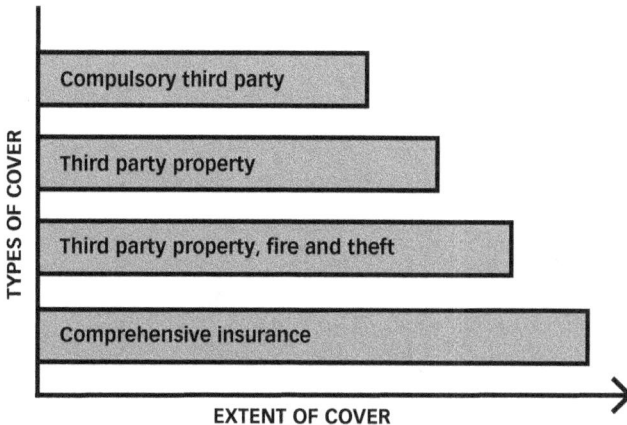

COMPULSORY THIRD PARTY

This is the type of insurance you are required to have by law, and as we mentioned it's a component of registering your vehicle. CTP insurance protects you in the event you, as the driver of that vehicle, are found responsible for an accident that results in the death or injury of someone else.

A word to the wise here . . . if your vehicle is not registered, it is not insured for CTP. That means if you have a serious accident you could be liable for the medical costs and compensation to the other party involved.

In some circumstances you can obtain interim compulsory third party insurance for an unregistered vehicle by contacting your motor registry or insurer. For example, you might do this if you have purchased an unregistered vehicle and are driving it to the mechanic for inspection.

But the bottom line is if a vehicle is not registered, and it's not covered by CTP, do not get behind the wheel!

THIRD PARTY PROPERTY

We'd argue this is the bare minimum type of car insurance that every driver should have. Third party property insurance covers you in the event you damage someone else's car or property in an accident. It does not cover damage to your own vehicle.

Some insurers also offer 'uninsured motorist extension' as part of this policy. This covers your vehicle if another driver is responsible for an accident but they're not insured.

Belle's carpark fender bender

Belle is backing out of a carpark when she runs into the car parked opposite, causing about $3,000 worth of damage to that vehicle and $2,000 to her own. Belle's third party property insurance covers her for the damage to the other vehicle. However, she has to pay a $500 excess for making the claim and is also responsible for paying for damage to her own car.

Total cost to Belle: $2,500

Costs Belle avoided: $2,500

THIRD PARTY PROPERTY, FIRE AND THEFT

Third party property, fire and theft is a slightly higher level of insurance. In this instance, you are covered for damage to another person's vehicle, and your car is covered in the event of fire or theft. That's a decent level of coverage, but it still doesn't cover you should you run into someone and damage your own car.

Steve's stolen car

Steve's $17,000 car was parked outside his house one night when it was stolen. Steve makes a claim, pays an excess, and his insurer offers a payout to the value of the vehicle.

Total cost to Steve: $500

Costs Steve avoided: $16,500

Will's total write-off

Will also has a $17,000 car, and one night he's driving home and hits a kangaroo, causing his car to roll. Fortunately Will's absolutely OK, but he's about to endure a massive financial headache. You see, with third party property, fire and theft, damage to Will's car isn't covered by insurance.

Total cost to Will: $17,000

Costs Will avoided: Zip

Could it be worse? Um, yes. What if Will had bought this car using finance? Now he still has to make repayments on a vehicle that he doesn't actually have anymore!

Total cost to Will: The value of the car ($17,000), plus interest on his loan.

Costs Will avoided: Still zip

COMPREHENSIVE INSURANCE

This is the most complete insurance you can have for your vehicle, and for younger drivers it's particularly worthwhile. Comprehensive insurance covers you for damage to another person's car or property as the result of an accident you are responsible for. It also covers damage to your vehicle along with fire and theft.

Sam's significant smash

Sam totally fails to see an oncoming car as she attempts to turn right at the traffic lights. Although everyone's OK, the accident writes off both Sam's vehicle and the other party's. (Their car happens to be a late-model Maserati, by the way, so this could potentially be a big, big financial hit.)

Fortunately, Sam happens to have comprehensive insurance, and this is about to make a huge difference to her life and financial future.

The insurer covers the costs of replacing both the Maserati ($125,000) and Sam's $10,000 Skoda.

Total cost to Sam: $500 in insurance excess

Costs Sam avoided: $135,000

So what would have happened if Sam didn't have insurance that covered the other party and herself?

Well, if you're not insured for damage to another person's vehicle, they or their insurer can potentially pursue you personally. For Sam, that might have meant spending the next 10 years paying back the other party for the loss of their Maserati. In the interim, Sam has also lost her own car to the value of $10,000.

IMPORTANT POINTS ABOUT CAR INSURANCE

The cost of car insurance can vary for a variety of reasons, including how experienced you are as a driver, whether you've been in an accident before or made an insurance claim, where your car is garaged and how many points you have against your licence.

It can also be impacted by your gender. Although that sounds sexist, the reality is young men statistically account for more accidents than young women, so chances are as a male your insurance will be slightly higher.

If you're looking to gauge what your insurance might cost, Canstar has an excellent rundown here, including a section on under-25 drivers: canstar.com.au/car-insurance/what-does-car-insurance-cost.

Meanwhile, your actions can potentially make your insurance null and void, and this is very, very important to understand because the ramifications can be dire.

So what type of things might reduce or negate your insurance coverage?

1. **Driving under the influence of alcohol or drugs** – Yep, sorry, no insurer will foot the bill for stupidity. What's more, if you're involved in an accident and found to be under the influence, you will also face court, be disqualified from driving and receive a traffic conviction.

2. **Driving an unregistered vehicle** – If your car is unregistered, your insurer is very unlikely to cover it in an accident, even if it wasn't your fault. And don't forget, if your car is unregistered it is not covered by CTP. Make sure you notify your state or territory's motor registry of any change of your mailing address or email address so that you never miss a registration renewal notice!

3. **Worn tyres** – As the driver of a vehicle it is your responsibility to ensure it remains in roadworthy condition, and that includes checking your tyres have adequate tread. If an accident is found to be caused by tyre wear, that's a claim that may not be honoured.

4. **Unroadworthy car** – On a similar note, if your car is found to be unroadworthy, any insurance claim may also be knocked back. Remember, cars should be regularly serviced, and things like brake pads, steering, shock absorbers and general condition should be regularly checked.

5. **Vehicle modifications** – A nice new spoiler or some extra horsepower might seem like a great idea at the time, but if you modify your vehicle and don't tell your insurer, their policy may not cover it.

6. **Lending your car to a friend** – You may be covered to drive your vehicle, but chances are your bestie is not. Some insurance companies are very strict about who exactly is covered under a specific policy.

7. **Driving for money** – If you intend to use your car as a rideshare service, you need to take out specific insurance. General insurance does not cover an accident that happens when you are a paid driver of a vehicle.

8. **Unlicensed** – Regardless of whether you simply forgot to renew it, lost it due to demerit points or are disqualified from driving due to a traffic conviction, if you drive your car while unlicensed, insurance will not cover you.

For more information about how your insurance could be made null and void, Canstar[43] has a great article here: canstar.com.au/car-insurance/7-ways-can-void-car-insurance.

Finder[44] also covers it here: finder.com.au/car-insurance-exclusions.

SOME SOBERING STATS

Just to drive home the point why insurance is so important, here are some very sobering statistics when it comes to young drivers and accidents:

- Drivers in their first year on the road are four times more likely to be involved in a serious or fatal accident. (Source: TAC Victoria[45])
- In 2018, people aged under 40 accounted for 46 per cent of all road fatalities. (Source: BudgetDirect[46])
- In 2018, 226 motorists aged between 17 and 25 were killed on Australia's roads. (Source: BudgetDirect[47])
- Males are more likely to be involved in a car crash that writes off the vehicle. (Source: Canstar[48])
- One in three drivers involved in a speeding incident or a crash are men aged 17–25 years. (Source: Canstar[49])
- The four major causes of accidents in 2016 were: speeding, alcohol consumption, driver fatigue and inattention/distraction while driving. (Source: BudgetDirect[50])

You can read more about car insurance at: moneysmart.gov.au/insurance/car-insurance.

Meanwhile, Canstar also covers the costs of car insurance for under-25s, along with access to quotes: canstar.com.au/car-insurance/car-insurance-under-25s.

CAR COSTS RECAPPED

Jodi's VW Golf

Jodi's pretty stoked when she picks up a bright red used Volkswagon Golf for the great price of $6,500[51] from a private seller. But has she accounted for the additional costs involved?

For a start, Jodi will need to transfer the vehicle into her name. She's a Victorian resident, so transfer will set her back $40.70[52]. Then she needs to pay the motor vehicle duty (which is a percentage of the vehicle's market value). That's another $277.20[53].

Therefore, purchasing the vehicle and simply getting it on the road in her name has actually cost Jodi $6,817.90.

Now what about those ongoing costs?

Jodi wisely decides comprehensive insurance is a great idea. That's going to cost her about $1,837[54] a year. (It will get cheaper for her once she turns 25, but for now she's in a high-risk category.) Then there's registration – that's $834.80[55] annually, including compulsory third party insurance.

So far Jodi's basic ongoing car costs per year are $2,671.80.

Now what about petrol, servicing and other costs like tyres?

According to BudgetDirect[56] in 2019, the average Australian driver spent $71.50 each week on fuel. That's $3,718 a year.

Servicing and maintenance costs are dependent on the type of vehicle and its age, but BudgetDirect notes in a two-car household they average $26.33 for regional areas and $28.24 for major cities. Jodi's in a city, and she only has one car, so let's halve those costs to $14.22 a week ($739.44).

Oh, and let's get her some roadside assistance too. After all, Jodi's only 18 and doesn't want to find herself stranded by the roadside late at night due to a flat car battery.

Jodi opts to go with the RACV and takes out the basic level coverage for $114[57] a year.

So what's her annual total?

Type of cost	Price per year
Registration	$834.80
Comprehensive insurance	$1,837
Fuel @71.50 per week	$3,718
Servicing and maintenance	$739.44
Roadside assistance	$114
Total per year	**$7,242.84**
Total per week	**$139.28**

As you can see, Jodi needs to budget $139.28 each week to keep her vehicle on the road. Of course, these costs vary depending on how much you use your car, what state it's located in, and its condition, but it gives you a great insight into just some of the commitment involved.

Those costs would also be higher if Jodi hadn't used her own money to buy a car. Otherwise she might be paying approximately an additional $35 per week ($1,820 a year) to the bank as well.

If you're looking for further information, there's a great guide to car operating costs here: budgetdirect.com.au/car-insurance/research/car-owner-cost-statistics.html.

MoneySmart also has further insight into the topic here: moneysmart.gov.au/life-events-and-you/under-25s/getting-a-car/ongoing-car-costs.

MOBILE PHONES

It's hard to imagine a world without mobile phones, but the luxury of remaining connected does come at a cost. That cost can be particularly high if only the latest model phone will do and you use your phone extensively.

So let's tap into the topic of mobile phones, including plans, terminology and costs.

TWO COMPONENTS

There are two basic costs when it comes to owning a mobile phone: the cost of the handset (the actual physical phone) and the cost of using it (making phone calls, texting, using mobile data).

Each of these costs can be covered by a plan or paid for upfront.

OK, let's investigate . . .

THE HANDSET

Ranging in price from $39 for a cheap basic model to thousands of dollars for a top-of-the-line iPhone or Samsung, mobile phone handsets are pretty much a mainstay of modern life. And there are a few ways you can buy them.

You can purchase them upfront using savings, you can buy them interest-free, or you can purchase them as part of a contract that also includes your phone calls and texts in one monthly bill.

The savings option is pretty straightforward, so let's skip ahead to interest-free and plans.

INTEREST-FREE

Many retailers allow you to buy your phone as part of an interest-free payment plan. We touched on interest-free purchasing earlier, but suffice to say it may not be the most affordable option in the long run, and it can put you at risk.

When you buy a phone interest-free, you are effectively taking out a loan with a credit provider. That means buying your phone goes on your credit record.

In addition, many interest-free credit providers also happily provide you with a credit card as part of your account. This puts you in jeopardy of spending money you don't have, often incurring a very high interest rate in the process.

Meanwhile, although these loans are called interest-free, the interest-free term has a time period attached to it (such as 12 months). If you do not make payments above and beyond the minimum monthly repayment, chances are you won't pay off the full amount within the interest-free period and you will then be subject to high interest.

Isla's not-so-interest-free iPhone

Isla simply has to have an iPhone 11 Pro Max – there's no talking her out of it. So off she goes to the local electronics retailer, who invites her to buy it interest-free for $1,899.

Isla fills out some paperwork and is instantly approved for interest-free credit. (That inquiry and the credit is now on her credit record, by the way.) Oh, and there's an establishment cost of $25, and a monthly fee of $5.95, so Isla's actually just signed up for almost $2,000 of debt.

Still, Isla's thrilled! Each month the credit provider asks her to repay just $90, and that's what Isla pays. But there's a problem here. At the end of 12 months, Isla's interest-free payments add up to just $1,080. So she still has $920 outstanding on the account, and the interest-free period is coming to an end.

The credit provider doesn't mind because they're about to start charging Isla an interest rate of 22.74 per cent. If Isla continues paying only $90 per month, it will now take her more than another year to pay off the balance, which will actually be about $1,011 (not $920) due to interest.

How could Isla have done it differently?

Interest-free really only works to your advantage if you pay above and beyond what your credit provider asks you to.

In Isla's case, in order to avoid incurring interest, she needed to make payments of $166.37 each month (not $90). Then she would have paid off her entire phone within the interest-free period.

MOBILE PHONE CONTRACTS

When you buy a mobile phone as part of a plan, you effectively sign up to pay for the phone in addition to phone calls, texts and data over a period of time.

That may sound convenient but convenience also comes at a cost. Although the price of the handset will be pretty much market value, you have to lock yourself into a contract for a number of months to pay for it.

What that means is that each bill you have to pay a portion towards the cost of the phone and a portion towards its usage.

You don't own that phone outright until you have met all those repayments, and if you lose or break that phone you are still liable for repayments. In the interim, the latest model is likely to be superceded. So by the time you actually own your phone it's probably a few years old.

Casey's contract

Casey is also keen on the latest iPhone, and right about now there's a contract available with a reputable phone company.

They're offering a 36-month contract that includes both the handset and the usage. The handset component of that plan alone is $52.75 a month (36 x 52.75 = $1,899) – that's the same price Isla found her phone for.

Then Casey needs to indicate the way she'll use it and select a plan. She opts for the cheapest option – a basic 15GB plan that includes unlimited standard national calls and texts. That adds another $50 to her monthly bill. Now Casey has a contract and plan that will cost her $102.75 per month.

In total, over 36 months, Casey's contract and plan will cost a minimum of $3,699[58], which could also change if the usage charges increase, and they can without much notice.

A year later, Casey's phone is stolen. Now, if Casey does nothing, she will still need to pay for the phone despite the fact she doesn't have it.

Alternatively, she could break the contract[59], but that's going to mean she still has to repay the outstanding handset charges of $1,266 and the phone provider might want that as a lump sum.

USAGE PLANS AND PREPAID SIMS

So what if you have a handset but need to connect to a network? Again, there are different options available. You can pay upfront via a prepaid SIM and recharge it by adding credit, or you can enter into a phone plan.

PREPAID SIMS AND RECHARGES

Basically, a prepaid SIM is effectively designed to allow you to pay for your calls, texts and data in advance. You physically buy the SIM and insert it into your device, and there's also the option of recharging it, which allows you to add credit to your account while still retaining your number.

Most big networks currently offer prepaid SIMs in various values, and often you have the option of recharging (topping them up) online, via an app or with a simple phone call.

The advantage of prepaid SIMs is that you never receive a bill. The catch is that data, calls and texts are a little more expensive, and you can run out of credit when you need it.

PREPAID PLANS

A prepaid plan sees you billed for your anticipated use of a phone each month in advance. If you exceed your expected usage, you are billed extra charges. If you do not use what you are entitled to, you are still billed the basic amount.

These plans are also available in increments.

So think back to Casey . . . In addition to her handset contract, she entered into a phone plan that entitled her to unlimited national calls and texts, along with 15GB of data. That cost her $50 a month in advance.

One month Casey was so busy streaming Netflix she went over her data limit. That cost her $10 extra that month.

If Casey consistently found she was going over her data limit, she might be better off opting for a more expensive plan that gave her 60GB rather than 15GB per month for $10 extra.

A WORD TO THE WISE ABOUT MOBILE PHONES

The cost of mobile phones can quickly add up, especially if you opt to take out a contract on the handset. Meanwhile, it's important to pay your bills on time. An unpaid bill can be listed on your credit report as a default if a payment of $150 or more is overdue by 60 days or more. This record will have a negative impact on your credit score.

Our top tips:

- Read your contract or plan carefully.
- Know the length of a contract and the costs involved, including any exit fees.
- Consider how you will use your phone, then use it wisely.
- Avoid interest-free handset purchases where you can, and only enter into them if you are prepared to make more than the minimum repayment.
- If you don't understand something your phone provider says, ask them.
- Know your excess fees. If you go above and beyond your intended usage on a phone plan, costs can quickly accumulate.
- Pay your bills on time.
- Only enter into a contract or plan that you are absolutely sure you can afford now and into the future.

More information about mobile phone deals and plans, including the questions you should ask, is available at: moneysmart.gov.au/life-events-and-you/under-25s/mobile-phone-deals-and-plans.

Given the ramifications of damage, theft or loss of your device, you may also consider insuring it. MoneySmart provide these helpful tips on mobile phone,

tablet and laptop insurance: moneysmart.gov.au/mobile-phone-tablet-and-laptop-insurance.

If you run into issues with high or disputed charges on your mobile phone, you can contact the Telecommunications Industry Ombudsman for help: tio.com.au/help/billing-and-payments/high-and-disputed-charges.

PROPERTY

From the moment you leave home, ensuring you have a roof over your head and a secure place to stay is one of the major responsibilities of adulthood.

For many, the first experience of property comes as a renter in share accommodation or university housing, then it might progress to property ownership as you embark on a career.

Regardless of whether you rent or own, property is a fascinating topic that will command a large proportion of all the income that you earn throughout your life.

Pennies that should drop in Chapter 5 . . .

Strap yourselves in because this is a hefty chapter for a weighty subject, and we're holding nothing back when it comes to all things property.

In this section, we're covering some major ground, including:

- Renting – how to rent a property, what's expected of a tenant and your rights as a tenant
- Different types of rental situations and the rules, rewards and liabilities that come with each
- Buying a property, looking at everything from the process to the finances and the legals
- Mortgages – how to obtain them, how they work, the role of interest rates, and different payment structures
- Types of property purchases (investor, owner-occupied) and what to look for in each
- Being a landlord
- Capital gains tax.

By the end of Chapter 5, you should have a firm grasp on the property market and how it works from almost all angles. You should also be clearer on how you can go about renting or buying a property and the financial obligations involved.

We're covering this topic extensively, because in Australia, the property market is almost a pastime. It's consistently talked about in the media, and many people aspire to the great Australian dream of owning their own home and perhaps a few investments on the side.

But before you get to the endpoint of a home you own outright, there's a big journey to consider along the way.

So, saddle up and let's take a ride through the ins and outs of home ownership, mortgages, renting and all things property related.

RENTING

Chances are, the first encounter you will have with the property market is as a renter. That might be through student accommodation or perhaps a share house. But there's a further chance at some point later in life that you will rent other properties as part of a lifelong relationship with the property market.

Renting a property comes with a number of responsibilities. And just as you should try to keep your credit history clean, you should also try to maintain a stellar rental history to ensure you're the type of tenant people want to have looking after their property.

RENTING A PROPERTY

Whether you are renting student accommodation, a share house or a luxury home, when you rent a property there is certain information that will be required at the outset and responsibilities that you need to meet once a property is entrusted to you.

When you apply to rent a property, a landlord or property manager will look to ensure you can afford to pay for the property you seek to live in, that you are an upstanding citizen who will look after that home, and that you've done the right thing in the past.

THE RENTAL PROCESS

When you go to rent a property, the process generally goes like this:

- The property is advertised for rent, with scheduled inspection times noted.
- You attend the inspection. If the property piques your interest, you fill out a rental application form.
- The person who has the best history and the proven ability to pay for that property will be offered a lease (a legal agreement) for a set period of time (usually six or 12 months).
- The lease will contain set conditions, such as the date when the lease starts and ends, who is renting the property and how much they are to pay each week.

- Once the lease is signed and the rental period begins, the renter is given keys to the property and it becomes the home in which they live.
- During the lease period they have the responsibility to keep the property in a respectable condition, pay the rent on time, meet any additional lease conditions and report any maintenance issues at the property. They will also need to have regular inspections (usually every three months) to ensure the property is being properly looked after.

Figure 6 – The rental process

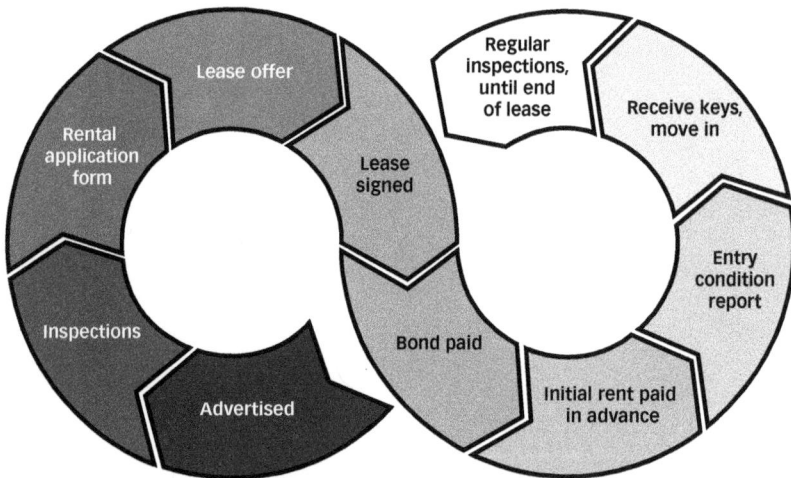

RENTAL APPLICATIONS

A rental application is a document that you fill out to indicate your interest in leasing a property. This document will ask for information about who you are, where you work, how much you earn and who you intend to live with at the property. It will also seek to understand your history and how reliable you are going to be as a tenant.

You will be asked to provide proof of your identity through the 100-point ID check, and the information you provide will be cross-checked.

WHAT MAKES A GOOD TENANT

When you rent a property, the landlord or property manager is generally looking for four things: proof that you can afford the property, stability, history and good character.

PROOF YOU CAN AFFORD THE PROPERTY

This is essentially proof of income, and it involves checking that you are employed where you say you are on the application, that you earn what you claim you do and that you will not suffer financial hardship if you take out a lease for a property.

To make sure of this, a property manager or landlord will usually ask for:

- Four to six payslips
- Financial statements or tax returns if you are self-employed
- Dividend statements if you have shares
- Proof of government allowances, like Newstart or Youth Allowance.

In addition, a property manager or landlord may call your employer to verify the information that you have provided.

STABILITY

Financial and general stability are also factors that property managers or landlords look for in any tenant application. This is about ensuring you can commit to a lease. It looks at historical information like:

- How long you lived at your previous address
- Your employment history (what jobs you've had and how long you were there).

If you've moved to a new area or recently changed jobs, that's OK, as long as your history indicates you were reliably employed and can settle somewhere for a reasonable period of time.

HISTORY

If you've rented a property before, your rental history is a critical indicator of exactly how you behave when entrusted with a property.

To check this, property managers and landlords will look at databases like TICA[60] to see whether you've been blacklisted for failing to pay rent or damaging a property.

They will also conduct reference checks with your previous landlord or rental agency to determine how well you looked after a previous property and whether you paid your rent on time.

GOOD CHARACTER

In addition to checking your finances, employment and history, a landlord or property manager may ask to speak to personal referees.

These are generally people you have known for a while (minimum of 12 months). They might be family friends, upstanding citizens you know or your employer, but the reason an agent may wish to contact them is to find out what sort of character you are and whether you're reliable, responsible, upstanding and held in high regard.

RENTING THE PROPERTY

Once you have been approved to rent a property, you will need to sign a series of documents and meet certain responsibilities before you can call your new accommodation home.

The most important of these documents is the lease – a legal document that sets out the period you can live there, who is entitled to stay, how much rent is to be paid and what items you and the landlord are responsible for.

TYPES OF LEASES

If you are renting a property such as a house or apartment for the long-term, there are two common types of leases available:

- **A fixed-term lease** – Establishes a set rental period, usually six or 12 months. This type of lease allows for security. The rent you pay over that period will not alter. You cannot be asked to leave unless there are special circumstances or either the landlord or tenant persistently does the wrong thing – this is known as a "breach".
- **A periodic agreement** – This type of lease isn't usually offered when you first go to rent a property; instead it might be offered after a fixed-term lease has expired. Rather than having a set period, it is a week-to-week or month-to-month agreement. With sufficient notice, the rent can be altered, the tenant can leave or the landlord can opt to no longer rent the property.

ENTERING INTO A FIXED-TERM LEASE

Should your application to rent a property be accepted, you will be required to sign the lease. This is basically a legal document that outlines what's expected of you, the landlord and any real estate agency.

Before you sign a lease, it's critical you appreciate that this is a really important piece of legal documentation that you should read in full.

The lease sets out:

- Who is entitled to live at the property

- What you need to pay, when (the weekly rental amount, the bond, who it's paid to, what happens if you don't pay, etc.)

- Conditions – like whether you or the rental agency is responsible for paying for excess water the property uses, who looks after the lawns and gardens, how often the property will be inspected by the property manager and whether pets are allowed

- How long the rental period goes for (six months, 12 months, etc.). The lease will have a beginning and end date. If you wish to stay longer than the end date, you may need to renew the lease. If you wish to leave at the end of a lease, you may need to let your property manager or landlord know in advance

If you wish to leave before the lease has officially ended, you need to give extra notice, and you may also need to pay for them to re-advertise and re-let the property. (We'll talk about that a bit more shortly.)

THE BOND

When you sign a lease to rent a property, you will be required to pay a bond. This is an amount designed to cover expenses should you fail to pay rent or damage the property.

Bonds can vary depending on whether you rent a property privately or through a real estate agent, but generally the maximum bond you will be required to pay is equal to four weeks' rent.

This money is held in a trust with a separate entity until the lease is up, and providing you have paid all rent and there is no damage to the property, it will be paid back to you when you leave.

RENT IN ADVANCE

In addition to paying a bond, you will also be required to pay rent in advance. Often this is two weeks' rent that must be paid upfront; then you pay rent every week after that.

THE ENTRY CONDITION REPORT

When you first take possession of a rental property your landlord or rental property manager will give you a form to fill in known as an entry condition report. This document can be quite lengthy and basically audits the condition of every single room and the exterior of the home you will be renting.

The agent will fill in one side of this report, indicating any problems with the property, like cracks in walls, stains on carpet, scratches on floorboards, etc.

The other half is for you to fill in to indicate you agree with their assessment of the property's condition. You need to return this document to the agent within a set period.

Before you move any furniture and start living in the property, fill out this report, documenting every single thing you see that is not quite perfect which the agent may have missed.

It's also a really good idea to photograph the areas in question.

Why is this so important? When you come to the end of the lease, this is the report that will be used to indicate whether there's any damage to a property that you may be required to pay for. And if that damage is significant, the cost of cleaning, fixing, repairing or replacing it could be taken out of your bond.

RENTING RIGHTS AND RESPONSIBILITIES

As a tenant you have responsibilities, as does the property owner and the real estate agent or property manager looking after where you live.

As we mentioned, your responsibilities include paying rent on time, looking after the property, not damaging it and ensuring activities that go on there are legal.

In addition, you should make sure any people who live there and pay rent are on the lease, and that any maintenance issues are reported in a timely manner.

In return, you should expect that you can live there with your privacy respected. There are strict conditions for when a landlord or property manager may visit and inspect the property – they must provide written notice in advance, and they must come within a set time frame.

More information about your rights and responsibilities as a tenant are available from your state-based tenant advocacy service.

ROUTINE INSPECTIONS

Under a lease agreement, routine inspections are a necessary part of the tenancy process. They allow a property manager or landlord to visit the property and make sure it remains in good condition, is neat, tidy and generally well cared for.

Although the law varies from state to state, there are generally a number of conditions that apply to these inspections.

The leasing agency must give adequate notice for a routine inspection (usually around 14 days in writing, but at least seven days), and there are a maximum number of inspections they can conduct within set periods each year. In Victoria, for example, routine inspections can be carried out every six months, but in Queensland and New South Wales it's every three months.

Inspections are carried out within business hours and the tenant can be there if they wish, but it's not necessary for them to attend.

During a routine inspection, the property manager will conduct a visual inspection of each room and area of the property.

These inspections are also designed to flag any potential maintenance issues or problems that could be emerging, so the property manager might look at trees that are overhanging the house, or check to see whether the gutters are in need of a clean. They might also note the paint is looking tired and suggest to the landlord it could use a spruce up.

As a general guide, when preparing for an inspection the tenant should ensure the property is neat, tidy and clean.

This involves:

- A routine clean (dusting, sweeping/vacuuming, and cleaning kitchen and bathroom surfaces)
- Removing any mould from surfaces
- Ensuring fans and air conditioners are free of dust
- Lawn mowing and gardening
- Tidying up outside areas (decks, patios, etc.).

AT THE END OF A LEASE

At the end of a lease period you will need to notify your agent or landlord about your intentions for the future. Meanwhile, your agent or landlord is also required to let you know what they want you to do.

They can offer you the chance to stay on either for another fixed term or an unspecified period based on a periodic agreement, or they can indicate that the property is not available for you to rent further.

LEAVING THE PROPERTY

Should you decide not to stay on at the property, you will need to indicate this in writing within a set period before the lease expires.

The time frames at present are:

- Northern Territory and Queensland: 14 days before the lease ends
- New South Wales: at least 14 days if the date is at the end of the tenancy agreement, or 21 days if the end date is after the fixed term
- Victoria: 28 days before the lease ends
- Australian Capital Territory: 21 days before the lease ends
- Western Australia: 30 days before the lease ends
- South Australia: 28 days before the lease ends.

STAYING AT THE PROPERTY

If you wish to stay at the property, the landlord and agent may give you the option to renew the lease. They can also alter the cost of the rent at that time and the rental agreement.

They may also give you the choice of a periodic agreement. This is a lease that has no definite end period. Basically it's week to week and allows you to give sufficient notice to leave at any time. On the flipside, it means your rent can also be changed with notice at any time.

ENDING A LEASE EARLY

If you need to end a lease before the term expires, things get a little more complicated. Not only will you be required to provide written notice, you may also need to compensate the landlord for the cost of re-letting the property. You may also need to cover the rent until another suitable tenant is found.

WHEN IT'S TIME TO LEAVE

When it comes time to leave a rental property, you will need to return it to its former condition, which involves fixing anything you may have broken, cleaning the property thoroughly and replacing things like dead light bulbs.

This is where that entry condition report comes into play. You will use this to return the property to the same state you found it in in order to get your bond back.

It's important to note that there's a clause in rental agreements called "fair wear and tear".

Although you are required to look after the property and not cause any damage, fair wear and tear is recognition that properties age over time. It covers things like carpets that become worn, blinds that start to yellow with the sun or paint that starts to age.

The bottom line is anything that is not likely to be considered fair wear and tear is your responsibility to fix and return to its former state.

GETTING YOUR BOND BACK

On the day your lease ends you will be required to finalise cleaning the property, have all your items removed and return the keys to the landlord or rental agency by a set time.

Armed with the entry condition report, the property manager or landlord will then conduct a thorough inspection of the property to ensure it's clean and in the same state it was in when you moved in.

You don't have to be there when this inspection occurs, but you may be notified that something's not quite up to par.

If that's the case, you will need to fix it to ensure you get your bond back.

In most circumstances, the rental agency will let the bond authority for your state know that you have vacated a property and that your bond is to be returned to your nominated bank account. If they haven't done that within a set period, you can apply in writing to have it returned.

If there's a problem with the property or your rent is not up to date, the agent or landlord can apply to have all or part of your bond withheld to cover these costs.

It's really important that you do everything in your power to ensure you get your bond back in full. In the future, having part or all of your bond withheld can affect whether an agency will consider you as a good tenant. A common question on rental applications is: have you ever had part or all of a rental bond withheld and, if so, why?

Meanwhile, if the amount owed exceeds your rental bond, there's a good chance you will be listed on a rental database.

TENANCY DATABASES

A tenancy database is a bit like a blacklist where agencies and landlords can record people who have failed to meet the conditions of a rental agreement, and if you are named on this list it will affect your chances of renting a property in the future.

In Australia there are a number of tenancy databases. These include: TICA[61], National Tenancy Database[62] and Trading Reference Australia[63].

You can be listed on a tenancy database following the end of a lease for a number of reasons. The most common are:

- The amount owing for repairs or rent on the property exceeds the value of the bond
- You have been served with a notice for rent arrears and have failed to pay that money to remedy the breach
- You abandon the property without legal reason
- You have repeatedly breached the rental agreement through behaviour, damage or failure to pay rent and a tribunal has ended the lease.

If a landlord or property manager has intentions to list you on a tenancy database, they must notify you in writing. They must also give you 14 days to object before listing you.

If you believe the proposed listing is incorrect or unjust, you can apply to the relevant tribunal in your state or territory.

TENANCY CONTACTS:

New South Wales
NSW Civil & Administrative Tribunal – 1300 006 228
NSW Fair Trading – 13 32 20

Queensland
Residential Tenancies Authority – 1300 366 311
QCAT – 1300 753 228

Victoria
Tenants Victoria – (03) 9416 2577
Victorian Civil and Administrative Tribunal (VCAT) – 1300 018 228

Western Australia
Tenancy WA – (08) 9221 0088
Commerce WA GOV – 1300 304 054

South Australia
South Australian Tenants' Information and Advisory Service (TIAS) – 1800 060 462
South Australian Civil and Administrative Tribunal – 1800 723 767

Australian Capital Territory
Tenants' Union ACT – (02) 6247 1026
ACT Civil and Administrative Tribunal – (02) 6207 1740

Northern Territory
Northern Territory Consumer Affairs – 1800 019 319

STUDENT ACCOMMODATION

If you are at uni or studying, another option that might be available to you is student accommodation.

This is often offered either by a private student accommodation provider or through your education institution, and often the lease conditions are different to what you experience in a standard rental property.

You will likely still be required to sign a lease and pay a bond, but the notice period that you need to give in order to indicate you are leaving might be different.

Often utilities like electricity and internet access will be included in the rent, along with some furniture.

Meanwhile, the living arrangements might range from shared rooms to studio apartments or shared bathrooms.

SHARE HOUSES

Share houses are another popular option when you are just starting out studying or have recently left home, and there are a number of options available.

You can move into an already existing share house and pay rent to those who already live there, or alternatively you and a group of friends can choose to rent a new share house together.

If the second option better suits, you need to be mindful of a couple of things. If you and a group of friends decide to apply for and rent a share house together, ensure all relevant parties are included on the lease.

If one person wishes to leave the share house, they will need to notify the landlord or agent, and if a new person moves in, they will need to be added to the lease.

Meanwhile, share houses can come with their own unique rewards and challenges, and you'll need to be clear on the rules and expectations from the outset.

Things to consider include:

- How will you collect the group rent and who is then responsible for paying it?
- What happens if someone fails to pay their share?
- Whose name will the electricity account go in?
- How will money be collected for shares in the electricity bill, and when will it be due?

- Whose name will the internet and telephone be connected in?
- How will money be collected for shares in the phone and internet, and when will it be due?
- How will you divide chores, like cleaning?
- What will you do if someone leaves, and how will the rest of you cover a larger share of the rent if this happens?
- What type of behaviour is appropriate and what is not?
- What about partners sleeping over, and when should they also be responsible for contributing to the costs of the house?

These things may not seem like a big deal at the outset, but laying down firm foundations early can really improve the share house experience.

It's also important to understand that if you are named on a share house lease or if you assume responsibility for the electricity bill or phone/internet bill, there are risks involved.

There's a chance you might be left holding the bag when it comes to rent and relevant bills, and yes, these could affect you financially in the future.

Share house shocker — Lea, Gina and Mel

Lea, Gina and Mel are a group of high school friends who can't wait to go to uni together in Brisbane. Come January of their first year, they find a great rental house near their uni campus, sign a lease together and each contributes to the bond.

Living with Gina isn't quite what Lea and Mel expect. Not only is she messy, her boyfriend frequently stays over and she's often late paying rent, leaving Lea and Mel to cover the shortfall to ensure they don't breach their rental agreement.

Then four months in, Gina drops out of uni. She's planning to travel Australia with her boyfriend – and she's set to hit the road tomorrow.

Now, not only is the friendship with Gina strained but Lea and Mel are left paying extra rent, a greater share of the electricity and internet, and they need to find a new flatmate.

We're not saying this scenario will happen, but we are reinforcing the fact that you need to be mindful of all potential outcomes. No matter the actions of others, as the person legally named on documents like leases, electricity accounts and phone bills, the buck ultimately stops with you.

> To avoid situations like this one, you might like to use an app such as 'easyshare' (geteasyshare.com). No more chasing housemates to pay rent and bills, they collect everyone's share and pay the total for you.

RENT ASSISTANCE

Renting a property can be a major expense, and it should be one that costs no more than 30 per cent of your income after tax.

To assist with covering this expense, the Federal and State Governments have a couple of schemes available. These include rent assistance and the National Rental Affordability Scheme (NRAS).

Rent assistance

If you receive certain payments or allowances from Centrelink, such as Youth Allowance, Newstart, ABSTUDY or more than the base Family Tax Benefit, you may be eligible for rent assistance.

This is an additional payment on top of your allowance that goes towards paying rent. The amount of rent assistance you can receive depends on how much rent you pay, but it is a portion of the rent, rather than the full amount.

There are strict conditions for rent assistance, which vary depending on the allowance you receive. You can learn more about your eligibility at: servicesaustralia.gov.au/individuals/services/centrelink/rent-assistance.

National Rental Affordability Scheme (NRAS)

In a bid to make rental accommodation more affordable, the Federal Government has also established something called the National Rental Affordability Scheme.

This program is designed to ensure affordable accommodation is available to people on low or medium incomes.

In short, the scheme sees the government offer incentives to businesses and corporations that build and lease quality rental accommodation. These properties then command a rental price at least 20 per cent lower than the market rate.

Currently there are 35,000[64] properties available around Australia that are part of the NRAS, and 1.5 million tenants are reportedly eligible.

NRAS tenancy applications are assessed by income thresholds, and these limits are intended to include key and essential service workers, for example, childcare workers, nurses, police officers and firefighters.

The Federal Government's NRAS website[65] notes:

"To be eligible to rent an NRAS property, potential tenants will need to provide the approved participant with evidence of their gross income for the previous 12 months before the day they enter the dwelling, both with their initial application and every year afterwards; and must not exceed the income limits for their household type by more than 25 per cent over two consecutive years.

"The total income of all tenants of an NRAS rental property is used to calculate the overall household income for that property."

NRAS application procedures vary depending on your state or territory, but further information is available here:

https://www.dss.gov.au/housing-support/programs-services/housing/national-rental-affordability-scheme/nras-tenants.

BUYING A PROPERTY

For many, having a home to call their own is the ultimate financial dream, while buying, owning and selling property can also be a way of building wealth throughout the course of their life.

That's not to say the property market is a sure-fire guarantee of making money, but the lure of bricks and mortar is popular for a reason. So let's take a look at the ins and outs of buying a property and the process involved.

THE PROCESS

Buying a property takes commitment. It involves saving for a deposit and generally requires you to take out a mortgage (a loan) with a bank or lender, which can take years to pay off before you can truly call that property your own.

In the interim, you have a place that's yours to enjoy and alter as you please, and chances are you are building financial equity, which gives you leverage to buy a better property in the future or further properties if you wish.

But to build this equity you need to fully understand the process involved and carefully research any property you intend to buy. After all, for many people buying a property is one of the biggest financial commitments you will make in your lifetime, and the more research you do in advance, the more likely you are to have success.

The reality is, property is also a journey. You don't tend to start by purchasing your dream home or acquiring a property portfolio. Instead, it's a series of steps that should ultimately allow you to reach your ideal destination.

The formal process of buying a property works like this:

- Talk to a mortgage broker or lending institution about your borrowing capacity and what may be required.
- Set a budget depending on your financial situation and goals, and save for a deposit.
- Search for a property that meets your criteria. (Do your due diligence.)

Figure 7 – The process of buying a property

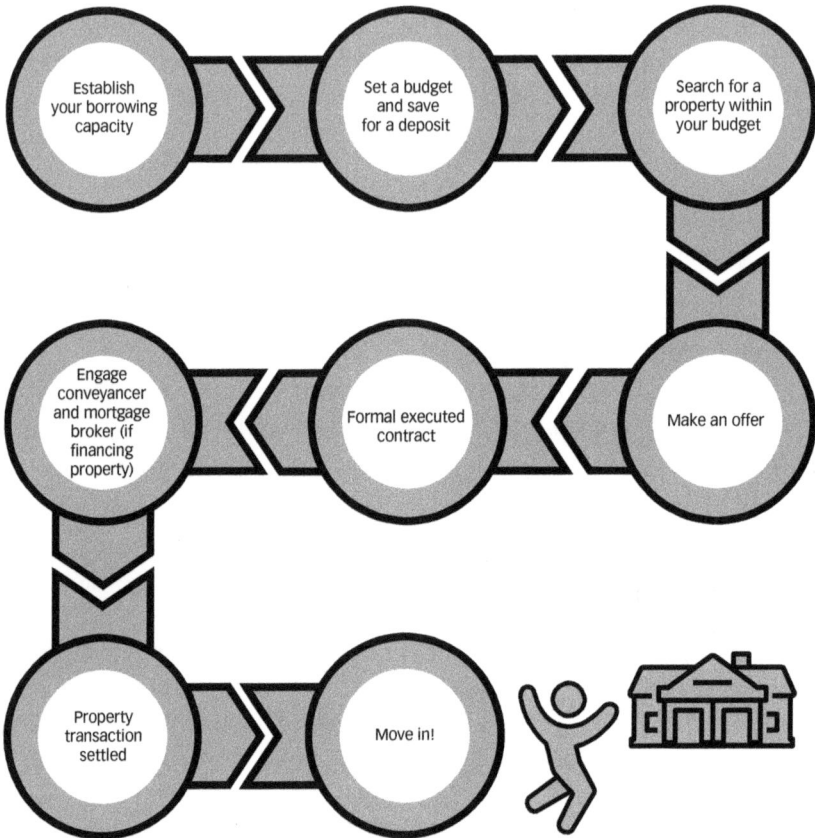

- Put in an offer on that property, come to an agreement with the seller and complete and execute the contract of sale.
- Immediately following going to contract, engage a skilled conveyancer to ensure a smooth transaction.
- Send a copy of the contract to your conveyancer and mortgage broker/bank manager to start the conveyance and loan application processes.
- Your conveyancer will manage all correspondence in relation to the transaction on your behalf and will liaise with you on property search options and results, and satisfaction of conditions.

- Once all conditions have been satisfied, the contract is deemed 'unconditional' and ready for settlement.
- Transfer documentation will be prepared by the conveyancer/lawyer and mortgage documents will be prepared by the bank. They will liaise with you regarding any execution requirements and fees.
- Prior to settlement, your conveyancer will confirm settlement figures with you, your broker/banker as well as the seller's conveyancer.
- At settlement, transfer documentation, money and mortgage documents are exchanged, and upon settlement ownership of the property will be transferred to you and your mortgage registered against the title of the property.

This is a brief summary, so don't worry – we take a deeper dive below.

So, let's start from the beginning . . .

YOUR BUDGET

If you're considering buying a property, the first thing you'll need to consider before scouring the internet for your dream home is your budget.

This is basically how much you will be able to afford to spend on a property depending on your income, equity, lifestyle and other financial commitments.

When you're young, there's a good chance your income isn't yet at its peak, and you're also likely to have limited equity, which means your first property will probably be on the cheaper side.

For example, in 2016 the Australian Bureau of Statistics[66] found the median value for properties bought by first-home buyers was $450,000. This compared to $580,000 for people who had previously owned another home.

DEPOSITS

The next thing you need to take into account is your deposit. This is an amount you've saved up before you apply for a loan. Basically, every lender requires a deposit. (If not, they will require some other form of additional collateral, such as a family guarantee, which we cover below.)

The deposit is the most expensive component of buying a property, and it serves a number of purposes.

A deposit gives a lender surety you're serious about the loan. It gives you an initial stake in a property and acts as a buffer for the lender should something go wrong. Often the deposit illustrates that you have the ability to save money. Every lender wants to know this if they're going to lend you a large amount.

When it comes to the amount of the deposit, it can vary depending on the type of loan you take out and the lender you go with, but as a rule of thumb, five per cent of the purchase price as a minimum is a good start. The more you have the better, and getting to a 20 per cent deposit will see you avoid paying lender's mortgage insurance. (We'll cover more on what LMI is and how it works later.)

That means if the median house price of a first home is $450,000, you will need to have a minimum five per cent deposit of $22,500.

You can come up with your deposit in a number of ways:

- Savings
- A gift
- First home owner's grant
- Family guarantee/family equity loan
- Equity in existing property
- First Home Loan Deposit Scheme
- First Home Super Saver Scheme.

Savings

If you are looking to take out a mortgage for a property, most lenders (but not all) will want you to satisfy their genuine savings requirement if you're borrowing above 90 per cent of the property's value.

To satisfy the genuine savings requirement, you can:

- Ensure you have five per cent of the purchase price held in savings or have built up five per cent through your income over a minimum three-month period. For example, if you are looking to purchase a $450,000 property, you will need to show $22,500 in genuine savings.

- Provide a satisfactory rental history with a real estate agent. This history must indicate regular rental payments for a minimum of three months. Some lenders want six months, and others require a 12-month history. A little catch here is that the lease must be in the same name as the borrowers applying for the loan. If two people are looking to enter a loan together, then both people must be on that lease.

- Draw on additional repayments you have made on loans, such as car loans and personal loans. These repayments must be in addition to your minimum repayments and must be able to be redrawn from the loan to use as a deposit.

Gifts

Any gifts that are to go towards the purchase of a property are usually non-repayable, and lenders often want the gift provider to sign a letter to that effect.

If the finance provided is not a gift, but rather a loan, the lender will need to confirm the loan terms. They will seek to understand the duration of the loan, the interest rate applied and the repayments required so this can be taken into account to calculate the borrowing capacity of the mortgage applicant. Any gift received does not count towards the lender's genuine savings requirement we mentioned above.

First home owner's incentives

In a bid to encourage young people into the property market, Australia's states and territories also offer a series of concessions and grants.

These include exemptions or concessions on stamp duty (the tax that comes with changing the ownership of a property) and actual First Home Owner's Grants (FHOG) that can be used towards your deposit. In some cases these grants only apply to new properties in order to encourage the construction of new homes. In others, they apply to all property purchases.

As we mentioned, these incentives vary from state to state, and they are subject to change. At the beginning of 2020, this is what is currently available:

NSW

Grant – $10,000 available for the construction or purchase of new homes

Conditions – purchasing a new dwelling complete and never lived in, the cost of the dwelling must be under $600,000. If you are buying land and building a new home, the combined value of land and construction must be under $740,000

Stamp duty – exemption from transfer duty on homes valued at less than $650,000, with concessions on homes valued between $650,000 and $800,000. If buying land, no stamp duty is payable up to $350,000 purchase price and concessions from $350,000 to $450,000.

VIC

Grant – $10,000 available for the purchase or construction of a new home in Melbourne. $20,000 available for the purchase or construction of a new home in regional Victoria

Conditions – only available for properties valued up to $750,000

Stamp duty – exemption for existing or new properties valued at below $600,000, with concessions on properties valued between $601,000 and $750,000.

In Victoria there is also a stamp duty concession for vacant land purchases for first home buyers up to $600,000.

QLD

Grant – $15,000 available for the purchase or construction of a new home

Conditions – available on properties valued at up to $750,000

Stamp duty – exemption on properties valued at up to $500,000 and vacant land up to $240,000, with concessions on properties up to $550,000 and vacant land up to $400,000.

SA

Grant – up to $15,000 available for buying or building a new home

Conditions – available for homes valued at up to $575,000

Stamp duty – no specific first home buyer stamp duty concessions available.

WA

Grant – $10,000 available when buying or building a new home

Conditions – available on properties valued at up to $750,000 which are south of the 26th parallel south latitude, and up to $1 million for properties north of the 26th parallel south latitude

Stamp duty – exemption for properties less than $430,000 and vacant land less than $300,000, concessions for properties between $430,000 and $530,000, and land between $300,000 and $400,000.

TAS

Grant – as at the beginning of 2020, there is a $20,000 grant available for buying or building a new home. In July 2020 this reduces to $10,000

Conditions – none set

Stamp duty – 50 per cent stamp duty concessions for first home buyers purchasing an established home valued at up to $400,000.

ACT

Grant – $7000 available for new or substantially renovated homes

Conditions – available on properties valued at up to $750,00

Stamp duty – exemption for buyers over 18 with a combined income of less than $160,000, with concessions then available depending on income and number of dependent children.

NT

Grant – $10,000 available when buying or building a new home

Conditions – none set

Stamp duty – a deduction of up to $18,601 when buying or building a new home.

Family guarantee or family equity loan

A family guarantee or family equity loan is a way for parents to help their children purchase a property, without the need to transfer any cash.

This type of loan can help you avoid the need to satisfy a genuine savings requirement, but you must still be able to illustrate to a lender that you can afford and service (pay off) the loan.

Also known as having a security guarantor, it sees a guarantor (usually parents) provide additional security either through equity in a property or cash in a term deposit. They are not there to guarantee the repayment of the loan, so in other words, if the borrower misses a repayment on the loan, the bank will not tap on the shoulder of the guarantor.

If possible the guarantor should seek to have a limited guarantee up to a maximum of 20 per cent. This means if things go wrong and the bank needs to foreclose and sell the property, the guarantor is liable for the least amount required.

It's also important to note this arrangement is not intended to be a long-term solution. Subject to the bank's lending criteria, generally when the debt level is at 80 per cent of the current value of the property, the guarantors can be released. This is usually achieved by a combination of paying down the debt and the value of the property increasing. Reviewing this annually with your mortgage broker is recommended so that the guarantors can be released as soon as possible.

Equity in existing property

Using equity in existing property is a great way to fund the purchase of another property. This essentially means that if you already have a property and you have either paid off a significant portion of the mortgage, or that property has increased in value, the lender will consider this equity in the purchase of another home.

You will still need to satisfy the bank that you can afford repayments on all the properties involved, but it means you don't have to save up a separate deposit.

Of course, this option only applies when you already have a foot on the property ladder!

First Home Loan Deposit Scheme

In 2019, the Federal Government announced they would assist a small number of first home buyers with saving for their deposit. Known as the First Home Loan Deposit Scheme[67], the initiative is available to first-time home loan applicants who have saved at least five per cent but no more than 20 per cent of the property's value. They can then apply to the government, which will guarantee up to 15 per cent of the property's value.

This doesn't mean the government lends you the money. Instead, the deposit balance is funded by your lending institution and the government underwrites it.

That means on a $450,000 property you will need to have savings of $22,500. If you have been approved for the First Home Loan Deposit Scheme (FHLDS), your mortgage would then be $422,500, with the Federal Government underwriting (guaranteeing) a $67,500 component of that figure.

The major benefit of the scheme is that you don't need to take out lender's mortgage insurance. The drawback is your loan will be higher than if you had saved the full 20 per cent deposit of $90,000.

This scheme comes with a series of conditions, and the government has also capped the number of people who its available to.

Available as of 1 January 2020, only 10,000 applicants a year will be allowed to take part. In real terms, that's a very small amount of first home buyers, considering more than 110,000[68] first homes were purchased in 2018.

To be eligible, the following conditions need to be met:

- You must have saved at least five per cent but no more than 20 per cent of the property's purchase price.
- As an individual, you have an income up to $125,000 per year.
- As a couple, you have combined earnings of up to $200,000 per year.

In addition, there are also different property price caps applied in different areas. This means you are only eligible to apply if your property is less than the threshold the government has set.

As of 2020, the thresholds[69] are:

State	Capital city threshold	Rest of state
NSW	$700,000	$450,000
Vic	$600,000	$375,000
Qld	$475,000	$400,000
WA	$400,000	$300,000
SA	$400,000	$250,000
Tas	$400,000	$300,000
ACT	$500,000	N/A
NT	$375,000	N/A

Source: nhfic.gov.au/what-we-do/fhlds/property-price-thresholds.

The First Home Buyer Loan Deposit Scheme is administered through the National Housing Finance and Investment Corporation (NHFIC), and this is where lenders will lodge the application for eligible participants. You should note, only certain lenders have been approved by the government to participate in the scheme.

In the 2020 Federal budget, the government added the New Home Guarantee to the FHLDS, with a further 10,000 places for new homes, only with an increased price cap. You can find out more here: nhfic.gov.au.

First Home Super Saver Scheme

The First Home Super Saver (FHSS) Scheme allows you to save money for the deposit on your first home as part of your superannuation fund. Introduced in 2017, it allows you to make voluntary contributions that can then be released when you go to purchase a property, but a series of conditions do apply.

In order to utilise the scheme you need to apply to the Commissioner of Taxation. You must be over 18, and you must be a first home buyer or suffering extreme financial hardship. You can only access up to $15,000[70] from any one financial year, and you cannot access more than $30,000 in total. The additional earnings you make in association with these contributions will also be released to you along with your contributed funds.

Meanwhile, it's assessed on an individual basis so, as a couple, each of you could potentially access up to $30,000 of voluntary contributions to help fund your deposit.

The Australian Taxation Office also explains there are other important things you need to know when using the First Home Super Saver Scheme:

- You should request the release of your FHSS amounts around the same time you start your home buying activities – for example, when you apply for a home loan.
- After you have requested the release, it may take between 15 and 25 business days for you to receive your money.
- You must apply for and receive a FHSS determination before signing a contract for your first home or applying for release of your FHSS amounts.

- If you've already received a determination and signed your contract to purchase or construct your home, you must make a valid release request within 14 days of entering into that contract. You can also sign your contract after you make a valid release request.
- The home must be located in Australia.
- You can only apply for release of your FHSS amounts once.

You have 12 months from the date you make a valid request for release of your FHSS amounts to do one of the following:

- Sign a contract to purchase or construct your home – you must notify ATO within 28 days that you have signed the contract.
- Recontribute the assessable FHSS amount (less tax withheld) into your super fund – you must notify ATO within 12 months of the release request date that you have recontributed.

If you don't notify the ATO that you have done one of the above or you choose to keep the FHSS money, you will be subject to the FHSS tax. This is a flat tax equal to 20 per cent of your accessible FHSS released amounts. This may not be the same as the total amount released.

You can learn more about this initiative at: ato.gov.au/Individuals/Super/Withdrawing-and-using-your-super/First-Home-Super-Saver-Scheme.

MORTGAGES

Because most people don't have hundreds of thousands of dollars simply lying around in their bank accounts, and it takes years to save that amount, the purchase of a property is usually funded through a mortgage.

This is basically a large loan that you take out with a bank or lender and pay back over an extended period of time. The length of time varies but can be up to 30 years.

Over that period, banks also charge you interest on the amount you borrow, which is basically a fee for the privilege of borrowing money.

And it works like this . . . If you're buying a $450,000 property and have saved a deposit of $90,000, you will need to borrow at least $360,000 from a bank. (Chances are, that borrowing figure will actually be a little bit higher, because there are extra fees attached to buying a property, but we'll come to those shortly.)

The bank will then calculate a regular repayment on that amount, which can be weekly, fortnightly or monthly, and they will also add a further amount for interest, which will be paid over the life of the loan.

This type of repayment is called principal and interest. You are paying back the loan (principal amount) at the same time as also paying off the interest attached to it.

So, if you borrow $360,000 at an interest rate of 3.19 per cent and your loan term is 30 years, you would pay:

- $359 weekly to repay the loan amount of $360,000, plus interest of $199,427, or
- $717 fortnightly to repay the loan amount of $360,000, plus interest of $199,530, or
- $1,555 monthly to repay the loan amount of $360,000, plus interest of $199,768.

The above interest figures are not the minimum required interest payable over the loan term. Typically interest on a mortgage is calculated daily on the outstanding balance of the loan and charged monthly. Any additional payments you make come directly off the principal, so the more you pay the more you save!

Using the example above, if you paid an additional $50 per week, it would cut five years and four months off the loan term and save yourself $38,621 in interest!

INTEREST RATES EXPLAINED

Interest is basically the fee you pay for the privilege of borrowing money from a bank, and it is charged at a percentage of the sum you have outstanding. Over the life of a mortgage this percentage rate can vary depending on economic conditions and a whole range of other factors.

In Australia, the interest rates that banks charge on mortgages are based on something called the cash rate, which is a figure set by the Reserve Bank of Australia (RBA).

You might have noticed there's been a lot of talk about the cash rate recently, because in October 2019, Australia's cash rate hit an all-time low of 0.75 per cent. Then, as a result of the coronavirus, on 4 March 2020 it dropped to 0.50 per cent. As part of an emergency meeting on 20 March 2020, it dropped again to 0.25 per cent.

In a nutshell, the cash rate is the interest rate the RBA charges for overnight lending, which then has flow-on effects to the major banks and lending institutions.

It works like this . . . Basically, banks move a lot of money around on a regular basis. From small transactions to major transfers, the volume of these can be unpredictable, and every institution is required to settle these transactions each night. To do so, banks will often borrow from each other or from the RBA.

When the cash rate is low, as it is at the moment, this borrowing is fairly cheap and banks can readily and affordably cover any shortfall.

This allows the banks to take greater risks, which in turn spurs on the economy because lending institutions are more likely to offer loans to individuals, households and businesses.

Therefore, a low cash rate is designed to stimulate the economy. When the cash rate is high, it's designed to slow the economy down, reducing borrowing, debt and expenditure. Australia's highest ever was an astounding 17.5 per cent in January 1990[71].

In deciding the cash rate, the RBA board takes a host of factors into account. These include employment, inflation, the global landscape, real estate prices and consumer confidence.

It's important to note that while the cash rate influences lender's interest rates, the figures are usually very different and banks tend to charge higher interest than the official cash rate.

In addition, the banks will charge different interest rates depending on the type of loan you take out, whether the rate is fixed or variable, the risk associated with your type of loan and the conditions attached to it.

This might factor in your income, your deposit amount and your loan-to-value ratio or your employment type.

That's why lenders tend to offer a number of loan types with different interest rates.

Different mortgage types

Most lenders don't just offer one loan type; they have a number of choices to accommodate people's different financial situations, their planned outcome with the property and the way they want to pay that money back. Different interest rates are then applied to these loans.

When looking at the different loan types, here's what you need to know . . .

Variable

A variable loan is one where the interest rate rises and falls in line with the cash rate and other factors. It's important to note, banks aren't necessarily obliged to pass on cash rate increases and cuts, but they do tend to reflect them.

If you have a variable loan, that means your interest rate may be 3.2 per cent initially but could rise to 3.25 per cent or more because the cash rate increases. It could also fall in line with reductions. The upshot is that your repayments will vary from month to month and year to year, so they're a little harder to accurately budget for.

On the other hand, variable loans are considered highly flexible in that they allow the borrower to make as many additional repayments as they like and redraw any additional funds. Many also offer an offset account that offsets the interest with savings or extra cash.

Variable loans are great for owner-occupiers who have little other debt and for people who are looking to pay more to reduce their loan.

Ruth and Ryan

Ruth and Ryan have just bought their own home to live in. They've borrowed $300,000, and it's a 30-year variable loan where they are paying both the principal amount and interest each month.

When their loan commences, their interest rate is 3.70 per cent. At this point their monthly repayments are $1,381. Later, the interest rates begin to rise, and soon they're at 3.9 per cent. Their monthly repayments are now $1,415.

But what if interest rates go down to 3.5 per cent, instead of going up? In that case, Ruth and Ryan only have to pay $1,347 a month.

Fixed loans

Fixed loans allow the buyer to set their interest rate at a specific amount for a period of time. This is designed to offer you certainty that your repayments won't change during the initial fixed term. Fixed terms are available for between one and 10 years, with prices varying depending on the term selected.

Cecilia and Tom

Cecilia and Tom also have a 30-year, $300,000 mortgage where they pay principal and interest, but they're on a tight budget so opt to fix their interest rate at 3.7 per cent for five years. That means their monthly repayments remain $1,381 each month for five years. After that the loan reverts back to variable and Cecilia and Tom will pay whatever the going rate is at the time.

In the interim, Cecilia and Tom may have avoided any additional expense of an interest rate rise. But if the rate had dropped to 3.5 per cent, they wouldn't have enjoyed any benefits. For the duration of the fixed period they would have been paying $1,381 per month when they could have been paying $1,347.

While a fixed loan offers certainty, it can reduce flexibility, with many lenders restricting the amount of additional repayments you can make as well as your ability to redraw those extra funds.

Usually offset accounts aren't available with fixed loans, and if you want to break the loan during the fixed period, you will incur a higher break fee to compensate the lender for interest lost.

Principal and interest repayments

In addition to giving you a choice in how you handle interest, in some cases lenders also offer a choice on how you pay back the loan, with the most common one being principal and interest repayments.

As we mentioned earlier, a mortgage comprises the principal sum (the money you borrow) and the interest (the fee the bank charges for borrowing money).

A principal and interest loan sees you pay both amounts off at the same time so you can pay your debt down efficiently. Almost all owner-occupied home loans are principal and interest, so it reduces the debt over time. Basically it means each month you are tackling both the actual debt and the interest, and building equity in your property.

On a 30-year, $300,000 mortgage with an interest rate of 3.7 per cent, monthly repayments would be $1,381 – $925 of that is interest, and $456 of that is repaying the principal sum.

Interest-only repayments

Interest-only loans are generally utilised by investors. This type of loan sees you only pay back the interest, not the principal amount of a loan, for a set period of time (usually between one to five years).

That means your monthly repayments are likely to be less at the beginning of the loan, but after the interest-only period expires you are then required to pay down the debt over the remaining term.

So the repayments will be higher than if you had opted for a principal and interest loan from the outset.

For example, if you take a loan out for $300,000 over 30 years with a five-year interest-only period, after five years the bank will work out what you need to pay weekly or monthly to pay the $300,000 down over 25 years.

When investing, interest-only repayments can be a handy strategy, but it is imperative you do your cashflow analysis to ensure you will be able to easily meet the jump-in repayments once the interest-only period ends.

Jane and Chris

Jane and Chris have bought an investment property and their loan is $300,000. It's a 30-year loan that currently has an interest rate of 3.7 per cent. They opt to pay interest-only amounts for five years. That means their monthly repayments are just $925.

After five years the loan reverts to principal and interest. Now their repayments jump to $1,534 monthly.

Some extras on the side

When you're offered some types of loans, you might also be given the option of extras on the side, such as offset accounts and redraw facilities. Both of these tend to be put forward with variable loans (as they offer the most flexibility) but in some cases can also be provided as part of fixed-interest packages.

Regardless, they work like this: a redraw facility allows you to channel extra funds into your home loan and then redraw them if required.

You can only redraw any additional repayments you make towards the loan; the minimum required repayments on the loan cannot be redrawn. Some lenders will charge a redraw fee, but most don't and we recommend finding a lender that doesn't. As interest on a mortgage is calculated daily on your net balance and charged monthly, the more you can pay into your loan the less interest you will be charged. This will in turn reduce your loan faster and save you thousands in interest!

It could also get you out of a tight squeeze should something go awry.

For example, Paul and Sarah have a redraw facility attached to their variable home loan. Since they've had the loan, they've been channelling $2,400 into the loan account each month, despite only being required to make minimum repayments of $1,300 monthly.

Suddenly, Paul is made redundant. Now Sarah is concerned about the mortgage. But courtesy of the redraw facility and the extra repayments, her loan account balance indicates she has funds available of over $8,800. (This is the extra money she channelled into the loan.) If she chooses, she can redraw this amount and use it to pay off the mortgage at $1,300 in the future, or for any purpose she desires.

Offset accounts work a little differently but are based on a similar principle. In the case of an offset account, your lender gives you an additional transaction account that is linked to your home loan but has normal transaction capability. The money held in this account is offset daily against your loan balance and can reduce the interest that you are required to pay.

For example, Jack and Joanie have an offset account linked to their $320,000 mortgage. When they receive a significant tax return of $5,000, they deposit it into this offset account. For the time that the $5,000 balance is kept in the offset account, Jack and Joanie only pay interest on a $315,000 home loan.

You can read more about redraw facilities and offset accounts at: canstar.com.au/home-loans/offset-or-redraw-whats-the-difference.

LENDER'S MORTGAGE INSURANCE

Although lenders often talk about a 20 per cent deposit, it is possible to get a loan with less than that amount, but special conditions and additional costs might apply. One of these is lender's mortgage insurance or LMI.

Lender's mortgage insurance works like this: when a lender offers you a loan, they look to minimise their risk, and they generally do so by requiring a 20 per cent deposit.

By lending only 80 per cent of the value of a property they have surety that, should the borrower fail to meet their requirements, the lender can reclaim the property and sell it to recoup the loan amount.

In an ideal scenario, every borrower would have that 20 per cent deposit at hand, but that's not always the case. When they have less than 20 per cent, lender's mortgage insurance can be used to help secure a loan with as little as a five per cent deposit, and a loan of up to 95 per cent.

The catch is, the borrower has to pay for it.

LMI is usually paid as a one-off fee at settlement, with many lenders opting to factor it into the loan amount. The cost depends on the value of your loan, your lender and your deposit.

LMI is not transferable between lenders, if you want to change lenders at a later stage. However, you will get a credit for what you have already paid if you increase your loan in the future, and the property and borrowers remain the same.

LMI example

John and Jane have their eye on a $400,000 property. Under normal circumstances, they would require a 20 per cent deposit of $80,000. While John and Jane can afford the repayments, they don't quite have that deposit in the bank. Instead, they have $20,000 (or five percent of the purchase price).

It turns out a number of lenders are willing to grant them a loan of $380,000 with the condition of LMI.

But six months down the track, John and Jane aren't faring so well. They've damaged the house, skipped out on the loan, and the bank is looking to recoup.

Now the bank needs to pay $20,000 to fix and sell the property, and when they do it's for just $370,000.

That's a shortfall of $30,000. Instead of the lender incurring that loss, the lender's mortgage insurer steps in and foots the difference. The insurer then pursues the borrower to cover the $30,000 cost.

HOW TO GET A LOAN

In order to get a home loan, you need to talk to a mortgage broker or financial institution, who will guide you through the entire process.

It's a great idea to speak with them sooner rather than later when it comes to the property search, as they can walk you through the options available, speak with you about your personal financial situation and offer advice on which options might suit you best.

Their guidance might also impact your property budget, giving you a better idea of the types of properties you are eligible to buy.

At this point in the property search, you could also get pre-approval for a loan.

What is loan pre-approval?

Basically, loan pre-approval is an agreement in principle that a lender will provide you with a required loan based on your circumstances.

Often considered the first step in the home buying process, it's not a guarantee but rather a gentlemen's agreement that, all things being equal, you will receive the loan you need.

In practice, pre-approval gives you peace of mind that you're in the financial position to make an offer on a property, but when push comes to shove, pre-approval is not an agreement etched in stone.

In terms of benefits, pre-approval allows you to understand how much a lender is willing to provide you with when buying a property and under what circumstances they will honour that loan.

It enables you to negotiate with confidence and bid at auction, and it can make you more attractive to sellers, indicating you're a serious contender when it comes to buying a home.

It's important to note that while pre-approval is valuable to serious buyers, a pre-approval will appear on your credit record as a credit inquiry, so a number of pre-approvals in quick succession with multiple lenders may indicate you're financially unstable or playing the system to suit your needs.

Meanwhile, although pre-approval means you may be more likely to have a loan approved, it does not guarantee that loan offer will be forthcoming.

Items that may affect your loan application include:

- A change in financial circumstances
- Changes in lender's credit policy or credit appetite
- A valuation on the property that is less than anticipated
- A property that the lenders deem too risky or uninhabitable.

Also, you should know that you don't require pre-approval to make an offer on a property, as most sales contracts include a series of conditions, one of which is 'subject to finance'.

The subject to finance clause is designed to give you sufficient time to get your loan application approved by a bank.

We'll come to sales contracts shortly, where we cover clauses like subject to finance in greater detail, but for now let's go back to the formal process of applying for a loan.

APPLYING FOR A LOAN

Once you've found the property you hope to buy, the loan process formally begins. At this point you and any other person who is applying for the loan with you will need to complete a series of documents and supply your mortgage broker or lender with detailed information.

This includes:

- Personal identification
- Proof of employment and income
- Proof of savings
- Approximate budget of what your living expenses will be (post-settlement)
- Proof of debts
- Proof of assets
- Bank statements
- A completed and current application form.

There may also be other documents the lender wishes to see, including rental history information or financial information from any family guarantor.

When applying for a loan, it's critical you provide the lender with all the information they are likely to need. Failure to do so may result in the loan application being delayed or rejected.

Once the lender has all the information they require, they begin to work through the process of analysing and verifying it.

They will also need information about the property to ensure the asset that they are lending against is worth what you and the real estate agent say it is.

That means a property valuation may be required. This sees the lender check available data or send out a valuer to look at the physical condition of a property.

The loan process timeline

During the loan application process, a day can feel like a week while waiting for approval. Lenders' response times can vary depending on their current volumes and the quality of the application submission. Here's a guide to what you can expect . . .

Step		Timing	Description
1		2 days	Initial meeting
2		Upon acceptance	Loan comparison & lending solution
3		4 days	Receipt of all requested documents & order valuation on properties
4		5 days	Submit loan application
5		3 – 4 days	Conditional approval from lender
6		4 days	Unconditional approval – celebrate!
7		2 days	Mortgage documents received to sign & return
8		3 days	Documents arrive back at lender
9			File is certified from the lender ready to book settlement
10			Settlement – PARTY!

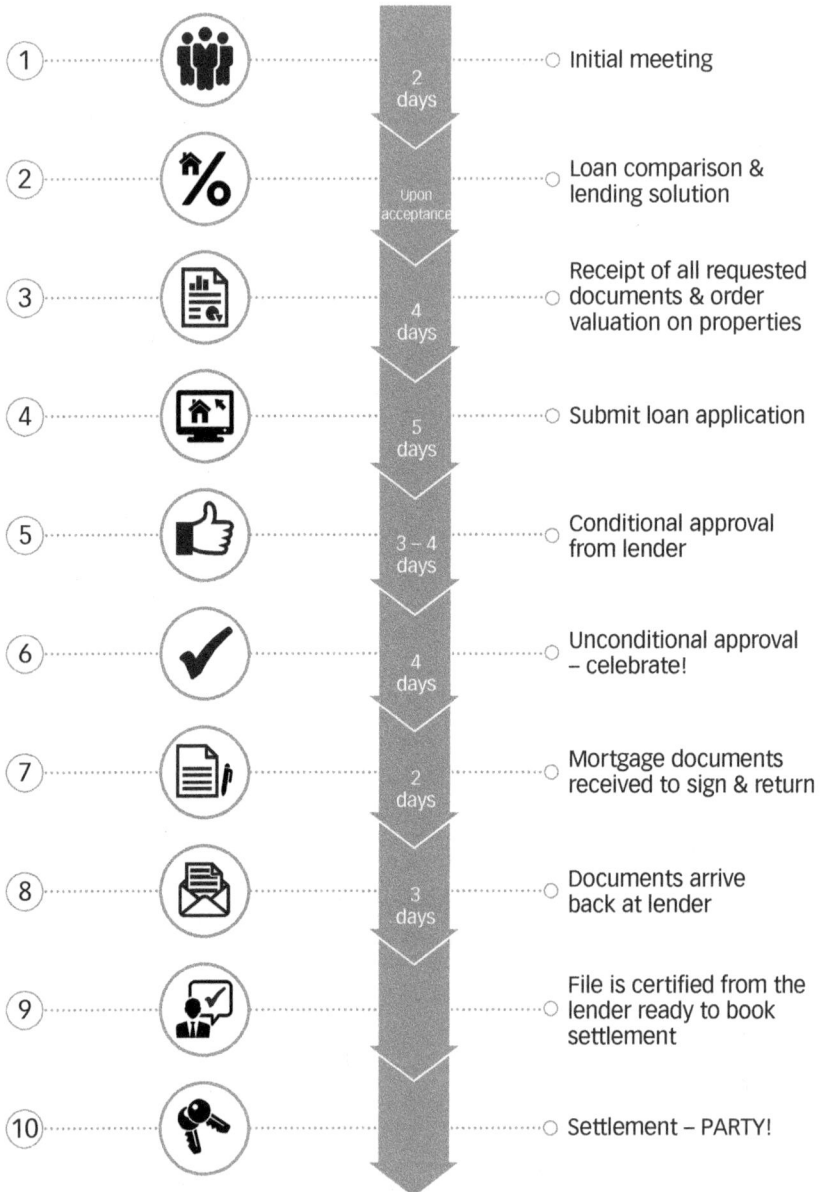

Meanwhile, there are specific things every lender looks for in a loan application . . .

What do lenders look for in an application?

When a lender seeks to make a decision about approving a loan application, they look at a series of key areas that are commonly referred to as 'three Cs'.

Capacity

In this first, critical C, lenders seek to ascertain what you earn and what you owe. In other words, the lender is looking to understand whether you can afford the loan amount proposed.

To facilitate this, a lender requires information about your income, including salary from your job, self-employed income, Centrelink payments you receive, investment income, etc.

They will also look at the regular financial commitments that you have and the expenses that you incur. This includes your existing financial commitments, such as loans and credit card repayments, as well as general living expenses.

It's important to appreciate that living expenses can vary greatly, and discretionary living expenses such as going out for dinner and entertainment can be reined in when you make the commitment to acquire a loan.

It's also important to consider that borrowing capacity differs between lenders.

Character

When a lender considers your character, they're looking to ensure you are reliable, stable and consistent. They factor in indicators like your employment history, your credit history and the length of time you have resided at current and previous locations.

Lenders believe a leopard rarely changes its spots, so they want to determine that your income is stable and any previous loans you have incurred have been paid back on time. Your credit history is a major factor in this assessment.

That said, many lenders are also aware that personal circumstances can and do vary. There are loan options for pretty much every person, and once again, it is just a matter of which lender suits your needs.

Collateral

Collateral sees the lender look at what equity you bring to the table for any loan. They will need to ascertain the value of the property you're buying to determine what it's worth, and they will also consider what deposit or equity is going into the deal.

Together, the three Cs of capacity, character and collateral all work to determine your eligibility for borrowing and the conditions that will be applied to any loan.

Abi and Simon

Abi and Simon are both in stable employment and have been with the same employers for a number of years. They can illustrate this with consistent payslips. They have also saved for their home deposit over a significant period of time, putting money aside each week. This is reflected in their bank statements.

They are looking to buy a $450,000 property, which is actually quite a good deal.

They have saved well, so they have a full deposit of 20 per cent, with $90,000 dedicated to it.

Abi and Simon meet criteria that allows the bank to feel very confident any loan they offer them will be paid back. That means they are eligible for the lowest current interest rate available from that lender, which is 3.2 per cent.

WHAT IF I CAN'T MEET MY PAYMENTS?

A mortgage is a major financial commitment, and not one you should take lightly, but sometimes things happen and circumstances change in life.

If you find yourself struggling to make repayments on your home loan, you need to contact your lender, explain your circumstances and come to an arrangement.

In some cases, your lender might allow you to make only interest repayments, or they may come to a temporary arrangement with you to only pay what you can manage.

Most lenders have a "financial hardship" department that will work with you. The important thing to note is that you cannot bury your head in the sand – you must proactively work with your lender to ensure you do not default on repayments and nothing is recorded on your credit record.

If you do come to an arrangement, you must also ensure you consistently meet the terms you have agreed upon.

THE CONTRACT OF SALE

The contract of sale is the most important document you will sign when purchasing a property. This is a formal and legally binding agreement between you and the current owner of the home, and it illustrates your intention to buy a property, should all conditions be met.

As it's a binding legal agreement, you should seek legal advice from either a solicitor or conveyancer and go through the document in detail.

Contracts of sale and their conditions vary a lot from state to state under the law, and they can also have conditions attached. They are also different if you purchase at auction compared to purchasing via private treaty.

In the case of a private sale treaty, the process works like this:

When you find a property you wish to buy, you put in a written offer to the real estate agent handling the sale.

This offer is then presented to the owner, who can accept it, reject it or come back with a counter-offer. Once the set sale price is accepted, the contract of sale is drawn up.

This document sets out all the details of the property transaction, including the sale conditions, the time frame in which the property will exchange hands and the formal information regarding the actual property that is to be purchased.

Before you sign this contract, you should have it looked at by your solicitor or conveyancer. If any changes or conditions are made to the contract of sale by the owner's legal team, you should also have these checked.

The process differs from state to state from this point forward. We will explain the process that occurs in Queensland, South Australia, Western Australia and Northern Territory first. Then we'll move onto how this differs in New South Wales, ACT, Tasmania and Victoria.

Once both you and the current owner have signed the document, the contract of sale becomes legally binding. This basically means each party has agreed to the information within the document, and once any conditions are met, the contract will become unconditional and the property is officially yours at settlement date.

Information contained within a contract of sale includes:

- Names and addresses: the initial area of the document contains the current owner's names and the property's address
- The chattels list: these are the things that are included in the sale of your home, such as fixtures and fittings, carpets, etc.
- Contract conditions: many property sales can be subject to a number of conditions, such as finance, building and pest report or an inspection, so these will need to be identified in this part of the contract of sale. Each special condition needs to be numbered and initialled by both parties
- Sale price of the property
- Any special terms and conditions
- Deposit amount and due date: there will also be a section on the agreement telling you how much of the deposit is due and what the remainder of the balance is
- Settlement date
- Whether the house will be a vacant possession or tenanted.

In some states and territories there is a cooling-off period for a contract of sale. This is basically a window of time where you or the owner can walk away from the contract and pay only a small fee. A vendor can ask you to waive this period.

As a buyer it is important you pay your deposit on time and meet your deadlines, such as finance and building and pest inspections on time. If you fail to do so you could be in default on the contract and the seller may be able to walk away should they choose too.

Once the contract of sale has been signed by the buyer and seller, and the buyer has received a signed copy, the clock starts ticking to meet any conditions of the contract by their due date.

That means you will need to have your finance application in and approved, inspections conducted, paid your deposit by the set time, and ensured that your funds will be ready for settlement by the date set out in the contract.

If you fail to meet these obligations within the required time frame, you may be in a position where you lose your deposit.

In Queensland, South Australia, Western Australia and Northern Territory, you have the ability to put the property under contract for a price and have it taken it off the market to give you time to sort conditions such as finance and building and pest inspection. In New South Wales, ACT, Tasmania and Victoria there is no such luxury.

The process differs in these states in that you can agree on a price with the seller at which time the real estate agent usually draws up a contract.

This contract is not signed at this stage, and you are expected to now obtain your unconditional finance approval and complete your building and pest inspection. Once you are satisfied you want to and can purchase the property, a contract is signed by both parties and becomes an "exchanged" contract.

If you're in the process of meeting your conditions and haven't yet exchanged the contract, another buyer can potentially come along and offer more. In this case the seller can exchange with that buyer, and you're right back to the drawing board, searching for another property.

To prevent disappointment, it's best to have your ducks in a row by ensuring your finance is pre-approved, your budget is confirmed and your building inspector is ready to go when you make an offer.

CONTRACT CONDITIONS

As we mentioned, contracts of sale can be subject to conditions. These will usually need to be met by a set date that is also documented in the contract.

Some of the more common conditions include:

Subject to finance – This basically denotes that if you cannot get a loan for the property you will not be required to purchase it. Any deposit you have put down when initially signing the contract will be refunded to you.

Subject to building and pest – Every buyer should conduct a building and pest inspection of the property they intend to buy. This sees you engage an independent building and pest inspector to thoroughly assess the property for problems that may not be immediately obvious, like structural issues, termites, renovations that are not to code, etc. This is a very small cost (usually under $1,000) but it could save you a LOT of money in repairs!

Subject to sale of buyer's property – If you are looking to sell your current property in order to fund the purchase of a new one, this clause may be required. It basically indicates that you will need sufficient time to sell your existing property and will not be able to proceed with the sale if you do not sell it by that date.

Subject to due diligence – This clause gives you time to carry out any necessary inquiries related to the property. So, for example, if it was a site you wanted to subdivide, due diligence gives you time to investigate whether that's possible with the local council.

ADDITIONAL EXPENSES

Along with actually financing the purchase of a home, there are additional expenses that come with any property transaction, some of which will come directly out of your pocket, while others will be factored into your mortgage.

We will cover some of the major ones below.

STAMP DUTY

Stamp duty is a government tax that is levied on all property purchases.

As a point of interest, stamp duty also applies to other major purchases, including motor vehicles and insurance policies.

In the case of real estate, the cost of stamp duty varies depending on which state or territory you reside in, but it is usually a percentage of the property sale price.

The amount you need to pay may also depend on:

- the type of property you are buying, i.e., a primary residence or investment property
- whether you are a first home buyer or not
- whether you're purchasing an established home, new home or vacant land, and
- whether you are classified as a foreign purchaser.

As we mentioned, first home buyers may be exempt from stamp duty in some states or may receive a concession. But on all subsequent property purchases, stamp duty will need to be paid – and it doesn't come cheap.

For example, if you were buying your second property in Queensland for a purchase price of $650,000[72] and you intended to live in it as your primary residence, stamp duty would cost you $16,984, including a transfer fee of $1,884, and a straight stamp duty levy of $15,100.

If you were buying a $650,000 investment property, that fee would be even higher at $24,159, comprised of a transfer fee of $1,884, and a straight stamp duty levy of $22,275.

If you're looking to calculate an estimate of the stamp duty you are likely to pay when purchasing a property, realestate.com.au offers a calculator at: realestate.com.au/home-loans/stamp-duty-calculator.

When buying a property, you'll generally need to pay stamp duty at settlement. Your conveyancer or solicitor will usually organise to pay your stamp duty on your behalf to your state revenue office.

If you're using a loan or mortgage to purchase a property, the lender will usually pay the transfer registration fee and mortgage registration fee out of the loan. This ensures the property is in your name and they can take a mortgage over the property for their security.

Stamp duty is an upfront cost that is usually paid from your cash or deposit towards the property. You should speak with your mortgage broker or lender about how this best fits into your situation and if it can be included in the loan or must be paid directly.

CONVEYANCING

Conveyancing is a necessary part of the process of buying or selling a property, and although technically you can do it yourself, a professional conveyancer or solicitor is often best suited to the task as they know exactly what to look for.

Conveyancers go through the legal documents associated with a property transaction, carefully analysing conditions and clauses to ensure both parties meet their legal obligations and each client's rights are protected.

Realestate.com.au[73] explains, for the buyer, a conveyancer will:

- Prepare, clarify and lodge legal documents – contract of sale, memorandum of transfer, etc.
- Research the property and its certificate of title – check for easements, type of title and any other information that needs addressing
- Calculate the adjustment of rates and taxes
- Book in settlement and arrange funds with you and your lender to ensure there are sufficient funds at settlement
- Settle the property – act on your behalf by attending settlement, liaise with the selling party to ensure funds are disbursed correctly, ensure the transfer is executed properly and the property is transferred into your name, advise when the property is settled
- Represent your interest with a vendor or their agent.

For the seller, a conveyancer will:

- Complete legal documents
- Represent you in dealings with the buyer – request to extend dates, ask title questions, etc.
- Attend settlement on your behalf to ensure all funds are received in accordance with the contract and any loans are paid out, and advise once the property is settled.

Conveyancing costs can vary depending on the professional you engage and the work required. There may also be additional costs, which include the expenses the solicitor or conveyancer has to pay to other parties on your behalf, such as a council for lot and easement searches. That means the cost of a conveyancer can be anywhere from $500 to over $2,000.

BUILDING AND PEST INSPECTIONS

As a property is one of the most substantial investments you will make in your lifetime, it's critical you ensure that it is in the condition you expect prior to purchase. That means you should have pest and building inspections completed prior to the contract going unconditional or sale.

Undertaken by a licensed professional, building and pest inspections involve a thorough examination of a property to look for hidden issues like structural problems and water damage or pest infestations, such as termites.

They are designed to find existing and potential problems that may not necessarily be obvious to the naked eye and give you the assurance that the property you are looking to purchase does not have any hidden issues that could be expensive to fix at a later date.

The inspector will assess all areas of the house including the roof, interior and exterior and some of the things they will look for include:

- Cracks in walls
- Mould and water leaks
- Ventilation issues
- The presence of termites and other pests
- Roof condition

- Electrical points
- Large trees which could potentially damage a home
- That all buildings/structures have the relevant council approvals.

Pest and building inspections can cost anywhere from $380 but are usually $600 to $1,000 to complete.

DUE DILIGENCE

In addition to formal inspections like building and pest, as part of buying any property you should conduct your own due diligence.

That involves visiting the neighbourhood at different times of the day to understand what it's like to live in, checking news reports to see if the local council has any plans for the area (such as new roads or highways that could affect the property), and researching the suburb and street in general.

As part of your due diligence, you may wish to contact the local council to ensure your proposed use of the property is permitted and get advice on any development applications required, and the costs and processes involved.

It may sound tedious but a little reconnaissance in the early stages of your property search can allow you to get a real feel for what the area is like and whether the intended property will suit your needs.

ONGOING PROPERTY COSTS

After you buy a property, the costs don't end there. Property ownership involves both regular payments each year along with ad hoc maintenance, repair and improvement costs associated with ensuring that the property remains a safe, appealing place to reside in.

Ongoing costs involved in owning a property include:

Your mortgage – Paid monthly, fortnightly or weekly to your lender.

Insurance – As this is your greatest financial asset, you should insure your property. If you live in the property, this insurance should cover both the building and the contents inside it. If you rent the property to another person, it should include building insurance along with landlord protection, which covers you financially for malicious damage from the tenant and in some cases loss of rent. If you live in a unit or townhouse, building insurance is usually covered by the body corporate (see section below).

Rates – Rates are a fee paid to your local council on a regular basis. They are intended to cover the costs associated with providing your property with services like sewerage and rubbish collection. They also include fees for maintaining the region where you reside with infrastructure like roads and water treatment plants.

Rates vary from council to council and can be charged annually or biannually. They are based on the unimproved capital value of your land, which is assessed every couple of years by your relevant state body.

Your local government will post or email you a rates notice outlining the breakdown of fees.

Water charges – In addition to charging you rates, your local government may charge you for access to water or the use of excess water.

Body corporate – If you live in a unit, townhouse or property where there is more than one residence on one title of land (strata title), you may be charged body corporate fees. These fees help maintain the building, now and into the future, and pay for council rates along with infrastructure that the property requires.

When buying a strata titled property, you should be fully aware of the body corporate costs prior to purchasing.

Repairs and maintenance – Over time, every property will require repairs and maintenance. Whether your hot water heater breaks, your roof gets a leak or you need to install air conditioning, these are the costs that ensure your property remains a viable investment and retains its value.

Repairs and maintenance can range from regular gutter cleans to purchasing a pool pump when required, replacing fixtures like blinds that break and having regular pest treatments.

PAYING YOUR MORTGAGE OFF FASTER

A mortgage is a major financial commitment, and it's one that can last decades, with standard loan terms being 25 or 30 years.

But in many cases you can pay that off faster, and by doing so you save yourself a lot of money and own your home outright sooner. Often this just involves a slightly larger repayment each week or month.

Here's an example of how that works . . .

Ben and Mel

Ben and Mel bought a $400,000 property with a 20 per cent deposit, meaning they have a 30-year mortgage of $320,000.

They negotiated well and managed to obtain a variable loan with an interest rate of 3.2 per cent. Their minimum monthly repayment is $1,384.

Over 30 years they will repay the bank a total of $498,200, including their mortgage, fees and interest of $178,200.

If, however, Ben and Mel decided to channel more than that into their mortgage each month, they would pay a lot less and own their home outright sooner.

Instead of paying what the bank suggests, Ben and Mel opt to channel $200 extra per month into their mortgage from the end of the first year onwards.

This will shave over five years off their 30-year home loan and see them pay $35,221 less in interest over the term of the loan.

So what's the key takeaway? Small amounts extra that you channel into your mortgage can really add up over time. That means you might want to consider making extra weekly or monthly repayments or even contribute lump sums, like tax refunds, when you receive them. The more you pay, the more you save!

TYPES OF PROPERTY OWNERSHIP

In property there are two main types of ownership: owner-occupied, where you live in the home yourself, and investment, where you rent out the property to a tenant.

With each type of ownership comes different responsibilities, tax implications and concessions. For example, as we noted before, first home buyers can receive grants for purchasing their own place of residence, but these do not apply to properties that you intend to use for investment purposes and rent out to a tenant.

Meanwhile, even the rates you pay to your local council each year can be different, depending on whether you are an owner-occupier or investor, and mortgages may also have different conditions and interest rates based on the property's use.

So, let's take a deep dive into the different types of property ownership, and the obligations and incentives that come with each.

OWNER-OCCUPIED

This is the property that you own and live in. Also known as your principal place of residence, it is yours to improve as you wish.

Benefits of owner-occupied:

- An owner-occupied property is your home.
- If it is your first property, you could be eligible for the First Home Loan Deposit Scheme, relevant first home buyers grants and stamp duty concessions.
- Typically lenders will offer lower interest rates and higher loan-to-value ratios (LVR) for owner-occupied loans.

Obligations:

- Your mortgage will likely involve principal and interest payments from the outset.
- You will need to pay council rates each year to your local government for services such as sewerage, garbage collection and

infrastructure. Rates vary from council to council and are levied based on a property's unimproved land value as determined by the relevant state government.

- If your property is a unit, you may have body corporate fees.
- Depending on your council area, you will also be responsible for using excess water.
- You are responsible for utilities costs, such as electricity and telephone/internet.
- Any ongoing maintenance costs will be borne by you.

Tax implications:

- The cost of maintaining your property or improving it cannot be offset against your taxable income. In short, this means any repairs or maintenance you have to undertake at your principal place of residence, or home, cannot be claimed as a tax deduction.
- On the flipside, your principal place of residence does not incur capital gains tax for as long as you live in it. This means any increase in the value of your property over the time you live in it is your profit. Should you live in your property and then later choose to rent it out, capital gains tax will be incurred from the time the property was rented.
- In many states, you can purchase a property as an owner-occupied property, receive all of the concessions, then rent the property out after living in it for 12 months. Once you own a property there are no further stamp duty costs, and you can claim the full tax advantages as an investment property. More about investing below . . .

INVESTMENT PROPERTIES

An investment property is one that you intend to rent out to a tenant, either through a long-term lease or short-term, such as holiday rentals or boarding-style housing.

Investment properties incur a number of responsibilities under the law when it comes to being a landlord. We'll look at that a little more closely later.

In the interim, here's a quick snapshot of their benefits, obligations and tax implications.

Benefits of investment property:

- You can have an investment property anywhere in Australia, regardless of where you live and work. In fact, there's a current trend in the market towards "rentvesting", where young people buy an investment property in an area they can afford but continue to rent in the area where they want to live and work.
- They can provide you with an income in the form of rent that the tenant pays.
- They can enable you to build financial equity in property due to increasing capital values over time. In other words, if your investment property goes up in value, you have equity to buy more properties.

Obligations:

- Mortgages associated with investment properties tend to have slightly higher interest rates attached to them; however, with an investment loan you may be eligible to pay interest-only for an initial period.
- You are responsible for the maintenance and repair of an investment property as the landlord.
- You are responsible for paying council rates to your local government, which may be slightly higher for investment properties (not in all cases).
- If your property is a unit, you may have body corporate fees.
- Depending on your council area, you may be responsible for excess water use, or you could incorporate it into the lease so the tenant is required to pay.
- You are NOT responsible for utilities costs, such as electricity and telephone/internet.
- Any ongoing maintenance costs will be borne by you, but they may be tax deductible.

Taxation implications:

- The income associated with your investment property is taxable and is assessed along with your employment and other income.

- Many of the costs associated with owning and maintaining an investment property are tax deductible. That means when it comes to tax time, the rental income of your property will be assessed along with your employment and other income, but investment costs may be offset against them. (We will have more on this a little later.)
- Your investment property will incur capital gains tax. That means if the property increases in value while you own it, when it comes time to sell, the government will take a portion of the profit. (We'll come back to this subject as it's both complex and important.)

NEGATIVE VERSUS POSITIVE GEARING

OK, at this point let's get stuck back into some taxation implications associated with investment properties, looking at what you can currently claim as a deduction and the topic of positive versus negative gearing.

In a nutshell, when you own an investment property it is likely to provide you with an income courtesy of the rent your tenants pay. This is taxable and is assessed by the ATO along with your employment income and income from any other assets, such as shares.

The costs associated with owning the asset of an investment property are also largely tax deductible. That means you can claim some of them when it comes to tax time as they are considered expenses associated with owning and maintaining an asset.

Types of things that can be offset against your tax include: interest charges on your mortgage, council rates, property management costs charged by your real estate agent, and the costs of having maintenance attended to around the property.

In addition, new items that you purchase for a rental property in order to maintain its value may allow for depreciation. This basically allows you to claim a little tax back on an item each year as it reduces in value. So say your investment property needs a new air conditioner, although you will bear the upfront cost of buying it, you can claim a bit back in the first year, the second and so on for the depreciative life of that item.

The building itself also depreciates, with newer properties attracting a higher rate of depreciation in the early years as opposed to older properties. Many investors looking to take advantage of these benefits opt for newer properties to maximise the depreciation and therefore the tax advantages.

Depreciation is a complex issue and we recommend you speak with a property-savvy accountant about possible deductions to maximise your investment.

At tax time your accountant will look at how much income you have derived from your rental property compared to how much you have paid in costs.

If you have paid more than the property earned, it is considered negatively geared. (This includes the depreciation figure mentioned above, even though you haven't actually paid that cost.) If you have earned more than you have paid, it is considered positively geared.

Or, as the Commonwealth Bank[74] succinctly puts it:

"A property is positively geared when the rental return (the amount of rent you receive from your tenants) is higher than your interest repayments and outgoings.

"A property is negatively geared when the rental return is less than your interest repayments and outgoings."

The key benefit of negative gearing is that the loss may also be offset against other income, like your employment earnings.

Many people successfully employ negative gearing to reduce their annual tax bill. However, it's important to understand that when your property is negatively geared you are losing money on that investment. Whether that's a viable option for you depends on your financial circumstances and tax implications.

How your property is geared is also just one of many considerations you need to be fully aware of when investing in property.

CAPITAL GAINS TAX

Due to the fact your investment property is considered a financial asset that is designed to make you money, it will be liable for capital gains tax.

This is basically a tax the government imposes on the profit you make on an investment when you sell it. Capital gains tax (CGT) also applies to other investments, like shares.

CGT only applies to assets purchased after 20 September 1985 and is calculated by subtracting the cost of acquiring and holding an asset from its price at sale.

While that sounds simple to calculate, it's actually quite complex. CGT takes into account a whole host of factors, like the costs involved in acquiring and disposing of an asset, and can also include some of the costs involved in owning it, such as rates, interest paid on your mortgage and improvement costs.

This is called your cost base, and it is subtracted from the sale price on the date you enter into a contract of sale, rather than the date that sale settles.

Also, if you have held an asset for less than a year you will pay the full percentage of capital gains tax on that item, but if you have had it over 12 months, that drops to 50 per cent.

Capital gain on the sale of an asset is then factored into your taxable income for the financial year in which you sold it.

Of course, not all things go up in value, and if they go down you may incur a capital loss. You can't deduct this loss from your taxable income, but you can carry it forward and offset it against any capital gains you have in the future.

The ATO[75] explains:

"There is no time limit on how long you can carry forward a net capital loss.

"You must offset your capital losses against your capital gains in the order in which you made them. You can't choose not to offset capital losses against capital gains if you have them, but you can choose which capital gains to deduct your losses from."

And, yes, this is complicated and a little hard to wrap your head around, but the ATO has more information here:

ato.gov.au/General/Capital-gains-tax

ato.gov.au/General/Capital-gains-tax/Working-out-your-capital-gain-or-loss/ Working-out-your-net-capital-gain-or-loss.

Figure 8 - Capital Gains Tax

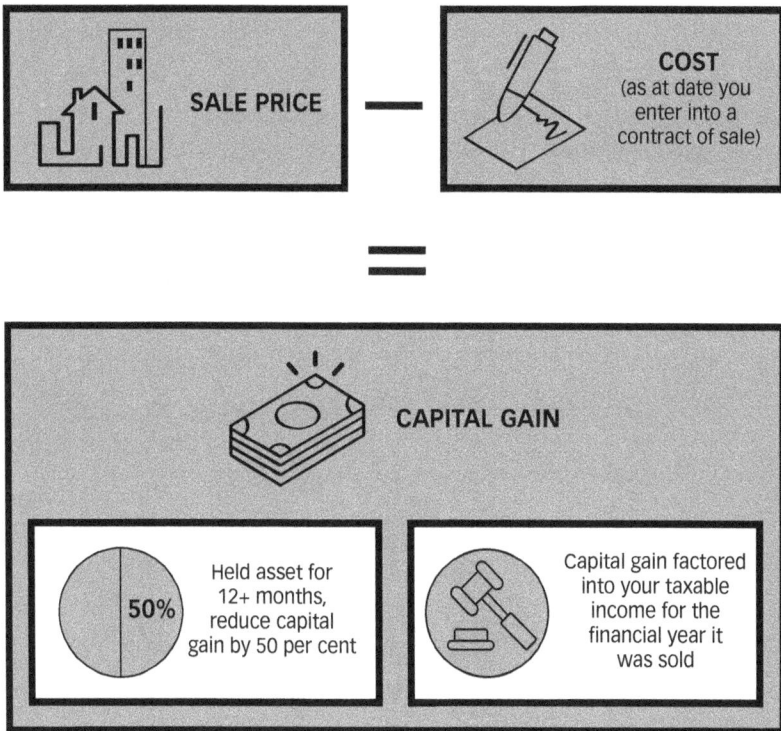

Chris's capital gain

Two years ago Chris bought an investment unit in Brisbane for $270,000. He paid legal costs of $1,500 and stamp duty of $7,875[76].

Recently, Chris sold the property for $350,000 and paid further legal fees and real estate agent costs totalling $12,000.

Therefore Chris's capital gain would be calculated as:

Sales price: $350,000

Cost: $270,000 + $1,500 + $7,875 + $12,000 = $291,375

Sale price $350,000 – cost $291,375 = capital gain of $58,625

This is a very simplistic example of capital gain, and your accountant is the best person to assist with calculating any gain or loss.

The ATO has further examples here: ato.gov.au/General/Capital-gains-tax/Working-out-your-capital-gain-or-loss/Working-out-your-capital-gain.

> **Sometimes on the way to your dream you get lost and find a better one.**
> Lisa Hammond

INVESTMENT PROPERTIES

Buying an investment property is an entirely different proposition to purchasing your dream home.

Why? Because unlike purchasing your principal place of residence, where it's about liveability and suitability, an investment property is about cold hard financial return.

So, if you're looking to purchase an investment property, here's a quick idea of what to look for:

Your financial big picture

Make no mistake, an investment property might be bricks and mortar, but its main aim is to improve your financial position.

For some people the main aim is providing rental income, for others it's through negative gearing and tax incentives, and for others still it might be long-term capital growth.

Whatever your financial aim or current situation, ideally an investment property should meet a stringent set of criteria.

Features versus research

The property market is ripe with discussion of features. These are things like a big backyard or recently renovated bathroom.

While features might be definite pluses, an investment property should see you dig a little deeper to look at the big picture of the region where you intend to buy.

In the case of an investment property, you're looking at demographics, economic indicators and long-term growth, asking:

- Who lives here now?
- What is the current and future population growth? Is there likely going to be ongoing population growth, which will in turn increase demand for more properties?

- What and how many industries underpin employment, and if one fails, how will that impact housing demand?
- Is the rental price currently affordable?
- What are the current vacancy rates?
- What are the government plans for infrastructure and services to this region?
- Is there a controlled supply of future housing? Or are there estates in the planning that could result in a potential property glut?

These questions allow you to gain a good idea of whether the area is currently in demand by tenants and whether it's likely to stay that way. It may also offer an insight into potential capital growth.

A property with appeal

When it comes to what to buy within the market of your choosing, look for properties that are appealing, yet low-maintenance.

Features that are likely to attract as many people as possible may include a second bathroom, off-street parking, proximity to schools, available transport and nearby shops.

And don't limit yourself to one market of prospective tenants. Ideally your investment would appeal not just to retirees or students but to families and professionals as well.

Maintenance

As a landlord, you will be responsible for ongoing maintenance and emergency repairs, and little things can soon add up.

That means you should have a building inspection undertaken before you purchase and select your investment property carefully, bearing in mind older homes, pools and high-maintenance gardens can require additional outlay.

ASIC's MoneySmart[77] website suggests landlords should put aside an amount each month to cover maintenance and repairs. And be mindful that every couple of years a major item like an air conditioner, oven or water heater might be among the property's items you need to replace.

Additional costs

In addition to ongoing maintenance costs and emergency repairs, investment properties also attract a range of ongoing expenses, such as letting fees to an agent, water charges and council rates.

While most of these items are tax-deductible, they will require an outlay of cash from time to time. Meanwhile, if you're considering a strata title property, there will be body corporate fees to consider.

Ensure you factor in all these extras when working out whether an investment property is affordable for you in the long term.

Affordability

On the note of affordability, it might be tempting to max out your borrowing capability for investment purposes, but circumstances can and do change.

That means you should "stress test" your investment.

This includes:

- Factoring in a market drop in rental prices – 10 per cent is a good buffer
- Basing your forecast rental income on 48 weeks' rent rather than 52
- Considering an interest rate rise – factor in paying your loan at an interest rate of six per cent
- Looking to the future when your repayments shift to principal and interest, rather than interest only. Keep in mind, the longer your interest-only period the bigger the jump when it finishes. If you are planning to keep the property long-term, principal and interest repayments from the start are a good idea
- Considering what happens if your personal situation changes (like you or your partner cease employment).

Maintaining a solid buffer when investing will see you in a position to ride out the bumps and enjoy the fruits of your hard work and discipline.

Insurance

An investment property is a significant asset and insurance is a must. To safeguard your investment, building insurance is highly advised. This covers you should the property be damaged in an event like natural disaster or fire. If purchasing a unit, the building is usually covered under the body corporate insurance. It's a good idea to always check when buying that this is up to date.

Meanwhile, landlord insurance is also recommended and very affordable. This protects you should your tenants damage the property or if they leave without paying rent.

USING EQUITY TO BUY MORE PROPERTY

If you already have a property, you can use the equity you have in it to purchase another. And building equity works in a couple of ways – through the repayments you have made on the loan to reduce the balance or the increase in capital value that your property has enjoyed.

So let's explore this a bit further.

WHAT IS EQUITY?

Equity is basically the difference between the current value of your property and the amount of debt you have outstanding on it.

So say you own a property that is currently valued at $400,000 and you have a loan of $250,000 – you have $150,000 equity in that property.

Equity can be attained in a couple of ways: by making principal payments in addition to interest payments on your mortgage, and when the value of that property increases.

How can you use it?

If you have enough equity in an existing property, you can use it as a deposit to buy another property. But when it comes to lending there's a difference between the full equity you have in a home and what's known as "usable" or "available" equity.

So what exactly is usable equity? Well, remember how lenders don't necessarily like to lend you the full value of a property – they stick to 80 per cent without lender's mortgage insurance and up to 90 – and some cases 95 per cent – with LMI. The difference between what you owe and what the lender is willing to lend is your usable or available equity.

Jonah and Liz – Additional loan repayments

Five years ago Jonah and Liz bought their first home together for $400,000. They started off with a mortgage of $320,000, which they've been working hard to pay off.

They were so keen to build equity in their property that they paid above and beyond what the bank suggested each month, and now they have a mortgage of just $270,000.

That means even without the value of their home going up, they have built $130,000 worth of equity in their home (the initial deposit of 20 per cent plus $50,000 in principal repayments over five years).

In the case of Jonah and Liz, their usable equity (without LMI) would be:

Current value of the property: $400,000
Value of the property at 80 per cent: $320,000
Minus their $270,000 mortgage

Jonah and Liz's usable equity is $50,000 (without LMI).

Luke and Sarina — Rising capital value

Luke and Sarina bought their first $400,000 home in what turned out to be a property hotspot, and the capital value of that property has increased a lot in the past five years.

In fact, their $400,000 home, which they bought five years ago, has now skyrocketed to $500,000. That means in terms of sheer capital growth, their home is worth $100,000 more.

In addition, Luke and Sarina started out with a $320,000 mortgage and were making principal and interest repayments as required by their bank. Their loan balance is now down to $295,000.

So now they have $100,000 in capital growth, $80,000 from their deposit and $25,000 in repayments, giving them $205,000 equity in their property at its current price.

In the case of Luke and Sarina, their usable equity would be:

Current value of the property: $500,000
Value of the property at 80 per cent: $400,000
Minus their $295,000 mortgage

Luke and Sarina's usable equity is $105,000 (without LMI).

While Luke and Sarina have enjoyed the benefits of a rising housing market, it's important to also understand that equity can reduce if the market falls, so let's look at Will and Amanda.

Will and Amanda — Falling capital value

Like the other couples, Will and Amanda bought a $400,000 home five years ago with a deposit of 20 per cent. That means their initial mortgage was $320,000. They have also made principal and interest repayments as required by their lender and have paid their mortgage down to $295,000.

However, the property market has not been so kind in their area, and five years later their house is valued at $380,000.

So they now have -$20,000 in capital loss, $80,000 from their deposit and $25,000 in repayments. Technically, they have $105,000 equity in their home, but due to the lowered value of their property, the usable equity has reduced.

Current value of the property: $380,000
Value of their property at 80 per cent: $304,000
Minus their $295,000 mortgage

Will and Amanda's usable equity is $9,000 (without LMI).

This highlights the importance of understanding the market you are buying in and looking for areas which show strong signs of future capital growth.

BUYING AN INVESTMENT PROPERTY USING AN EXISTING PROPERTY

If you are looking to buy an investment property, the banks will lend against it just as they have already lent against your existing property, requiring a standard deposit of 20 per cent (or less with lender's mortgage insurance).

Therefore, on a $400,000 investment property you will need a standard deposit of $80,000, which you can acquire by accessing the usable equity you have in your existing property.

However, when it comes to buying an investment property, you also need to factor in additional costs like stamp duty, legal fees, and pest and building inspections. Unlike when you buy your first home, there is no rebate, concession or grant available to cover these items, and they can equate to an additional five per cent of the property's total cost (or $20,000 in the case of a $400,000 investment).

That means in total you will need about $100,000. The National Australia Bank[78] describes this as the "Rule of Four", meaning when investing you have to have access to funds that equal about a quarter of the value of a property rather than just 20 per cent.

In the above examples, you'll note Luke and Sarina have more than enough usable equity to do that, Will and Amanda do not, and Jonah and Liz might be able to secure a second mortgage if they took out lender's mortgage insurance.

It's important to also note that a lender doesn't just look at available equity when deciding whether to offer you an investment loan. They'll also consider your ability to repay it, taking in factors including potential rent, your income, discretionary expenses and the number of dependent children you have before deciding whether you can afford it.

A bit of a wrap-up

Using equity in an existing property can be a great way to start building yourself a property portfolio. But it's not without risk, and before you start planning out which investment you buy, you should ensure you understand your goals and what you want to achieve from the property, borrowing capacity and what markets fit your budget and goals. Seeking trusted advice is recommended, but be careful of the sharks in the industry. Unfortunately in property, there are many circling.

Speak with a reputable mortgage broker about your borrowing capacity, and be careful about calculators online advising of your borrowing capacity – none are accurate and all are designed as a sales tool.

There are some reputable property investment businesses, but ensure you understand how they are paid and if this affects which properties they recommend. As it is your financial future, it is best to spend the time educating yourself on what is a sound investment so you can be comfortable making the decision with the assistance of your advisors.

BEING A LANDLORD

Being a landlord comes with responsibilities under the law, which vary depending on the state or territory where your property is located.

As a landlord, you can choose to have a property manager (real estate agency) help you meet these legal obligations and manage your rental property, collect the rent, ensure the paperwork is signed and conduct inspections, or alternatively you can manage the property yourself.

Either way, the same laws apply, and by far the greatest responsibility involves ensuring your property remains safe and habitable for your tenant.

As Tenancy Check[79] explains:

Of utmost importance is that no injury or damage is caused to the tenants, neighbours or public as a direct result of the landlord neglecting their responsibilities.

In addition to common law there are regulations specific to rental properties – these fall under landlord responsibilities and must be followed to the letter.

Landlord responsibilities include:

- Maintaining the structure and exterior of the house
- Ensuring all 'installations' are working, such as gas, electricity and heating
- Installation and appliance maintenance and safety of all landlord-owned appliances
- Treating potentially health-threatening issues, such as rising damp
- Anything else that's stipulated in the tenancy agreement.

OK, so what does this all mean?

As we mentioned earlier, when a property is rented the tenants and landlord (or their agent) sign a rental agreement. This is a binding legal document between a landlord (or their representative agency) and a tenant. It stipulates what's included under the lease conditions, how much rent is to be paid weekly and how long the property is to be rented for.

As the landlord, you have responsibilities under this agreement, with the biggest one being maintenance.

If something breaks at the property, like your water heater or air conditioner, you as the landlord have an obligation to fix it. Basically you have to maintain the property so it remains in the same condition and is as liveable as when the tenant entered it.

Meanwhile, the tenant has an obligation to look after the property, notify you of any maintenance issues and keep it tidy and damage-free.

There are two types of maintenance issues that landlords generally have to deal with: emergency repairs and ongoing maintenance.

An emergency repair is the urgent repair of an essential item, like the hot water heater, any dangerous electrical faults or water supply to the property.

Ongoing maintenance is other things that might need tending to over time, like a bit of a paint refresh, replacing blinds, etc. This second type of maintenance is about ensuring the tenant remains happy in their home and the property retains its value.

If you have an investment property, you need to budget for these emergency repairs and ongoing maintenance, because even in new homes issues do arise.

That's why when you consider the rental income that will be derived over the course of a year, you should budget for 48 weeks rather than 52 weeks of rental income.

Meanwhile, as a landlord, there are a wealth of other decisions to be made. These include selecting the right agency to manage your property, setting the rent, deciding whether or not to allow pets and agreeing on the length of the lease.

So let's look at a few . . .

SELECTING THE RIGHT PROPERTY MANAGER

Although you can manage your own rental property, in most cases it's easier and more efficient to engage a property manager to do that for you.

They look after the tasks associated with renting a property, including:

- Advertising the property
- Suggesting the rental price, based on the market and property type
- Opening it for inspections by prospective tenants
- Filling out an entry condition report

- Drawing up the lease agreement and having it signed by the tenants
- Collecting the bond and lodging it with the relevant state or territory body authority
- Collecting rent on the agreed payment schedule
- Handling maintenance requests from the tenants and organising repairs
- Conducting routine inspections
- Dealing with any lease breaches or issues, such as unpaid rent and property damage
- Liaising with the landlord over lease renewals.

You'll need to pay a property manager for this service, with most deducting a management fee out of your monthly rent in addition to other costs, like letting fees, administration charges and more.

Just some of the costs associated with a property manager are:

Management fees

This is an ongoing fee that a property manager charges for looking after your property. It covers things like collecting rent and handling maintenance requests.

The management fee is usually a percentage of the weekly rent and varies depending on the agency and state or territory. In general, property management fees are five to 12 per cent[80] of the weekly rent.

Letting fees

The letting fee is the charge associated with drawing up a new lease and securing a new tenant for your property. Depending on which state or territory the property is in, it can vary from one to two or even three weeks' rent.

Lease renewal fee

This is the fee charged when an agency draws up a new lease for an existing tenant, and it usually equates to about one week's rent.

Marketing fees

Not all agencies charge this but some do, and it's the cost associated with advertising your property online, in local newspapers, etc. It might also include the cost of photographing your property for advertising purposes. This can be around $200[81].

Monthly administration fee

This is a small amount charged for the paperwork involved in managing a property, like distributing monthly statements. It can be around $10 or in some cases slightly higher.

Annual statement fee

At the end of each financial year, your property manager will issue a statement recapping your rental income and expenses, including the cost of any repairs and maintenance. This might command an annual statement fee, which also varies from as little as $30 to over $80.

Routine inspection fees

Some agencies include routine inspection fees within their management fee, but others charge for this, with the price ranging from $40 to over $100.

Other fees

In addition, depending on where the property is, a property manager might charge ongoing inspection fees, outgoing inspection or bond inspection fees and a percentage on all maintenance and repairs.

If there's a problem with your property and the property manager is required to represent you in court, they are also likely to charge court or tribunal representation costs.

How it looks on paper

Adam and Sandra have a rental property in Queensland, rented for $370 per week. At the end of the month their statement from a property manager has the following charges and income itemised.

- Rent paid by tenants: $1480

- Invoice for gutter clean: $270

- Routine inspection fee: $55

- Management fee (10 per cent): $148

- Administration fee: $11

Amount paid into Adam and Sandra's bank account: $996

Remember, Adam and Sandra will still have to pay any mortgage out of this income, and many of the charges are able to be offset against tax. Together, this indicates whether their property is negatively geared (making a loss) or positively geared (making a gain, which will be assessed as part of their taxable income).

Many investors choose to manage their investment properties themselves. While you can save on the cost of paying a property manager, you need to ensure you follow the relevant laws, execute all documents correctly and carry out routine inspections to ensure your asset is being looked after. If you have the time, knowledge and skill to do this effectively, great. If not, then paying for a professional property manager is money well spent so you can focus on what you do best.

TO RENT OR BUY?

A home to call your own has long been considered the great Australian dream, but that doesn't mean everyone embraces the idea of home ownership.

For some, the benefits of renting far outweigh the cons. For others, the allure of owning your own personal patch of Australia is a vision they actively pursue.

Each has its strengths, so let's look at the question of whether to rent or buy, weighing the pros and cons of each.

THE RENTING PROS

By renting instead of buying a home you avoid the costs of maintaining a property and have greater freedom to move when and where you wish without the encumbrance of selling or renting out your property.

Property maintenance and repairs are the responsibility of the landlord, rather than coming out of your own pocket.

The deposit you require to rent a home is also significantly smaller than the deposit required to buy a property, and renting may allow you to channel those savings into other investments, like an investment property, shares or lifestyle options.

THE RENTING CONS

Like most expenses in life, the cost of renting tends to increase over time, and your landlord is within their rights to increase the rent of your property at the end of each lease term.

They are also within their rights to end a lease agreement with you should you breach the lease terms repeatedly or if they wish to take possession of the property. In each instance sufficient notice is required; however, it does mean renting offers less security than owning your own home.

Altering the property you rent also requires permission, so that outdated kitchen colour scheme may be something you have to live with.

Meanwhile, the money you spend on rental payments does not work towards building up your personal wealth. It's purely an outgoing each and every week.

Figure 9 – Renting pros and cons

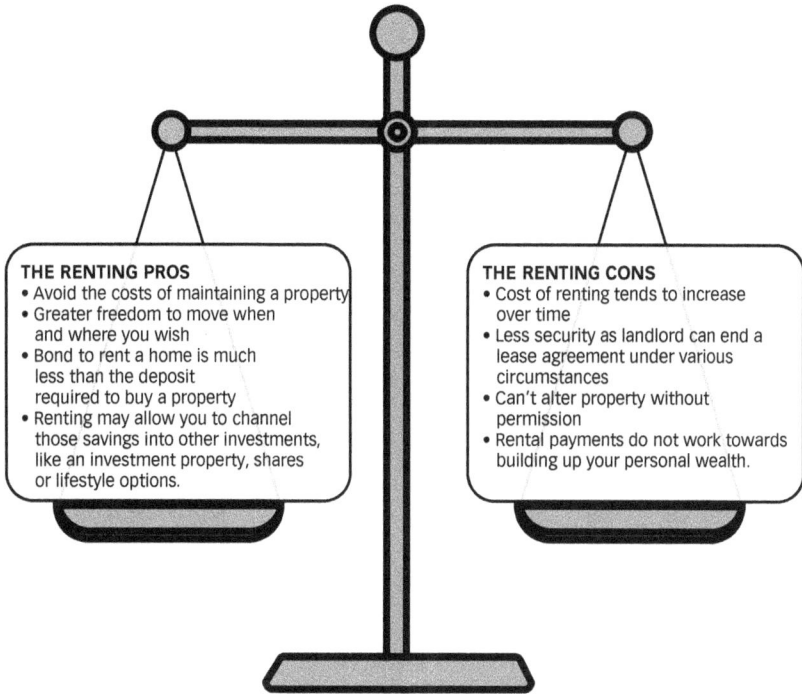

THE RENTING PROS
- Avoid the costs of maintaining a property
- Greater freedom to move when and where you wish
- Bond to rent a home is much less than the deposit required to buy a property
- Renting may allow you to channel those savings into other investments, like an investment property, shares or lifestyle options.

THE RENTING CONS
- Cost of renting tends to increase over time
- Less security as landlord can end a lease agreement under various circumstances
- Can't alter property without permission
- Rental payments do not work towards building up your personal wealth.

HOME OWNERSHIP PROS

A home to call your own is just that: you can renovate, alter it and improve it at will.

The property market in Australia has also seen significant capital gains over extended time. That means the asset you buy now will likely be worth more in the long run, even if there are financial glitches like market downturns along the way.

That mortgage you pay monthly is also like an enforced savings policy, building your stake in an asset over time. Most mortgages have terms of around 30 years, and by and large people pay their homes off within that time.

Loans are structured so that over the course of their term you pay interest and principal amounts, gradually reducing the amount you owe and increasing your ownership of the property.

For many, that means by the time they reach retirement and their income decreases, they own their own home outright, with no outgoings for accommodation.

The equity you build in a property can also feasibly be used to buy additional investment properties, allowing you to build wealth through property ownership.

HOME OWNERSHIP CONS

Buying a property requires you to save a significant deposit, with the minimum amount being about five per cent of the property value. To avoid lender's mortgage insurance you would need 20 per cent plus the purchasing costs, such as stamp duty, legal fees, etc.

That's a significant sum to save and then have tied up in an asset. There are also costs associated with taking out a loan, such as interest payments and annual fees. And you should be prepared for those interest rates to fluctuate over the life of your loan.

Even if you opt for a fixed loan initially, all mortgages revert to flexible interest rates after a set period of time that can be anywhere from one to five years depending on the loan conditions you choose.

In addition to the costs associated with servicing the loan, there are also costs associated with owning a property. From repairs and maintenance to council rates and water or body corporate fees, these additional expenses need to be taken into account.

Meanwhile, should you choose to sell your property, there are costs involved in the buying and selling process, with agents charging commission and advertising fees.

Figure 10 – Home ownership pros and cons

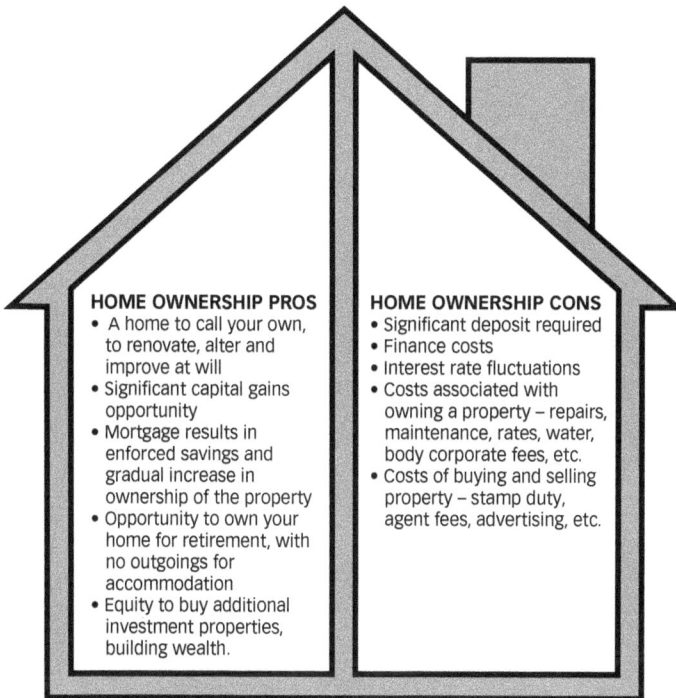

HOME OWNERSHIP PROS
- A home to call your own, to renovate, alter and improve at will
- Significant capital gains opportunity
- Mortgage results in enforced savings and gradual increase in ownership of the property
- Opportunity to own your home for retirement, with no outgoings for accommodation
- Equity to buy additional investment properties, building wealth.

HOME OWNERSHIP CONS
- Significant deposit required
- Finance costs
- Interest rate fluctuations
- Costs associated with owning a property – repairs, maintenance, rates, water, body corporate fees, etc.
- Costs of buying and selling property – stamp duty, agent fees, advertising, etc.

A DIFFERENT OPTION – RENTVESTING

Just when you thought the decision to rent or buy the property where you live was becoming a little more clear-cut, there's also another option that is becoming increasingly popular: rentvesting.

This snappy little term has popped up a lot in recent years and it has a simple meaning. Rentvestors are people who buy property where they can afford yet continue to rent accommodation where they wish to live.

In major markets like Sydney, Melbourne and Brisbane, it's a particularly popular move for young professionals trying to get into the property market but who desire to live close to their workplace or social circles.

According to Domain[82], rentvesting is also a strategy on the rise. In 2014, 20 per cent of investors were rentvestors, while in 2016 that figure had climbed to a third.

And, yes, rentvesting has some benefits, along with some compromises that should be considered . . .

The benefits

It's no secret major metropolitan housing markets present some serious affordability challenges, with houses and units close to the city often commanding the highest purchase prices.

Rentvesting sees these investors seek out property within their budget to buy, while remaining tenants in the properties that offer them access to their workplace, lifestyle and social network.

Ideally, the rent from their investment property pays the majority of the mortgage costs while investment tax incentives also work in the investor's favour.

These incentives range from depreciation for improvements and equipment replacements, to negative gearing tax breaks that allow owners to offset their taxable earnings against any shortfall between the income the property provides and the costs of owning that property.

Meanwhile, choosing the right area and property will also attract capital gain, increasing in value over time, thereby "growing" overall wealth and future borrowing power.

In the interim, the investor still lives in rental accommodation where the landlord bears the cost of maintenance and upkeep.

The downside

Being a landlord comes with responsibility, and there are additional costs that need to be considered.

For example, first home buyer grants are often issued on the premise that the buyer intends to live in the property. That means rentvestors are ineligible for these grants.

Meanwhile, lender interest rates for investors are also slightly higher, while some councils charge higher rates for investors than owner-occupiers.

If you're considering rentvesting, you also need to factor in ongoing upkeep and maintenance costs involved in owning a rental property. While you may get a tax break, it's unlikely these costs will be fully recouped, and the money will need to come out of your pocket over the course of the year.

If the rental income from your property falls short of your mortgage repayments, you need to be mindful of your weekly expenses, which will also include your own rental outgoings for the property that you lease.

The final tally

For some, rentvesting may indeed be the best of both worlds, allowing them to step onto the property ladder while continuing the lifestyle they enjoy.

But as with any financial decision, rentvesting involves research and consideration, and you need to fully consider the pros, cons, your personal circumstances and financial position before you make a commitment.

What's right for you

In the end, whether you buy your home, rentvest or choose to rent comes down to you, and may be influenced by your financial resources, your stage of life, your job security and your lifestyle.

The best advice is to make an informed choice, understanding the pros and cons of each, the long-term scenario and the costs involved.

SELLING A PROPERTY

Whether you're upsizing, downsizing or just looking to embrace the next exciting chapter in life, when it comes to selling a property there's also a process and financial implications involved.

The likelihood is that you will engage a real estate agent who will charge a fee, and there may also be capital gains implications or mortgage exit fees involved.

So let's start at the top . . .

SELLING WITH AN AGENT

Although you can sell your home yourself, most people engage an agent to handle the negotiations, documentation, advertising and some of the legal side of things.

This agent will usually charge a commission or in some cases a flat fee for the sale of your property, along with marketing fees. In return, they will help you set the price based on their market knowledge, advertise the property on the internet and elsewhere, host inspections at the property and negotiate with potential buyers.

They will also draw up the required contract of sale, take any deposit on your behalf and keep you updated throughout all stages of the sales process.

The commission an agent charges will vary depending on where the property is, and the value they believe they provide, but generally it's in the vicinity of about two to three per cent.

This is really a rule of thumb because as Agent Select[83] notes, an agent can propose different fee structures, such as:

- Higher commissions, which include some or all advertising
- Guaranteeing the sale by not getting paid a cent if there's no sale
- Conversely, requiring signage and advertising costs even if the property doesn't sell
- Flat fees
- Scale of commission on the sale price of more expensive real estate
- Any mix of the above, balancing out commission and upfront costs on advertising and signage.

In this instance, we'll base our sums on three per cent. So if your property sells for $600,000, you might pay an agent commission of $18,000 when the property sells.

CONVEYANCING

Just as you required legal assistance when you bought a property, you will need it again when you sell one. This is usually in the form of a conveyancer or lawyer who guides you through the sale process, making sure the documentation is up to par.

As we mentioned earlier, a conveyancer can cost anywhere between $500 and over $2,000, however costs are less for a sale than for a purchase.

MORTGAGE EXIT FEES AND DISCHARGE FEES

Not so long ago, exit fees were often charged by lenders when a home owner either repaid their loan or sold their property and exited their mortgage early. The period was usually restricted to the first five years, but in some cases it was longer.

In 2011, the Federal Government banned this practice on all new loans, but some lenders who entered into a mortgage before this date may still have fees associated with ending your mortgage.

The law now states that these charges cannot exceed the losses incurred by the lenders resulting from the early termination.

These fees may include:

A discharge fee – This is a fee charged by the bank for completing the paperwork on your mortgage. It can range from $150 to $500 depending on your lender.

Early repayment adjustment – If you decide to sell your property during the fixed term of a mortgage, the lender is going to charge you. While there is no set fee, it is calculated by your loan amount, fixed interest rate, current interest rate and fixed term remaining.

Mortgage release fee – This is a government fee for releasing the mortgage the lender has on your property. The fee differs from state to state and is reviewed each financial year. At the time of writing, they range from $110 to $200.

CAPITAL GAINS TAX

As we mentioned before, if you are selling an investment property that has risen in value since you first bought it, you will incur a capital gain, and this will need to be assessed in your taxable income in the year you sell your property.

The home you reside in is exempt from capital gain, but one that you rent out is not. If you have owned the property for less than a year you will pay capital gains tax on the total profit, but if you have had it over 12 months, you receive a concession in only paying capital gains tax on 50 per cent of the profit.

OTHER INVESTMENTS

Bricks and mortar residential property isn't the only way that people choose to invest, with many also diversifying into other arenas, like the share market, antiques, commercial real estate and more.

With the right knowledge and guidance, some of these avenues also have potential for you to put your hard-earned money to work on your behalf, and a couple can also earn you income along the way.

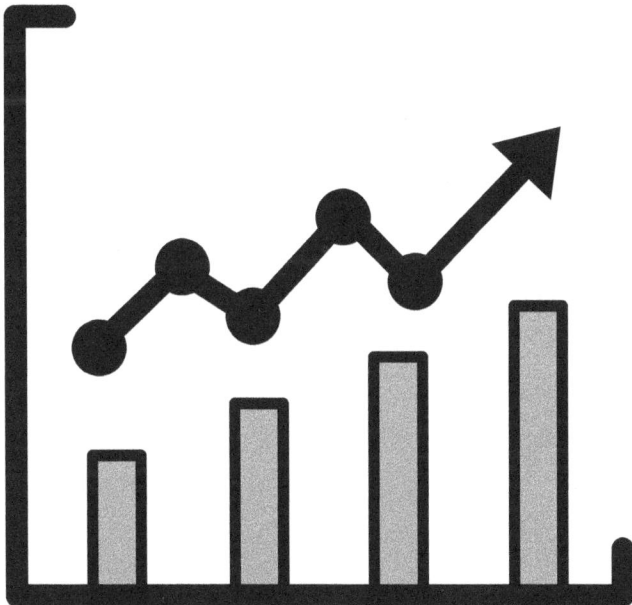

6

Pennies that should drop in Chapter 6 . . .

In Chapter 6, we'll take a look at just some of the other types of investments available, including:

- The share market and how it works, along with dividends and franking credits
- Real estate investment trusts
- Collectibles
- Non-traditional investments, like blockchain
- Seed-funding and angel investing
- Superannuation
- Financial planning and advice
- Scams to watch out for.

By the end of this chapter you'll have a broad appreciation of the many investment options available and some of the risks associated with each, along with potential rewards. You should also be better positioned to consider which types of investments you might want to look into further to make your hard-earned money work for you.

So let's take a brief tour through some of the other investment options available, kicking off with the share market . . .

> *Wings are like dreams. Before each flight, a bird takes a small jump, a leap of faith, believing that its wings will work. That jump can only be made with rock-solid feet.*
>
> J. R. Rim

Figure 11 – Other investment options to consider

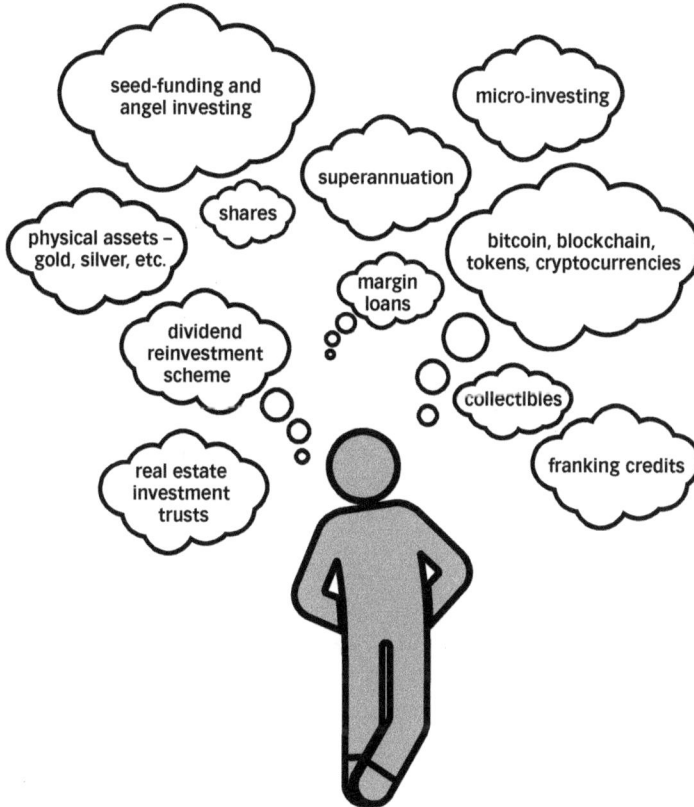

THE SHARE MARKET

You've probably caught a bit about the share market on the news each night courtesy of the daily report, and it's a really fascinating but slightly complex subject matter.

Basically, it works like this . . . Around the world there are 60 stock exchanges. This includes big names like the New York Stock Exchange (NYSE), the London Stock Exchange (LSE) and the Australian Securities Exchange (ASX).

These are places where publicly listed companies offer people the opportunity to invest by purchasing shares in a company. A share is akin to buying a tiny slice of the publicly listed business. Or in other words, the business is divided into tiny components that an investor can buy. There is no set number of shares that a publicly listed company can offer – it's simply determined by how much money the business would like to raise and how many people they would like to offer a stake in ownership to.

For example, the Commonwealth Bank of Australia has 1.77 billion shares available, while the National Australia Bank has 2.95 billion.

When the company does well, the value of each share increases, when it doesn't fare well, the value falls.

As an example of this, in January 2018 Commonwealth Bank shares were valued at over $82 each, but as the housing market fell and the Banking Royal Commission generated negative news about the big banks in the headlines, that share price fell to around $67 in July of that year.

Shares have since picked up again, but it illustrates how their values can rise or fall depending on the company's performance, the economy and other factors.

You can invest in shares of all types of sectors, which the ASX[84] breaks down into 11 broad categories and tracks using indexes that show how well each sector is performing.

These sectors are:

- Consumer discretionary – media, retail and household goods
- Consumer staples – food, beverage and non-durable household goods
- Energy – oil, gas and coal
- Financials – banking, asset management and insurance
- Healthcare – drug developers and healthcare facilities
- Industrials – machinery, airlines and defence
- Information technology – internet providers and online applications
- Materials – glass, paper and steel producers
- Telecommunications – phone carriers
- Utilities – gas, power and water.

DIVIDENDS

Along the way, publicly listed companies can choose to pay a dividend on the shares an investor holds. This is a small return that you get for backing the business involved when the company makes a good profit. So, for every share that a person has, the company might give the investor a slice of the company's earnings based on the company's half-year and end-of-financial-year profit.

For example, throughout the 2018/19 financial year the National Australia Bank made decent earnings.

As a result, it paid a final dividend of 83 cents on each share on 12 December 2019 following its financial results for 2018/19. Six months earlier, It also paid an interim dividend of 83 cents based on its half-year results for 2018/19.

That meant every eligible shareholder received a total of $1.66 per share on that investment during 2019.

Interestingly, the dividend amount dropped to 30 cents in May 2020 due to the economic impacts resulting from the coronavirus.

Publicly listed companies are not required to pay a dividend, but they often do to make investing in their business more appealing. Meanwhile, even those companies that do generally offer a dividend can choose not to pay them if the company fails to make a profit or they feel it could be improved by using the dividend money elsewhere.

For example, between 2014 and early 2019 Origin Energy was having a bit of a tough financial time and recorded consistent losses. This affected both its share price, which dropped, and its dividends. As a result, investors were not paid dividends for about three years.

Dividends are announced when the company involved issues its half and full-year results, and they are paid on a set date after that announcement. To receive the dividend, you must hold the share before something called ex-dividend date.

That's the day before the company works out exactly which shareholders are entitled to a payment (record date). If you buy a share after ex-dividend date, it comes without the dividend attached and the previous shareholder is entitled to it.

And the information looks like this:

Record Date	Ex-Dividend Date	Date Payable	Dividend Amount
13/05/2016	12/05/2016	30/05/2016	90.4c

Source: asx.com.au/prices/dividends.htm

If you're looking for more information about how dividends work, along with a much deeper insight into the share market, the Australian Securities Exchange website is packed full of great resources, which you can access at: asx.com.au.

SHARE INVESTING IN PRACTICE

Investing in shares in Australian-listed companies can also come with some additional tax perks, which we'll get into later. But in the interim, some of Australia's largest companies are publicly listed and many, many people are shareholders.

For example, all major banks, including the Commonwealth Bank, National Australia Bank, Westpac and ANZ are publicly listed companies, as are Woolworths and Coles, and lots of major mining companies, like Rio Tinto and BHP.

As we mentioned, these shares can increase or fall in value in both the short and long term.

Here's a quick example:

On 19 September 2011, Therese had some spare cash and decided to purchase Commonwealth Bank shares. At that time the market was low due to the attack on the World Trade Center and she picked them up for $43.69 each and bought 100 shares for $4,359.

The market continued to fluctuate, but a year later Therese's 100 shares were worth $54.40 apiece ($5,440 in total). At the end of 2019, those same shares were worth $81.65 apiece ($8,165 in total) – a profit of $3,806, if she chose to sell them.

Along the way, Therese received dividends[85] every six months from the shares, depending on how well the company was doing at the time.

Her payments were as follows:

September 2019: $2.31 per share = $231
March 2019: $2.00 per share = $200
September 2018: $2.31 per share = $231
March 2018: $2.00 per share = $200
October 2017: $2.30 per share = $230
April 2017: $1.99 per share = $199
October 2016: $2.22 per share = $222
April 2016: $1.98 per share = $198
October 2015: $2.22 per share = $222
April 2015: $1.98 per share = $198
October 2014: $2.18 per share = $218
April 2014: $1.83 per share = $183
October 2013: $2.00 per share = $200
April 2013: $1.64 per share = $164
October 2012: $1.97 per share = $197
April 2012: $1.37 per share = $137
October 2011: $1.88 per share = $188

So, in the eight years that she has held them, Therese's shares have earned her dividends of $3,331, in addition to increasing in value by $3,806.

In Australia, many major companies also earn something called franking credits, which impact your annual tax, and these too have worked to Therese's advantage.

So what is a franking credit?

FRANKING CREDITS

In a nutshell, a franking credit[86] is a tax imputation credit. (Yes, yes, we know that does not make it simpler.) Basically, a franking credit is a kind of rebate that Australia recognises when it comes to tax and shares.

In short, our taxation system acknowledges that most major companies pay a lot of tax before distributing dividends (a slice of the profits) to share holders. So they don't think it's fair that shareholders get taxed again on dividends, depending on the shareholder's financial circumstances.

The top Australian companies offer fully franked shares. This means a shareholder can receive up to all the tax back that a company would pay on profits, which is usually in the vicinity of 30 per cent.

Therefore, if your income allows for it and your shares are fully franked, you would receive $30 back come tax time on $100 worth of dividends.

And what about Therese? Well, CBA shares are indeed fully franked and she hasn't been earning much other income. That means, since she bought them, she has also received around $1,000 back over the years in tax refunds.

DIVIDEND REINVESTMENT SCHEMES

While Therese was happy to take the modest income each year that she received from dividends, she could also have used them to build a greater share portfolio via dividend reinvesting, and this is a pretty neat way of building equity in shares.

Basically, rather than the shareholder banking the proceeds, many companies offer them the chance to reinvest by buying more, and it allows them to build share equity over time.

So, let's examine Therese's situation slightly differently . . .

In October 2011, Therese received $188 in dividends from her initial 100 CBA shares, but rather than banking the proceeds, she elected to reinvest and purchase three more shares at the October 2011 share price of $47. So then she had 103 shares. In April 2012, she then used her $137 dividend to buy two more shares at $50.25 each. Then she had 105 shares, and so it goes on as this following chart reflects:

Therese's shares	Share value	Dividend	Reinvestment purchase
October 2011 (100 shares)	$4,700	100 @ $1.88 = $188	3 shares @ $47
April 2012 (103 shares)	$5,175.75	103 @ $1.37 = $141.11	2 shares @ $50.25
October 2012 (105 shares)	$5,932.50	105 @ $1.97 = $206.85	3 shares @ $56.50
April 2013 (108 shares)	$7,419.60	108 @ $1.64 = $177.12	2 shares @ $68.70
October 2013 (110 shares)	$8,045.40	110 @ $2.00 = $242.00	3 shares @$73.14
April 2014 (113 shares)	$8,728.12	113 @ $1.83 = $206.79	2 shares @ $77.24
October 2014 (115 shares)	$8,813.60	115 @ $2.18 = $250.70	3 shares @ $76.64
April 2015 (118 shares)	$10,923.26	118 @ $1.98 = $233.64	2 shares @ $92.57
October 2015 (120 shares)	$9,067.20	120 @ $2.22 = $266.40	3 shares @ $75.76
April 2016 (123 shares)	$9,025.74	123 @ $1.98 = $243.54	3 shares @ $73.38
October 2016 (126 shares)	$9,351.72	126 @ $2.22 = $279.72	3 shares @ $74.22
April 2017 (129 shares)	$11,083.68	129 @ $1.99 = $256.71	2 shares @ $85.92
October 2017 (131 shares)	$10,131.54	131 @ $2.30 = $301.30	3 shares @ $77.34
March 2018 (134 shares)	$10,048.66	134 @ $2.00 = $268.00	3 shares @$74.99

Therese's shares	Share value	Dividend	Reinvestment purchase
September 2018 (137 shares)	$9,751.66	137 @ $2.31 = $316.47	4 shares @ $71.18
March 2019 (141 shares)	$10,205.58	141 @ $2.00 = $282.00	3 shares @ $72.38
September 2019 (144 shares)	$11,645.28	144 @ $2.31 = $332.64	4 shares @ $80.87

As you can see from the above chart, simply reinvesting her dividend payouts into purchasing more shares allowed Therese to build a solid shareholding that has now increased from an initial outlay of $4,359 to almost $12,000.

That's a pretty good outcome, but not all share investments pay off. Like property, shares can decrease in value as a result of external factors, like recessions or poor consumer confidence, and internal factors, like company decisions, acquisitions and management changes.

It's also important to note that if Therese chose to sell those shares they would be liable for capital gains tax, because she purchased an asset that has now increased in value.

Like an investment property, this tax would factor in the cost base of the initial purchase and weigh it against other costs associated with managing the shares, like transaction costs, administration, advice and management fees, and the length of time she had them along with the price at sale.

Remember, once you have owned an asset for more than one year, capital gains tax halves to 50 per cent of the total gain.

MARGIN LOANS

Another way people build equity in shares is through something called margin lending, which is basically taking out a loan on the shares or cash you already have and using that borrowed capital to buy additional shares.

This has long been a popular self-managed superannuation strategy that allows people to build large share portfolios, but again it's not without risk.

A margin loan sees you use cash, a managed fund or your existing shares as security for the loan, and the amount you can borrow is based on your loan-to-value ratio (LVR). The LVR is the amount of your loan divided by the value of the shares or managed funds being used as security.

In the case of existing shares, each has an LVR. This can vary over time, depending on how well the company is doing.

For example, CBA shares currently have an LVR of 80 per cent, which means you can potentially borrow up to 80 per cent of the current value of those CBA shares to reinvest in other shares. Origin has an LVR of 75 per cent, so you can potentially borrow up to 75 per cent of the value of your existing shares, while Village Roadshow has an LVR of 50 per cent.

Borrowing up to the maximum amount isn't advised, however, because of something called a margin call, and Investopedia[87] explains how this works:

"A margin call occurs when the value of an investor's margin account (that is, one that contains securities bought with borrowed money) falls below the broker's required amount.

"A margin call is the broker's demand that an investor deposit additional money or securities so that the account is brought up to the minimum value, known as the maintenance margin."

In other words, if the value of the existing shares falls below a certain point, the investor must either deposit more money in to top it up and ensure it's above the threshold, or sell some shares.

If you have a margin loan, that means you need to pay very close attention to the value of the shares you have borrowed against, and be able and prepared to take action should a margin call be triggered.

The benefit of a margin loan is that it gives you access to more funds to invest. It can also have tax benefits, as you may be able to claim the interest on that loan as a tax deduction. But as we mentioned, you need to treat this strategy with extreme caution and educate yourself thoroughly. It may not suit your financial circumstances.

As CommBank[88] notes: "There is additional risk in borrowing to invest. If the market or your investments drop in value, then you won't only be dealing with that loss – you'll also have to repay the loan.

"Although the additional market exposure has the potential to magnify returns, it also has the potential to magnify losses. In addition to this, any positive returns need to outperform the cost of borrowing, which can fluctuate with interest rates."

OTHER INVESTMENTS ON THE SECURITIES EXCHANGE

In addition to investing in shares in companies on the Australian Securities Exchange, you can also invest in other asset classes, like commodities, and government and corporate bonds. Slightly different to the securities discussed above, which represent a stake in a company, investing in commodities represents ownership of actual physical products while buying shares in government bonds represents the ownership of a loan.

In the case of commodities, these tend to be raw materials, like gold, crude oil, wheat or sugar.

Meanwhile, bonds are issued by a government or corporation when they wish to raise money. Basically, when you buy into a bond, you become that entity's lender, and they agree to pay you back the loan at a specific date, while also making interest payments along the way.

SHORT-TERM INVESTING

Investing in the share market is generally considered a long game. You buy an asset, hold it for an extended period to achieve capital gain and also reap the benefits of dividends along the way. You can of course take a short-term view, should you wish.

This involves investing in a share that you believe has a low value now but will quickly increase.

This is much much riskier and has far greater tax implications, and it's like betting on the fact the market will do something in the short term.

In this case, for example . . .

Mani knows there's been some pretty negative news in the headlines about the big banks. That's likely to see the CBA share price plummet when the ASX opens at 10am tomorrow. So he sets up a trade, using his online trading account, to buy 100 CBA shares should their price hit $70 (a $7,000 outlay, plus broking costs).

Once purchased, he further 'bets' on the fact the market will rally and those shares will quickly increase in value to $80 apiece. He sets up a trade, noting he will 'sell' his entire holdings of 100 shares when this happens.

If it comes off, Mani stands to make $1,000 (minus broking fees). He will also be liable for full capital gains tax, as it's likely he has held those shares for less than 12 months.

Although this sounds simple, there are very real risks involved. The share price could drop further, which would see Mani either required to hold the shares or make a loss. Meanwhile, that 'quick trade' may actually take years to pay off.

If you have a look at the historic CBA share price in the chart below, you'll note they were valued under $80 for a very long time. So, the bottom line: only invest what you can afford to lose or outlay and be fully aware of the tax implications involved.

Source: asx.com.au/asx/share-price-research/company/CBA

This also brings us to the concept of short-selling, which is a pretty contentious topic, made famous by movies like *The Wolf of Wall Street* and *The Big Short*.

So what is short-selling?

SHORT-SELLING

Let's start with a quick disclaimer – short-selling is a very risky strategy that is generally reserved for very experienced and professional investors who know the market incredibly well, and it is not something we would advise.

Also, most brokers in Australia do not facilitate short-selling, so it's not like you can open an NAB or CBA trading account and undertake this risky activity. In most cases, short-selling is facilitated by hedge funds or brokers trading on behalf of a firm.

But, just so you know, it works like this:

Short-selling is when an investor borrows shares (for a fee) then immediately sells them in the hope their price will drop. They then buy the shares back at this lowered price to return them to their rightful owner. In the interim they make a profit on the price difference between the sale and the repurchase.

Being 'short' is the exact opposite strategy to normal share investing ('being long'), where the aim of the game is for the share price to rise.

The problem with short-selling is that it's a bet – it's a wager that a share will plummet, and the results are far from guaranteed. It can also be a very costly punt.

With a standard share purchase, the worst that can happen is that you lose the asset you own and reap no financial return, say, if the company goes bankrupt and you lose 100 per cent of your investment.

With short-selling, there is no limit to the amount of money you could lose if the share price doesn't drop and instead increases.

Say, for example, you borrow a share then sell it for $2 in the hope it will drop to $1. Instead, it doubles to $4. Now you need to repurchase that share at twice the price you sold it for so you can return it to its rightful owner, and on top of that you still pay them for the privilege. Ouch.

There's also no set time frame for when you have to 'close out your position' and return the shares to their owner. Basically, if they want their shares back, you need to oblige.

That said, there are advantages for seasoned investors who often short-sell in addition to buying stocks for the long term. When successful, short-selling can allow them to make a profit regardless of whether the market rises or falls.

But if you're not a seasoned investor, this is definitely not something to try at home!

HOW CAN YOU INVEST IN SHARES?

There are a number of different ways to invest in shares. You can buy them through a broker or broking service and manage them yourself, purchase them directly when a company first goes public or join a managed fund.

Let's look at the options . . .

Buying and selling via a broker

In Australia, all existing shares in publicly listed companies are bought and sold via a broker. This person or service is a member of the stock exchange and is authorised to conduct transactions.

These days, most major banks offer broking services that allow you to set up a trading account then buy or sell shares online. This is considered a non-advisory broker – they don't provide any advice on what you should buy or sell, or when, but they simply facilitate the transaction for a low fee.

In addition to that there are also full-service brokers. These companies or people tend to be more expensive, as they offer advice and recommendations on securities to invest in and can provide tailored investment plans suited to your circumstances.

The ASX has some great resources and tips that offer an introduction to the stock market, including how to find a broker, and you can access their wealth of information at asx.com.au/education/first-time-investors.htm.

Initial public offerings (IPOs)

When a company first goes public or wishes to release new shares as a way of raising capital, it will undertake an initial public offering (IPO). Also known as a float, this sees shares directly available for purchase.

How to apply for the shares in question is contained in the company's prospectus, which must be lodged with the Australian Securities and Investment Commission (ASIC). This document should also contain information about what the company intends to do with the capital, how many shares are available, who the company directors are and the company's financial position.

If you're considering investing in an IPO, you should read this document very closely and fully understand it before proceeding.

Crowd-sourced funding

Generally restricted to start-ups and small to medium companies, crowd-sourced funding (CSF) is another way to invest in shares. The process usually occurs through a CSF website and allows you to invest up to $10,000 per annum per company.

Crowd-sourced funding of shares is often considered riskier, as the company usually lacks a track record; the value of the shares may fall; and the investment is considered illiquid. This means you could be required to hold your shares for a set period and may not be able to sell them when you want to.

If you're considering this as an investment option, it's critical to do your research and also check that the CSF website the company uses is run by a licensed intermediary. You can ascertain this at ASIC Connect's professional services register: asic.gov.au/online-services/search-asics-registers/professional-registers.

Employee shares

If you work for a publicly listed company, you may be given shares or offered the opportunity to purchase shares at a discount rate or minus broking fees.

These shares may come with conditions about when they can be bought, sold or accessed.

Managed funds

When you invest in a managed fund, your money is pooled with other people's. Each fund has a manager who then makes investment decisions on your behalf. Their aim is to outperform the market, buying and selling based on research, knowledge and insight.

They may just invest in shares, but they could also invest in other assets as well. In return you should receive income or periodic distributions.

Fees for investing in a managed fund can be high, but it can also be a good way of putting your money to work on the share market without the pressure of making the decision of what to buy and sell by yourself.

You can also regularly contribute to a managed fund to build your wealth, and they tend to offer diversification.

Superannuation funds are a type of managed fund.

More information about managed funds is available at: moneysmart.gov.au/investing/managed-funds.

Exchange-traded funds

Bought and sold in a similar manner to shares, exchange-traded funds or ETFs are an increasingly popular way of investing in the share market.

Rather than investing in a single company, buying into an ETF sees you purchase components of an investment fund that has a portfolio of shares or bonds.

The value of an ETF on the stock exchange represents the value of underlying investments that the ETF holds, and they can be either active or passive.

Passive ETFs are the most common and tend to track in line with an asset or index, like the ASX200. So their value goes up and down in line with the market.

Active ETFs attempt to outperform the market, which makes them slightly riskier. In this instance, the fund manager is attempting to predict what the share market will do and capitalise on its rise or fall.

The benefit of an ETF is that the fees are lower than a managed fund but they still allow you to diversify into different company holdings. You can also invest in them with only a small amount of cash.

It's important to note when you invest in an ETF that you don't actually own the shares they buy and sell. Instead, you own a unit of the ETF.

Meanwhile, an ETF will generally cover just one type of asset class, and there are different types available that extend beyond shares to include commodities such as wool, precious metals (like gold) or foreign currencies.

More information about ETFs is available at: moneysmart.gov.au/investing/managed-funds/exchange-traded-funds-etfs.

Index funds

Index funds are a type of managed fund that allows you to hold a selection of stocks. However, in this case the fund directly reflects a stock market index (such as the ASX200 or ASX300). Effectively, that means you invest in a fund that has shares in the largest 200 or 300 companies in Australia (by market capitalisation) at that time.

When one company leaves the index, the fund manager sells shares in that company and replaces them with new ones. This makes index funds very easy to oversee for a fund manager. They are also considered a generally safe investment option and have historically performed well compared to many other types of investments.

In Australia, many ETFs behave like index funds by tracking companies within an index. However, there are a few distinct differences between an ETF and an index fund.

For example, ETFs are traded like shares and listed on the stock market. Index funds are not listed – they are a type of managed fund. Index funds are also priced differently to ETFs. The price paid for an ETF reflects its value on the stock market, while the price of an index fund reflects the value of its underlying assets.

On the subject of price, while an ETF can cost less than $100 to purchase, an index fund tends to require more capital, with funds typically commanding a minimum investment of $5,000[89].

Meanwhile, an ETF can be bought or sold at any time during the trading day, while an index fund is priced at the end of the trading day.

Warren Buffet, considered by many as the greatest investor in history, says in his book *The Little Book of Common Sense Investing* that "a low-cost index fund is the most sensible equity investment for the great majority of investors".

You can learn more about index funds at: finder.com.au/how-to-invest-in-index-funds-in-australia#whatif

morningstar.com.au/etfs/article/head-to-head-index-funds-versus-index-etfs/186787.

INVESTING IN ASSETS LIKE PHYSICAL GOLD

As we mentioned above, you can buy shares in gold, silver and platinum through the ASX, but you can also buy physical gold in coin form or certificates in gold, silver and platinum through the Perth Mint.

In the case of the Perth Mint, they offer the only government-backed certificate program in the world. It allows you to own investment-grade gold, silver or platinum. They give you a certificate of ownership and store the precious metals in their storage facility.

You can then trade this gold, silver or platinum when you wish, using an authorised distributor. You can learn more about the Perth Mint's certificate program and how it works at: perthmint.com/storage/certificate-program.html.

INVESTING IN COLLECTIBLES

In other cases, people also choose to invest in physical items, like collectibles.

Collectibles generally encompass valuable items that are likely to rise in value over the period of time that you hold them.

Examples include artwork, classic cars and antiques. Investing in collectibles involves a sound knowledge of the asset involved, and they may take some time to increase in value.

Heather's classic car

Heather has always had a love of classic cars, especially Holdens. So when she finds a 1959 Holden FC available for sale for $5,000 she's keen to snap it up.

Heather owns the car for 10 years and really takes care of it while still enjoying a regular drive. In that time, Heather's classic car has increased in value because Holden FCs are becoming increasingly rare.

When she chooses to sell it, her car is valued at $20,000 (an increase of $15,000 above her purchase price).

It's important to note, Heather got a little bit lucky here. She managed to pick a car that became rare, she looked after it, and it was in demand by the time she came to sell.

REAL ESTATE INVESTMENT TRUSTS (REITS)

We talked a lot about property earlier, but another way of gaining exposure to the property market is through a real estate investment trust or REIT. Real estate investment trusts work a bit like a managed fund, but instead of shares in companies, you invest in a slice of the property pie.

It works like this: when you invest in a REIT, your money is pooled with that of other investors, and the trust manager then makes investments on your behalf. You receive a slice of the profits and earnings that this fund makes.

There are two main types of REITs, each with slightly different strategies.

The first and most common is an equity REIT. This sees the fund buy physical property. Often different REITs will specialise in different areas of the property market, like residential housing, apartments, shopping centres or pubs and hotels. They might also offer diversification, where they span a couple of these sectors.

Money is then generally made from leasing these properties out, with the income distributed to the REIT members.

The second type of REIT invests in mortgages, and this one's a little more complex. Canstar[90] explains: "These types of REITs loan money to the owners of real estate for mortgages or mortgage-backed securities. Typically, mortgage REITs generate income through the interest paid on the loan."

REITs can offer benefits for people looking to gain exposure to the property market without taking out a mortgage or saving for a deposit. They can also allow you to invest in property types that would normally be unavailable, such as commercial developments.

Like a managed fund or ETF, they can also be a source of income. Meanwhile, the investment you make could also grow in capital value as the value of the property increases.

Another benefit of a REIT is they are relatively easy to invest in. REITs are traded on the stock market just like a share, so you can buy into them and sell your holdings when you choose. That means they are considered a "liquid" asset, unlike property, which takes time to sell and can be costly to transact.

Generally, the minimum investment capital for a REIT is $500, and there are a large number of Australian REITs currently listed on the share market.

You can see a list of REITs here: listcorp.com/asx/sectors/real-estate or learn more about them at https://www.asx.com.au/products/managed-funds/areits.htm.

SEED FUNDING, ANGEL INVESTING AND CROWD FUNDING

Seed funding or angel investing involves investing in a start-up company. You and often a group of others provide initial investment in a company for a share of the business and profit if they succeed. Generally, the threshold to enter investments like this is quite high – you need to have a fair bit of wealth behind you.

It's also considered an illiquid asset – you have to hold your investment for a lengthy period of time, and there may be barriers to cashing out.

It can also be quite risky. Start-ups can and do fail, quite often. For every Atlassian, Facebook and Microsoft out there, thousands of companies have never progressed beyond start-up. But if the idea of being an angel investor piques your interest, the *Financial Review* published a useful article on it here: afr.com/wealth/investing/how-to-be-an-angel-investor-20151210-glkcwd.

Meanwhile, there are angel investing clubs where people pool their money and look at companies to invest in.

In contrast to angel investing, which often requires large amounts of capital to invest, crowd funding sees projects get off the ground courtesy of small investments from a large number of people.

Crowd funding can also involve just pure donations, so if you're considering this as an investment strategy, be sure you understand exactly what's on offer in return.

It's also considered risky, so make sure you thoroughly research the organisation seeking funding and the project they are looking to undertake.

DIGITAL TOKENS AND CRYPTOCURRENCIES

OK, this topic is considered quite contentious, so we'll be clear from the outset – we are not talking about mining Bitcoin or investing your life savings into cryptocurrencies. Instead, we will explain a little about what digital tokens and currencies like Bitcoin, Litecoin, Ripple and Ethereum are and give you a quick 101 on blockchain.

Bitcoin and blockchain

Made famous by the likes of Bitcoin, blockchain is basically a virtual distributed ledger system containing digital blocks of time-stamped information. Each block of information on the chain adds to the previous one. They are only added to by the consensus of a group allowing an entire asset's history to be tracked and the transfer of ownership to take effect immediately.

Blockchain has a host of applications beyond cryptocurrencies like Bitcoin. In fact, there are now hundreds of other ways blockchain is employed, and it's popping up in highly reputable areas.

As another way to think about this, just as email is one use of the internet, Bitcoin is one application of blockchain.

The advent of blockchain is seeing banks, the real estate sector and many more industries look to use the system as a way to exchange ownership of products, goods and even shares.

In the meantime, a number of digital tokens have sprung up, which people can buy. These tokens basically represent the different applications of blockchain, so Bitcoin is one of these tokens representing a blockchain that acts as a currency to buy and sell items.

As we mentioned, some people mine Bitcoin and other tokens. In the case of Bitcoin, they do this through a complex mathematical computer process that allows the currency to change hands. That's not what we are talking about here, but you can learn more about it at: dummies.com/software/other-software/bitcoin-mining-works.

In addition to Bitcoin, there are other cryptocurrencies and digital tokens, some of which represent an investment in the technology that's driving blockchain.

OK, so what exactly do we mean by that? Well, let's look at Ethereum for example.

Ethereum and other digital currencies

Ethereum is both a digital currency and a blockchain technology platform. As an open software platform it allows developers to create and run software and also facilitates transactions.

One of Ethereum's major strengths lies in smart contracts, which are a neat way of meeting regulatory compliance and executing the terms of contracts. Basically, it's a code that only allows something to change hands when specific conditions are met.

That means Ethereum has a potential role to play in a lot of different areas, like real estate, asset exchange, loan terms and finance.

People invest in Ethereum's digital tokens, which are known as Ether (ETH). Like shares, Ether can be bought and sold, while Ether is also used to pay for services on the Ethereum network.

As you can imagine, if Ethereum's usage increases and blockchain becomes more mainstream, the value of these tokens might rise. That value might also fall depending on its popularity and how many tokens in total are available.

As an insight, ETH tokens were first available as an Initial Coin Offering (we'll explain a bit more about that later) in 2015, and tokens were valued at USD$0.31.

As of January 2020, their value was $170.14. That might seem like a solid investment, but make no mistake – there have been peaks and troughs along the way, and buying into digital currencies is far from a sure thing for a host of different reasons.

Other big names

Ethereum is just one example of a digital token and blockchain technology. There are other big names:

Ripple (XRP) – A blockchain-based technology that facilitates real-time settlements and transfers of currencies and can store their value.

Litecoin (LTC) – A cryptocurrency and payment system that's much like Bitcoin but is able to be processed faster.

Tether (USDT) – A way of anchoring digital currencies to fiat (traditional currencies). It's designed so users can transact traditional currencies in a digital manner.

Meanwhile, new digital tokens and currencies roll out all the time.

How digital tokens and currencies are traded

Just like shares, digital tokens and cryptocurrencies can be bought and sold on an exchange. But here things start to get very different. For one, unlike the Australian Securities Exchange or New York Stock Exchange, these exchanges aren't regulated. That means if they fail or are hacked your investment might simply disappear.

To start trading, you transfer real money into a digital wallet and then purchase the digital currencies you would like to hold.

Bear in mind, these tokens are virtual. Crypto and digital currencies are not anchored to a real-world product, nor are they guaranteed by a government or bank.

Instead, their value is based on their popularity at that moment in time, and it's a volatile playing space. MoneySmart[91] explains that popularity can rise or fall for a host of reasons, "such as the number of people using it, the ease with which it can be traded or used and the perceived value of the currency and its underlying blockchain technology".

That makes it highly speculative, while you also run the risk of your tokens being stolen. Just as your real wallet can be taken by a thief, your digital details could feasibly be hacked, and as cryptocurrencies and digital tokens are by nature anonymous, there's no way of proving ownership and getting them back.

Initial Coin Offerings

Another way to acquire digital tokens is through Initial Coin Offerings. These take place when a blockchain start-up is looking to raise some capital. At this point they will offer a number of coins for sale, encouraging investors to back their endeavour.

The value of that investment will then be based on whether their technology succeeds or fails and how popular it becomes. If successful, these tokens can be traded for cash or other digital currencies. If it fails, they may be worth . . . nothing.

Bitcoin ATMs

In rare cases you can also exchange cash for cryptocurrencies like Bitcoins at ATMs, and these days you can also use the currency to buy some real-world goods.

A TAXATION WORD TO THE WISE

Like all assets, buying and selling digital currencies and tokens has tax implications. Although the regulations are in their infancy, MoneySmart[92] explains the ATO's proposed treatment of crypto and digital currencies like this:

- **Goods and services** – If the cost of your digital currency is less than $10,000 and you are only using it to pay for personal goods or services, it is not taxed.
- **Investment** – If you hold digital currencies as an investment, you will pay capital gains tax on any profits when you sell them.
- **Trading** – If you trade virtual currencies for profit, the profits will form part of your assessable income.
- **Carrying on a business** – If you use cryptocurrencies to pay for (or accept them as payment for) goods or services, the transactions will be subject to goods and services tax (GST).
- **Mining bitcoin** – If you are mining bitcoins or other digital currencies, any profits you make will be included in your assessable income.
- **Conducting an exchange** – If you are buying and selling cryptocurrencies as an exchange service, you will pay income tax on the profits and transactions will be subject to GST.

MICRO-INVESTING

One of the newest trends currently available is something called micro-investing. Made possible with technology, micro-investing generally utilises an app that allows you to designate small change towards investments. A good example is Raiz (raizinvest.com.au), which helps you invest spare change automatically from everyday purchases into a diversified portfolio.

You can set these apps up to take regular amounts from your bank account for investment purposes, or to round up the small change from purchases.

For example, you can specify that every time you buy a coffee (for, say, $4.50), the app will round the purchase up to the nearest dollar ($5) and deposit the change ($0.50) into your investment strategy.

At present, micro-investing apps cover a range of assets, including share market exchange traded funds and indexes.

They also encompass new investments, like blockchain and cryptocurrencies, allowing you to invest a small amount in things like Bitcoin, Litecoin, Ripple and Ethereum.

The benefit of micro-investing is that you don't require a large pool of cash to start putting your money to work, and you can build your investment strategy over time.

As always, it's important to carefully consider what types of investments you are putting your money into.

> **It's amazing what you can accomplish if you do not care who gets the credit.**
> Harry Truman

SUPERANNUATION: MANAGED AND SELF-MANAGED

For many people, the investments they make throughout their life are designed to give them access to wealth in both the short and long term, with one of the primary aims being to ensure they have enough income to retire comfortably.

This brings us neatly back to the topic of superannuation. Earlier we mentioned that when you have a job your employer will be required to contribute part of your salary to a superannuation fund on your behalf in order to set money aside for your retirement.

The reality is that there are two types of superannuation schemes available: managed superannuation and self-managed super. So, let's take a look at the difference between the two.

Managed superannuation

In many ways, managed superannuation is a bit of a set-and-forget scenario. You either pick a super fund that you believe suits your needs or you are directed to one as part of your industry agreement. Once you start contributing to that fund, they take care of the rest.

They pool your money with other super fund contributors and make investments on your behalf in a bid to increase your money over time. They may invest in shares, real estate investment trusts, etc., but the aim of the game is for your net worth to grow.

Although you can't pick what investments your managed super fund will make on your behalf, if you are able to select your own super fund, you can do so based on the type of investments they are likely to consider, such as ethical investments or high returns.

Selecting your managed fund

When it comes to managed super, it's important to remember the following:

- In certain jobs, you may not be able to pick your own fund – your industry agreement may dictate which super fund is used.
- You should base your decision on which fund to go with based on their long-term performance (five years at least, not just one). Sometimes the investments super funds opt for do not pay off.
- All funds charge fees, but the lowest fees may not equal the best fund. Funds may also charge fees for different actions (advice fees, exit fees, rollover fees, etc.), so be sure you know exactly what you're up for.
- Different funds have different levels of risk and you should ensure you are comfortable with the risk involved.
- If a new job brings with it a new fund, you need to consolidate your super. More than one fund means more than one set of fees.
- You can consolidate your funds using a rollover form from the ATO, which is available at: ato.gov.au/forms/rollover-initiation-request-to-transfer-whole-balance-of-superannuation-benefits-between-funds.

You can learn more about managed funds, including choosing your super fund at: moneysmart.gov.au/superannuation-and-retirement/how-super-works/choosing-a-super-fund.

Self-managed funds

Unlike managed super, where you simply name a fund and they invest on your behalf, self-managed superannuation is more of a do-it-yourself affair. You choose the level of risk, you choose the investments, and you bear the responsibility should something go wrong.

You also have some serious obligations under the law, and self-managed super funds can be expensive to establish. That means self-managed super funds are often best suited to people with significant financial knowledge and a large balance at the outset.

In short, a self-managed super fund (SMSF) is a legal tax structure established with the sole purpose of providing for your retirement. A SMSF is private, can have up to four owners and is regulated by the Australian Taxation Office. It operates under the same rules and restrictions as an ordinary super fund, but each member must be a trustee.

MoneySmart[93] explains when you run your own SMSF, you must:

- Carry out the role of trustee or director, which imposes important legal obligations on you
- Set and follow an investment strategy that is appropriate for your risk tolerance and is likely to meet your retirement needs
- Have the financial experience and skills to make sound investment decisions
- Have enough time to research investments and manage the fund
- Budget for ongoing expenses, such as professional accounting, tax, audit, legal and financial advice
- Keep comprehensive records and arrange an annual audit by an approved SMSF auditor
- Consider insurance, including income protection and total and permanent disability cover, for super fund members
- Use the money only to provide retirement benefits.

You can engage a licensed advisor to assist with the decisions you make on behalf of your SMSF and the financial or tax obligations, but MoneySmart also notes, "If you decide to set up an SMSF, you are personally liable for all the decisions made by the fund – even if you get help from a professional or another member makes the decision."

Benefits of an SMSF include:

- The ability to choose your own investments and level of risk
- Tax strategies
- Flexibility
- Transparency
- Cost
- The ability to consolidate superannuation assets.

Risks of an SMSF include:

- Personal liability
- Responsibility
- Potential increased exposure to risk
- Time-consuming and administratively intensive.

Wrap accounts

In addition, normal super, which is managed on your behalf, and self-managed super, which you look after, there's also the option of what's called a wrap account.

This option allows you to store all your investments in one place, including managed funds, shares and cash, and term deposits.

You can then track how all your investments are performing using one platform and work with a financial advisor or choose to select which investments you hold yourself. Note that most wrap account providers have an approved product list that you must stay in between.

Choice[94] offers an insight into the pros and cons of wrap accounts, with this explanation:

Pros

- Access to a wide range of managed funds, investments and fund managers
- A single, consolidated report instead of individual reports for every investment or account
- Potentially lower management fees if you have access to wholesale funds
- Online access
- A single report at tax time, plus fees may be tax deductible with certain platforms.

Cons

- Fees can be charged for wrap fund administration, moving money in and out of the fund, management of different investment options and performance reports, plus an overall service fee from your financial adviser.
- You may be locked into a particular adviser's firm and have to liquidate the account as well as pay capital gains and an exit fee if you want to take your business elsewhere.
- Advisers may be recommending these funds for their own convenience, not yours.

You can read more about wrap accounts here: choice.com.au/money/ financial-planning-and-investing/managed-funds-and-trusts/buying-guides/ wraps-and-master-trusts.

FINANCIAL ADVISORS AND PLANNERS

Not all of us have the time or perhaps the inclination to become an expert in all areas of our finances, which is where the assistance of a financial planner or advisor might come in handy.

These two terms are often used interchangeably but are actually a little different.

A financial advisor is someone who helps a client manage their finances, and their role can be one-off advice or an ongoing relationship.

A planner tends to have more long-term expertise in areas like retirement and superannuation. Their role is often ongoing and they re-evaluate the best course of action over time.

Each works with you to identify your financial goals and then devise strategies to achieve them. They tend to start this process by looking at what you earn, what you own and what you owe, along with analysing your typical expenditure each month or each year.

Then they'll work with you to come up with strategies to achieve these aims. Areas they might advise on include budgeting, investing in shares, investing in property, paying down loans and more.

If you're looking at long-term planning, they'll also take your life goals into account, like travel, holidays and time off work to be with children, and the type of risks you'd be willing to take to achieve your financial dreams.

It's a bit like putting together a map for your financial future with the stepping stones marked out clearly.

If you're looking for the expert assistance of a financial planner or adviser, there are a couple of things to keep in mind:

1. **Check their credentials** – Professional advisors are registered and licensed to offer their financial expertise. You can check whether someone is registered at the MoneySmart advisors register, which can be found at: moneysmart.gov.au/investing/financial-advice/financial-advisers-register.

    This register contains information like the advisor's qualifications, their licence number and the type of finances they advise on, along with any previous disciplinary action.

2. **You need to be honest** – There's no point giving a planner or advisor only half the story. Give them all the information they ask for and be honest about what you want to achieve.

    Only then can an advisor or planner devise strategies that are right for you and your circumstances.

3. **Find someone you trust** – You'll be working closely with an advisor and offering up all your financial information, so in addition to finding someone who is licensed and registered, ensure you feel you can work with them and trust their decision-making.

    If you're not gelling with an advisor or their suggestions don't sit well with you, seek out another alternative.

4. **Consider the services you're after** – Different advisors have different areas of specialty. Some might have a broad overview; others might lean towards specific areas, like superannuation, share investing or property.

    Consider the aims you're looking to achieve and the type of services you might be after. For example, it's no use consulting a superannuation advisor if your aim is to simply reduce debt here and now.

5. **Consider your level of risk** – An advisor might come up with different types of strategies to help you achieve your aim, and some could be riskier than others. For example, they might look at more

aggressive share investing where the rewards will be higher but the risks could also be greater.

Make sure you understand the strategies your advisor is suggesting and that you are comfortable with that level of risk.

6. **Know the cost** – Advisors come at a cost, so be very clear about exactly how much you will need to pay them and when. Your prospective advisor should clearly inform you of this, but make sure they do so in writing and you read the information provided, including any ongoing commissions or management fees.

Once your advisor has met with you and understands your current financial situation and future goals, they will provide you with a document called a statement of advice (SoA). This document will contain a series of strategies and options that they recommend.

Be sure to read this closely, including all disclosure information. Ask yourself whether you feel the advisor understands your situation, whether you're comfortable with the strategies they outline, and whether they suit your needs.

Also consider whether these strategies are balanced or push too heavily in one direction.

Only when you are fully acquainted with this document, understand it and are completely happy with it should you sign it.

MoneySmart has some more great advice available for selecting the right advisor, and you can find it at: moneysmart.gov.au/investing/financial-advice/working-with-a-financial-adviser.

The reality is that many people have worked very successfully with financial advisors to set themselves up financially in both the short and long term. Whether it's an option that suits you comes down to your stage of life, your personal preferences and whether you consider it a worthwhile investment.

SCHEMES TO BE WARY OF

There's a great old saying that, "If it looks too good to be true, it probably is," and nowhere is this more true than when it comes to your personal finances.

At any given time there are a wide variety of 'get rich quick' schemes circulating on Facebook or via email scams. Others use the tried-and-true old-school methods like phone and post.

The truth is, for as long as people have had money, others have tried to fleece them of it, so if something looks even *slightly* suspicious, think twice.

Never give your bank account details or personal information to people you do not know well, and be wary of the promise that someone can make you rich.

For example, one of the most prominent scams currently doing the rounds on Facebook involves Bitcoin. This scheme looks for all intents and purposes like a news item from a reputable publication, which talks about how celebrities have made a killing investing in cryptocurrencies.

Any investment, whether it's blockchain, shares, super or property carries risks. No reputable entity will make a surefire promise that it will deliver, because they can't – legally or ethically.

If in doubt about an offer you receive or advice you are given, always research the information, seek reputable advice and reconsider.

This applies to cryptocurrencies especially, as that sphere is yet to be regulated, the asset is not tangible, and the market is volatile.

There are also numerous scams where fraudsters are posing as reputable entities like Telstra, internet providers, Woolworths and the Australian Taxation Office.

The reality is the ATO will contact you in writing, not via the phone. Telstra will have details, like your customer reference number, and your internet provider will say who they are. If this information cannot be provided or if it does not ring true, chances are it's a scam.

You can find more advice on current scams or report one at: scamwatch.gov.au.

7

STARTING A BUSINESS

Australia is a small business nation, accounting for 35 per cent of the nation's domestic gross profit and 44 per cent of all employment, according to the Small Business Ombudsman[95].

This nation of entrepreneurs is also growing courtesy of both Millennials[96] and Generation Z[97], who have the freedom of being their own boss in their sights and the technology to drive their independence.

So how do you go about establishing yourself in small business? What's involved? What are the risks? And what do you need to know?

Pennies that should drop in Chapter 7 . . .

This chapter is for the entrepreneurs among us, and chances are there are a few. It's a broad-brush perspective of what it takes to start a business and run one, covering topics like:

- Due diligence
- Business structures
- Business rights and responsibilities, including registrations, licenses, tax, GST, insurance, and Workplace Health and Safety
- We'll also look at staffing and funding your business.

By the end of Chapter 7 you might have a better idea whether starting or buying a business feels right for you, along with the boxes you need to tick as you grow in business and attain success.

> **All things are difficult before they are easy.**
>
> Thomas Fuller

THE SMALL BUSINESS REALITY

People enter small business for a whole range of reasons: independence, opportunity, a great idea or simply to be their own boss. And small business can be a hugely rewarding experience, allowing you to manage your own time, provide employment for others, secure your financial future and establish an empire.

But it's not without risk or, in some cases, sacrifice. Although the statistics vary and in many instances are grossly exaggerated, small business failure is far from uncommon. In 2019, the Small Business Ombudsman put the average survival rate of all small business at 64.5 per cent, and in the case of non-employing small business, the rate is slightly lower at 59.6 per cent.

According to the Australian Securities and Investment Commission[98], nominated reasons for failure include:

- Inadequate cash flow or high cash use (46.7 per cent of reports)
- Poor strategic management of business (45.6 per cent of reports)
- Trading losses (35.5 per cent of reports).

The success of small business can also be affected by a range of factors beyond your control, such as consumer confidence, the wider economy and simple supply and demand.

But still, for many the potential rewards far outweigh the risks, and careful planning and management go a long way to achieving your business goals.

So, if you're considering embracing the entrepreneurial spirit and starting up your own small business, what's the process involved?

RESEARCH AND RECONNAISSANCE

Any business start-up should commence with serious research and reconnaissance, looking at demand for your products or services, potential and existing competition, who your customer is, their spending habits and lifestyle, whether their purchase of your products or use of your services will be recurring, and if so, how often and at what price?

This research should involve both a qualitative and quantitative approach, where you find statistics and demographics, but you should also speak to potential clients and actively look into other existing businesses in your prospective sector.

There's a great old saying, "Time in reconnaissance is never time wasted," and in small business that's definitely the case.

This information will then be compiled into a business plan that identifies the cost of start-up, the equipment you'll need, whether staff are required, the intended price of your products and much more.

A business plan is imperative because it helps you ascertain whether your idea is viable and provides a map to establishing your start-up. Meanwhile, a well-written business plan can also help you gain the funding you might need to commence your business.

This is just a brief snapshot of the research involved before you begin any business. If you're looking for more comprehensive insights and step-by-step guides, the government's business website (business.gov.au) should be your first port of call.

They have a wealth of resources available, including a 'starting a business guide', which can be accessed at: business.gov.au/guide/starting.

Meanwhile, in addition to general research, if you're serious about going it alone in business there are a number of administrative boxes you need to tick.

BUSINESS STRUCTURES

Businesses generally fall into four different categories: sole traders, partnerships, companies and trusts. Each has slightly different reporting criteria, obligations and structures. You'll need to decide which one you wish to use when you start your business, and you can change that structure as your business grows.

So, let's take a quick walk through each.

SOLE TRADERS

Most start-ups involve the sole trader structure, and there's a good chance this is the category you might fall into. As a sole trader you are in full control of your operation. You own all assets, you are responsible for all debts, and you use your individual tax file number to lodge your annual tax return.

This structure is also considered easier to set up, with fewer reporting requirements.

The government's business website[99] sums it all up neatly with this explanation:

A sole trader business structure:

- *is simple to set up and operate*
- *gives you full control of your assets and business decisions*
- *requires fewer reporting requirements and is generally a low-cost structure*
- *allows you to use your individual tax file number (TFN) to lodge tax returns*
- *doesn't require a separate business bank account, although this is recommended to make it easier to keep track of your business income and expenses*
- *requires you to keep financial records for at least five years*
- *has unlimited liability and all your personal assets are at risk if things go wrong*
- *doesn't allow you to split business profits or losses made with family members*
- *makes you personally liable to pay tax on all the income derived.*

Although it might be termed 'sole' trader, this business structure also enables you to hire the staff you need when you require them.

These staff members can be casuals, part-time or full-time. When you hire staff, you will need to ensure you pay them properly. You will need to meet superannuation requirements and minimum wage obligations in addition to providing a safe workplace that complies with relevant Workplace Health and Safety guidelines and has adequate insurance, like public liability and workplace compensation.

Again, there's a bit more to this than we've just covered here, but you can find out more at: business.gov.au/New-to-business-essentials/ Hiring-people.

Taxation obligations

As a sole trader, you can employ other people, but you do not pay yourself a wage. Instead, the business income you earn is considered your personal income and taxed using your personal tax file number. You are also responsible for your own superannuation contributions.

The Australian Taxation Office[100] notes:

As a sole trader, you:

- *use your individual tax file number when lodging your income tax return*
- *report all your income in your individual tax return, using the section for business items to show your business income and expenses (there is no separate business tax return for sole traders)*
- *apply for an ABN and use your ABN for all your business dealings*
- *register for Goods and Services Tax (GST) if your annual GST turnover is $75,000 or more*
- *pay tax at the same income tax rates as individual taxpayers and you may be eligible for the small business tax offset*
- *put aside money to pay your income tax at the end of the financial year – usually, you will do this by paying quarterly Pay As You Go (PAYG) instalments*
- *claim a deduction for any personal super contributions you make after notifying your fund.*

As a sole trader you can't claim deductions for money 'drawn' from the business. Amounts taken from the business are not wages for tax purposes, even if you think of them as wages.

You can read more about sole trader tax implications at: ato.gov.au/Business/ Starting-your-own-business/Before-you-get-started/Choosing-your-business-structure/Sole-trader.

PARTNERSHIPS

A partnership is made up of two or more people who distribute the business income or losses between them. A partnership is still relatively easy to set up but has very different tax obligations to sole traders.

Partnerships have their own business tax file number, the business is required to lodge a tax return, and it falls under different laws in different states.

When it comes to each individual's tax return in a partnership, each partner pays tax on the individual income they have received from the business, and they are responsible for their own superannuation.

If the business turns over more than $75,000, it must also register for Goods and Services Tax – GST – which we'll talk a little more about later.

The government's business website[101] explains there are three different types of partnerships:

1. *General partnerships where all partners equally share responsibility for running and managing the business, including responsibility for debts and losses.*

2. *Limited partnerships where the partners are usually passive investors who don't play a role in the business's day-to-day running. Their liability is limited to the amount of money they have contributed.*

3. *Incorporated limited partnerships where one general partner has unlimited liability for all the business's debts and losses, but others are limited to the money they have contributed to the business.*

COMPANIES

Companies are a separate legal entity. They are more expensive and complicated to set up. As a legal entity, the company is liable for any debts and losses. They are controlled by directors and owned by shareholders.

As a member of that company, you are not personally liable for those debts (unless you are a director and have provided a personal guarantee), and you cannot be sued (unless you are a director and the company is found to be in breach of legal requirements). A company must comply with the Corporations Act 2001, which you can learn more about here: legislation.gov.au/Details/C2018C00424.

A company must also lodge its own tax return each year, and it is taxed differently to both sole traders and partnerships.

The Australian Taxation Office[102] explains that a company:

- *must apply for a tax file number (TFN) and use it when lodging its annual tax return*
- *is entitled to an Australian business number (ABN) if it is registered under the Corporations Act 2001. A company not registered under the Corporations law may register for an ABN if it is carrying on an enterprise in Australia*
- *must be registered for GST if its annual GST turnover is $75,000 or more*
- *owns the money that the business earns – the individuals who control the business cannot take money out of the business, except as a formal distribution of the profits or wages*
- *must lodge an annual company tax return*
- *usually pays its income tax by instalments through the pay as you go (PAYG) instalments system*
- *pays tax at the company tax rate or lower company tax rate (if a base rate entity)*
- *may be eligible for small business concessions*
- *must pay Superannuation Guarantee Charge (SGC) for any eligible workers. This includes you, if you are a director of the company, and any other company directors.*

TRUSTS

A trust is an entirely different business structure altogether and is also more expensive to operate and establish than other business types. Considered a relationship rather than a legal entity, trusts are often used when a business is a multi-generational family affair and can include other assets, like property and shares.

Trusts are overseen by trustees, which can be individuals or a company. Trustees are legally responsible for the business operations, along with administrative tasks such as managing the trust's tax affairs. This includes registering the trust in the tax system, lodging trust tax returns and paying some tax liabilities.

Meanwhile, beneficiaries receive income from that trust. In terms of tax obligations, all beneficiaries (except minors and non-residents) need to declare their share of the trust's income as part of their personal income. (In the case of a deceased estate, family trust or super fund, these rules can vary).

The government's business website[103] notes that trust structures:

- *can be expensive to set-up and operate*
- *require a formal trust deed that outlines how the trust operates*
- *require the trustee to undertake formal yearly administrative tasks.*

You can learn more about trusts and their taxation implications at: ato.gov. au/General/Trusts.

WHICH STRUCTURE SHOULD I CHOOSE?

The reality is that most people starting a business simply opt for the sole trader structure, which is what we will dive into a little more deeply below.

But if the above has you thinking another structure might be better, we recommend you speak with a qualified and reputable accountant or check out business.gov.au, which has a nifty tool available called 'Help me decide'. You can access it here: register.business.gov.au/helpmedecide.

BUSINESS NUMBERS

If you're looking to start a business, one of the first things you will need is an Australian business number (ABN). This is an 11-digit number that is unique to every registered business in Australia.

It helps identify you for taxation purposes, and you'll also need it to invoice your clients. Obtaining an ABN is simple, quick and free, but first you need to ensure that you're eligible.

The Australian Business Register[104] explains that to be entitled to an ABN you need to be carrying on a business, providing products or services to clients. Your unique ABN will then allow you to:

- Identify your business to others when ordering and invoicing
- Avoid pay as you go (PAYG) tax on payments you get
- Claim Goods and Services Tax (GST) credits
- Claim energy grants credits
- Get an Australian domain name.

Once you have an ABN there are obligations you need to meet. You must keep it up to date and ensure the information attached to it (like your address) is current.

You will also need to file business activity statements (BAS) if required. (We'll touch on these shortly.)

GETTING AN ABN

Obtaining an Australian business number involves applying for one with the Australian Business Register at abr.gov.au.

You'll find the link on the home page under 'Business, Super Funds and Charities'. Click the 'Apply for an ABN' link, then scroll down and click the 'Apply or Reapply for an ABN' button.

This takes you through the application process and asks questions about your business structure for taxation purposes and the type of business activity you intend to carry out. You will also be asked to input your tax file number to link your ABN to, along with your name and address.

Once you have filled in all the details and declared the information true and correct, you will be issued your ABN almost immediately.

This information is then added to the Australian Business Register and is available for public view.

BUSINESS NAMES

In addition to an Australian business number, you might also need to register a business name. A business name registration is required when you are looking to trade under any entity other than your personal name.

So, for example, if your legal name is Jack Taylor and you are calling your business Jack Taylor Mowing, you won't need to register that as a business name. If your name is Jack Taylor and you call your business A Cut Above Mowing, that name will need to be registered.

Registering a business name is also simple, but it does come at a small cost, currently $36 per year. First up, however, you'll need to check that your intended name is available and not already being used by another business. You'll also have to already have your ABN.

You can check whether a business name is available or has already been registered at the Australian Securities and Investment Commission website: asic.gov.au.

On the home page, head to the menu on the right-hand side, click the link to 'business names', select 'search business index' in the dropdown menu beneath 'search business names register' then enter the name under that and click 'go'.

The next page will tell you whether your proposed business name is currently registered. If it is you'll need to come up with a variation or something else. If not, you can begin registering your intended name.

REGISTERING A BUSINESS NAME

To register a business name, go to the ASIC home page: asic.gov.au, click the link on the left that says 'registering a business name'. This takes you to a great step-by-step page that walks you through the registration process, along with providing further insight on business names.

If you're looking to shortcut this, scroll down until you see the blue tab that says 'Use the Business Registration Service' and select the link.

Click on the box that says 'register your business' then on the next page, tick the box alongside 'business names' under 'select new registrations to apply for'.

This begins the business name registration process, where you fill in your name, address and details of the business, the personal details of all other people associated with it (like partners or directors), your proposed business name and your credit card details.

Once complete, you will receive an email confirming payment and your registration details.

Remember, you will need to renew your business name before it expires, otherwise it could be registered by another business! ASIC offers the choice of registering a business name for either one or three years.

GST AND BUSINESS ACTIVITY STATEMENTS

Goods and Services Tax (GST) applies to most goods and services sold in Australia. In short, it's a 10 per cent tax that the government applies. If your business turns over enough of these products and services, you, the business owner, collect GST on the government's behalf and then pay it to them. To do this you have to register for GST.

In turn, you can claim deductions on the items that you buy as a business, which also incur GST.

Sounds complicated, doesn't it? Well, it kind of is, so let's walk through the process with a little assistance from business.gov.au[105], who explain this well.

Let's start with some basics. If your business turns over less than $75,000 per annum, you do not have to register for GST, but you can if you want to.

If your business turns over more than $75,000 per annum, you will generally be required to register for GST, but it depends on the type of services and products you sell or provide.

For example, basic foods like bread and milk are often exempt from GST, as are some education courses and medical, health and care products and services.

Pretty much all other goods and services are liable for GST, and when you turn over more than $75,000 worth of these a year, you must register your business for GST with the Australian Taxation Office.

The ATO[106] clearly maps out exactly when you should register for GST and other reasons outside of turnover when you may need to. They note you must register for GST:

- *when your business or enterprise has a GST turnover (gross income minus GST) of $75,000 or more*
- *when you start a new business and expect your turnover to reach the GST threshold (or more) in the first year of operation*
- *if you're already in business and have reached the GST threshold*
- *if your non-profit organisation has a GST turnover of $150,000 per year or more*
- *when you provide taxi or limousine travel for passengers (including ride-sourcing) regardless of your GST turnover – this applies to both owner drivers and if you lease or rent a taxi*
- *if you want to claim fuel tax credits for your business or enterprise.*

WORKING OUT YOUR GST TURNOVER

As the ATO notes, you need to register for GST once your business has a GST turnover of $75,000 or more.

They further explain that you work out this figure by calculating your total business income (not your profit), minus any of the following:

- *GST included in sales to your customers*
- *sales that aren't for payment and aren't taxable*
- *sales not connected with an enterprise you run*
- *input-taxed sales you make*
- *sales not connected with Australia.*

Your business accounting software, your bookkeeper or your accountant can assist with working out when you might reach the GST threshold.

HOW TO REGISTER FOR GST

Registering your business for GST is simple and free, and you can do it at register.business.gov.au or alternatively by calling the ATO or through your registered tax agent.

Once your business is registered you have obligations you need to meet and ways of incorporating GST into your business.

GST REPORTING AND OBLIGATIONS

If you have a GST-registered business, your main obligation is to collect GST and pay it to the ATO when due.

And it works like this . . . GST is added to products or services you provide. As the tax is 10 per cent of a product's total value, that means you add one-eleventh of the sale price to it.

Yep, that is slightly confusing, but in other words if you sell $100 worth of products, the customer will actually pay $110. That extra $10 is GST you collect and pay to the ATO.

Meanwhile, as a GST-registered business you can also claim the GST you pay on goods and services back. So if you purchase $110 worth of products or services for your business, you can claim the $10 as a GST credit.

To adequately account for all this incoming and outgoing GST, you will need to file a business activity statement. This is usually filed quarterly (just after the end of September, end of December, end of March and end of June) or perhaps even monthly if you have a high-turnover business or find it easier to budget monthly in your business.

At this point you submit a document to the ATO that outlines all your GST sales and the amount of GST collected. You then indicate the amount of GST you have paid and subtract this from what you have collected.

The final figure is your net GST, which will be payable to the ATO.

In addition, as part of everyday business operations, you need to indicate to your customers when they are liable for GST and how much it is, so they can claim a tax credit if they're eligible.

This is done via your invoices or receipts and is a requirement when a purchase is more than $82.50. Your invoices need to indicate very specific information. The ATO[107] notes they must display the following:

- *that the document is intended to be a tax invoice*
- *the seller's identity*
- *the seller's Australian business number (ABN)*
- *the date the invoice was issued*
- *a brief description of the items sold, including the quantity (if applicable) and the price*
- *the GST amount (if any) payable – this can be shown separately or, if the GST amount is exactly one-eleventh of the total price, such as a statement that says 'Total price includes GST'*
- *the extent to which each sale on the invoice is a taxable sale (that is, the extent to which each sale includes GST).*

Should the invoiced amount be above $1,000 the obligations become even more stringent. Meanwhile, if your customer asks for a tax invoice, you are obliged to provide one within 28 days of the request.

You can learn more about tax invoices, what they should look like and the information they need to include at: ato.gov.au/Business/GST/Tax-invoices.

In the interim, this has been a very basic explainer of GST. If you're looking for more comprehensive advice, your tax accountant can assist, along with a wealth of resources at the ATO: ato.gov.au/Business/GST.

BUSINESS INSURANCE

If you have built yourself a business, you need to protect it, and that starts with having the right insurance in place to cover yourself, your staff and your assets. So what type of insurance might you need?

Let's start with the basics and public liability insurance.

PUBLIC LIABILITY INSURANCE

Public liability insurance is designed to protect you if you are found to be legally responsible for any personal injury or property damage that might be caused to a third party. It is arguably the most important insurance any business can have, saving you a whole lot of heartache and costs when you least expect them.

Marcus the car detailer

Marcus has a car detailing business. One day he's dutifully detailing a client's car when the wax he's using reacts with the paintwork, causing thousands of dollars worth of damage.

Marcus is deemed responsible, but public liability insurance will cover the costs that Marcus would otherwise have legally been required to pay.

Julie the eBay seller

Julie has a great little business on eBay selling handmade jewellery. Each week suppliers deliver her jewellery craft items directly to her door. But one day a supplier falls on the concrete path outside her house and suffers a back injury.

Julie is found to be responsible because her home is her registered place of business, and the concrete path was uneven. Public liability insurance covers the associated costs.

Sammy the baker

Sammy runs an inner-city cafe with some funky umbrellas out front. One day a gust of wind lifts one of the umbrellas and it strikes a nearby car.

If Sammy didn't have public liability insurance, he would personally be required to pay for the associated costs of fixing that vehicle.

WORKERS' COMPENSATION INSURANCE

If you employ staff, you are legally required to have workers' compensation insurance. The exact terms vary from state to state, but this insurance protects you (the employer) should one of your staff be injured in the course of their duties or on your premises.

PROFESSIONAL INDEMNITY

If your business provides advice or recommendations, you might require professional indemnity insurance in addition to public liability. This insurance protects you should a client sue you for losses that stem from advice your business provided.

BUSINESS VEHICLES

Whether you have one business vehicle or a fleet of 50, you should protect them with insurance. Business vehicle insurance covers you should a business car be damaged, damage another vehicle or worse – injure a person.

BUSINESS BUILDINGS AND CONTENTS

If your business has premises, the likelihood is you will need business premises insurance. This insurance is designed to protect you from the costs associated with damage to your property and loss. It generally covers things like natural disasters, such as fires and flooding, along with break-ins and theft, or damage due to equipment failure.

SICKNESS AND INJURY

When your livelihood depends on your ability to work, sickness and injury insurance is another type of coverage you might want to consider. This insurance protects you and your family should you be injured, be too sick to work or in the event of your death.

A QUICK INSURANCE RECAP

The type of insurances you take out for a business will depend on the type of business you have and your personal circumstances. In some cases, public liability is the only insurance you may need, or if you have staff you might only require public liability and workers' compensation.

In other instances, you might need those two basics plus business premises and business vehicle insurance. You can learn more about the type of insurance you might require at: business.gov.au/Risk-management/Insurance. Or you can speak with a reputable insurance broker who can advise on what cover would best suit your business.

STAFFING

When a business has staff, you will need to meet certain obligations as an employer. These extend from basics like protecting your staff against injury to paying them in accordance with the law and withholding superannuation.

So let's look at what's involved with bringing staff into a business.

SAFETY

As an employer, you have a legal requirement to ensure that your workplace is safe. That means you will need to meet relevant Workplace Health and Safety requirements both in terms of the jobs that your staff do and the premises where they work.

To do this, the government's business website[108] notes you must:

- *provide a safe work environment*
- *provide and maintain safe machinery and structures*
- *provide safe ways of working*
- *ensure safe use, handling and storage of machinery, structures and substances*
- *provide and maintain adequate facilities*
- *provide any information, training, instruction or supervision needed for safety*
- *monitor the health of workers and conditions at the workplace.*

In addition (and as we mentioned earlier), you must also insure your business to protect your workers with workplace compensation insurance.

This covers you financially should an employee be injured, become sick or die as a result of working for your business.

You can learn more about ensuring the safety of your staff here: business.gov. au/risk-management/health-and-safety/work-health-and-safety.

> ## *Find something you're passionate about and stay tremendously interested in it.*
> Julia Child

SALARIES

As an employer, you must pay your staff the correct wage and any entitlements they are eligible to receive, depending on their age, the industry, their qualifications, and their duties and responsibilities.

Different industries command different pay rates (awards), and you can learn more about them here: fairwork.gov.au/awards-and-agreements/ awards.

TAX AND SUPERANNUATION

When you hire staff, you are also required to withhold tax and superannuation and pay it to the government.

This includes:

- **PAYG withholding** – This is designed to collect employees' tax. It is usually documented and paid as part of your quarterly business activity statement.
- **Payroll tax** – This is a state tax on wages paid by employers. It is calculated on the monthly wages a business pays and only comes into play after a business exceeds the exemption threshold set by their state or territory.

- **Fringe benefits tax** – If you provide certain benefits to your employees or their families, you might need to register for and pay fringe benefits tax.
- **Superannuation** – If you pay your staff more than $450 in a calendar month, you will be required to contribute money from their wage into their nominated superannuation fund.

This is just a brief rundown of some of the requirements that come with having staff work in your business. You can learn more at: business.gov.au/people/pay-and-conditions/employees-pay-leave-and-entitlements.

FUNDING YOUR START-UP

So you have a brilliant business idea and are looking to get it off the ground. Awesome! Now what about some funds to bring that business to life.

Well, there are a number of options available. You could continue to work and start your business on the side. You could save to start a business with your own personal capital. You could also seek funding or a loan from family and friends.

In addition, you could seek government sponsorship, or you could apply for a loan. So let's look a little further into these two options.

GOVERNMENT ASSISTANCE

The government is actively looking to embrace entrepreneurship in the knowledge that small business is the backbone of Australia.

To accommodate this, they have programs available to assist, such as NEIS.

Also known as the New Enterprise Incentive Scheme, NEIS is a government-backed program available to individuals who are not currently in employment, education or training and who are interested in starting their own business.

The program provides training, business mentoring and support, including an allowance of $555 per fortnight for up to 39 weeks and rent assistance for up to 29 weeks.

The NEIS program has been running for over 30 years, and more information is available at: employment.gov.au/self-employment-new-business-assistance-neis.

BUSINESS LOANS

Start-up loans are also available from banks and credit unions, but they tend to involve a more rigorous application process that includes a detailed business plan.

Bear in mind, if you do successfully secure a business loan, you will be required to pay back the money borrowed regardless of whether your business succeeds or fails.

The loan may also impact your ability to borrow further funds for other endeavours.

ANGEL INVESTORS

Angel investors are individual investors who can help finance your start-up in exchange for a stake or share of the business.

Again, when it comes to the type of enterprises they're interested in, the selection process is rigorous and usually requires a proof of concept, white paper or detailed business plan. You can connect with angel investors at start-up hubs, meetups or investment groups.

VENTURE CAPITALISTS

Venture capitalists are individuals, groups or firms who actively seek investment opportunities in new ideas. Like angel investors, they tend to require a stake in any start-up, and they will need detailed information about your idea or business, including a plan or indication of potential revenue.

If you're interested in obtaining venture capital, the government has some venture capital initiatives here: business.gov.au/Grants-and-Programs/Venture-Capital. There are also many private firms, but we recommend doing your homework first, as this can be very complex.

CROWD FUNDING

Over recent years crowd funding has emerged as a new way for start-ups to gain access to the capital they need. Generally done through a crowd funding website, the concept sees everyday people offer loans, finance or funds in exchange for a stake or portion of your business.

The government business website has more information on exactly what's involved and what you should be aware of here: business.gov.au/Finance/Seeking-finance/How-to-crowdfund-your-business.

8

PROTECTING YOUR FINANCIAL FUTURE

Regardless of what stage of life you're at, it's important to protect yourself or prepare for events you may not see coming. Life can change in the blink of an eye due to circumstances far beyond your control. Accident, illness or misfortune can have major ramifications for both your physical and financial wellbeing.

So how do you arm yourself against something unexpected? By planning for the best yet preparing for the worst. And that's where insurance, wills and legal agreements like power of attorney come in.

Pennies that should drop in Chapter 8 . . .

In this section we look at how to protect yourself and your loved ones financially when it comes to the unexpected, including sickness, injury, accidents, death or even the breakdown of a relationship.

Often these are potential issues many of us either don't consider or delay thinking about because they fall into the "too hard" basket. They are also things many of us are guilty of putting off because life changes can be tough to envisage.

This chapter is designed to make that a little easier, covering topics like:

- Health insurance, life insurance and asset protection
- Wills, testaments, power of attorney, health directives and the differences between them
- Superannuation and how to ensure it goes to the right people should you pass away
- Handling the financials should a relationship turn sour
- Risky business, including the responsibilities of going guarantor on a loan or lending loved ones money
- The costs associated with having children.

By the end of Chapter 8 you'll have a clearer idea of how to protect the assets you acquire over a lifetime, along with the implications of life decisions that we often enter into without thought.

So, let's commence with a liberal dose of insight into health insurance.

HEALTH INSURANCE

In Australia, we are fortunate to have a healthcare system that's designed to look after us in the event we become ill or are injured. Known as Medicare, it allows us to seek medical treatment and emergency care, and covers some or all of the costs of doctors' visits, non-elective surgery and public hospital stays.

But that doesn't mean it covers everything. When it comes to further health services, like dental treatment, orthodontics, psychology, physiotherapy, elective surgery, rehabilitation and buying glasses, private health insurance can be hugely beneficial.

So, let's take a quick look at Medicare – it's benefits and limits, and why you might also require private health insurance as well.

MEDICARE

Medicare is a public, universally funded health insurance scheme designed to cover some of the costs associated with healthcare.

First introduced in 1984[109], it allows all Australian citizens to access primary healthcare, and it is funded through a levy on each resident's personal taxable income (with some exceptions).

At the moment that levy is two per cent, meaning when you do your tax return, two per cent of your taxable income goes straight to funding public healthcare.

In addition, there's also a surcharge for high income earners. This 1.5 per cent extra charge applies to individuals earning over $140,000 per annum, and families earning over $280,000 per annum who do not take out appropriate private hospital cover.

These levies and surcharges do not cover the full cost of Medicare, however. In 2013–14, for example, the levy and surcharge raised $10.2 billion[110], accounting for 53.4 per cent of Medicare's total cost. The rest of the funding was provided by the Federal Government.

In return for the Medicare levy, all Australian citizens receive a Medicare card and have access to basic healthcare. This includes being treated as a public patient at a public hospital by a doctor of the hospital's choosing.

Some or all costs of visiting your general practitioner may also be covered by Medicare as part of a bulk-billing process. This depends on whether your GP is a registered bulk-billing provider.

Meanwhile, Medicare can also cover additional costs of healthcare services that are listed on the Medicare Benefits Schedule (MBS)[111]. This schedule changes regularly, with services being added and removed.

To give you an example of what Medicare does and does not cover, the government's private healthcare website[112] (privatehealthcare.com.au) breaks Medicare down into areas, including 'hospital' and 'medical'.

HOSPITAL

Under Medicare you can be treated as a public patient in a public hospital, at no charge, by a doctor appointed by the hospital. You can choose to be treated as a public patient, even if you are privately insured.

As a public patient, you cannot choose your own doctor and you may not have a choice about when you are admitted to hospital, because you may be placed on a public hospital waiting list.

When it comes to hospital, Medicare does not cover:

- Private patient hospital costs (for example, theatre fees or accommodation) – you can purchase private hospital insurance to cover this item
- Medical and hospital costs incurred overseas
- Medical and hospital services that are not clinically necessary, or surgery solely for cosmetic reasons
- Ambulance services.

MEDICAL

When you visit a doctor outside a hospital, Medicare will reimburse 100 per cent of the MBS fee for a general practitioner and 85 per cent of the MBS fee for service provided by a specialist. If your doctor bills Medicare directly (bulk billing), you will not have to pay anything.

Medicare provides benefits for:

- Consultation fees for doctors, including specialists
- Tests and examinations by doctors needed to treat illnesses, such as x-rays and pathology tests
- Eye tests performed by optometrists
- Most surgical and other therapeutic procedures performed by doctors
- Some surgical procedures performed by approved dentists
- Specific items under the Cleft Lip and Palate Scheme
- Specific items under the Enhanced Primary Care (EPC) program
- Specific items for allied health services as part of the Chronic Disease Management Plan.

In terms of medical, Medicare does not cover:

- Examinations for life insurance, superannuation or memberships for which someone else is responsible (for example, a compensation insurer, employer or government authority)
- Ambulance services
- Most dental examinations and treatment
- Most physiotherapy, occupational therapy, speech therapy, eye therapy, chiropractic services, podiatry or psychology services
- Acupuncture (unless part of a doctor's consultation)
- Glasses and contact lenses
- Hearing aids and other appliances
- Home nursing.

You can learn more about what is and isn't covered by Medicare at: privatehealth.gov.au/health_insurance/what_is_covered/medicare.htm.

If you are seeking to have further costs of your healthcare covered beyond what is eligible under Medicare, you will need private health insurance.

PRIVATE HEALTH INSURANCE

Private health insurance is designed to fill the financial gap between what Medicare covers and other health-related costs.

Depending on your stage of life, it can help with the costs of orthodontics, elective surgeries, maternity, buying glasses and even preventative health measures like remedial massage or yoga.

But what's covered all comes down to the policy you take out. It's a very competitive arena where each provider may offer something different and the cost of insurance can quickly add up.

In the interim, private health cover is broken down into three general areas:

Hospital cover

Hospital cover allows you to choose whether you will be treated as a private or public patient. It may allow you to select the hospital you wish to attend and could give you more flexibility about when you wish to be admitted to a private hospital. It also enables you to pick the specialist practitioner of your choosing. Waiting times for operations and procedures may also be reduced with private health cover.

General treatment

Also known as extras cover, this allows you to select from a range of services that you may be more likely to use, depending on your stage of life. It can include options like:

- Dental treatment
- Chiropractic treatment
- Home nursing
- Podiatry
- Physiotherapy, occupational therapy, speech therapy and eye therapy
- Glasses and contact lenses
- Prostheses (e.g. hearing aids).

Generally, these services are only covered to a certain extent, and there may be some out-of-pocket expenses or limits on the number or value of services you can access within a set time frame.

Ambulance cover

Depending on where in Australia you live, you might require ambulance cover as part of your private health insurance. Some states offer free emergency ambulance transport, while others do not. Medicare does not cover ambulance transport.

For more information on private health insurance and to compare policies, visit privatehealth.gov.au.

> **In a growth mindset, challenges are exciting rather than threatening. So rather than thinking, oh, I'm going to reveal my weaknesses, you say, wow, here's a chance to grow.**
> Carol S. Dweck

INCOME PROTECTION

When you're just starting out, it's hard to imagine that illness or accident might take away your ability to earn an income.

Income protection insurance is designed to protect you and your immediate family in these circumstances. It helps you manage your expenses and meet your financial obligations if you fall ill or are injured and are unable to work.

The period of time and percentage of your wages that income insurance will potentially cover depends on the premium you take out.

However, you usually have the option to cover up to 75 per cent of your total wage before tax and can set time coverage periods that range from two years up to the point you reach the age of 60. Each premium also has definitions of the injuries and illnesses eligible for protection, and the higher the level of coverage you opt for, the more you pay for your premium.

As part of income protection, many insurers also offer redundancy insurance. This covers you for a limited period of time if your employer makes you redundant.

Income protection is often paid for from your superannuation fund. However, income protection premiums outside of your super fund are generally tax deductible and won't eat away at your super balance in the long term. Where possible, it is a good idea to pay for income protection outside of super.

As MoneySmart[113] notes, income protection is especially valuable for self-employed people, professionals and business owners who rely on their ability to work.

You can learn more about income protection, including what to look for in a policy here: moneysmart.gov.au/insurance/life-insurance/income-protection.

LIFE INSURANCE

While income protection covers you if you can't work, insurance like life cover protects your family financially should you die. In this case, you insure yourself for a set amount of money that is paid to your immediate family in the event of your death.

It's important to note, life cover is considered different to accidental death cover. Life cover protects your family more broadly should you pass away from illness, disease or accident, but accidental death cover only protects your family financially should you suddenly die in an accident.

Accidental death cover has a long list of exclusions, or situations where coverage won't be paid. So, as always, read the documentation carefully.

Life cover is considered a particularly good insurance to have should you be supporting a family, as it minimises the trauma they would endure at a highly emotional time by reducing their financial burden.

MoneySmart[114] notes, when considering life insurance, you should take into account the number of dependents you have (a spouse, children, etc.) and the amount of money required to cover all your existing debts. Then weigh this against the amount of money your family would receive from other investments in the event of your death (superannuation, shares, property sales, etc.).

The difference between the two is the amount of cover you should get.

Life cover is also often paid from your super fund, and it often comes at a discount when you opt to take it out with them. Some life insurance providers will require a detailed medical history from you, and some pre-existing illnesses may make you ineligible.

You can learn more about life cover and what you need to consider at: moneysmart.gov.au/insurance/life-insurance/life-cover.

TOTAL AND PERMANENT DISABILITY COVER

Usually available in conjunction with life cover, total and permanent disability cover protects you should you suffer a serious and permanent injury that prevents you from being able to work. It helps manage the cost of rehabilitation, debt repayments and living.

MoneySmart[115] explains that total and permanent disability cover falls under two categories:

- Inability to work in **any** profession
- Inability to work in your **usual** profession.

Each insurer will have different inclusions, exclusions and definitions of what equates to a disability, so read the fine print of any documentation carefully and also consider other protection you might have, like health insurance and life cover when it comes to working out the level of total and permanent disability cover you might need.

More information about total and permanent disability cover, and whether it's right for you, is available at: moneysmart.gov.au/insurance/life-insurance/total-and-permanent-disability-cover.

BUILDING INSURANCE

If Australia's natural disasters of the past few years have taught us anything, it's the value of property insurance.

Building insurance protects you should the property you own be damaged by circumstances beyond your control. It covers you for some of the costs of rebuilding or repairing your home, but its costs and coverage can vary depending on where you live and the type of threats your home might be prone to.

There are two types of home insurance available: sum insured and total replacement cover. It's important you understand the difference between the two when selecting the right coverage.

Sum insured – This type of coverage is the most common. It covers a set amount that you nominate to replace or repair your home. The risk here is that you might undervalue what it could cost to rebuild, meaning you will be out of pocket should the worst happen.

If you opt for a sum insured policy, make sure you take the time to revisit your policy every couple of years and clearly understand what exactly is covered and the true cost of rebuilding.

Total loss – As MoneySmart[116] explains, only a few insurance companies offer total loss coverage, and it can be slower to access in the event of a disaster. Total loss covers the cost of rebuilding your property to the condition it was in prior to an event. Should the worst happen, an assessor will need to visit your property to gauge the extent of damage and the full cost of making repairs or rebuilding.

Meanwhile, all insurance policies have exclusions, caps and excesses, and it's critical you understand these when deciding which policy is right for you. When you receive an insurer's product disclosure schedule (PDS), you should read it, looking for limits on your coverage and any events that may not be covered.

A very public example

In 2011, Queensland endured a major flooding event that saw a number of Brisbane suburbs inundated with water. In the weeks that followed, many insurance holders found that while they had home insurance, they were not covered for flooding.

To make matters more complicated, some insurers covered the type of flooding that results from rising stormwater[117] or flash flooding, but not general flooding.

"With most insurance companies not providing automatic cover against 'riverine' flood, their rulings on whether damage was caused by rapidly falling rain or slowly rising rivers and creeks are crucial for the peace of mind and financial security of hundreds of families," News Corp[118] reported at the time.

As a result, many residents who had suffered significant damage to their homes spent weeks in limbo, trying to understand whether they were covered, while some were not covered for that type of event at all.

The bottom line? Know your policy. If it seems unclear or if you are unsure of what's covered and what's not, ask your insurer to clarify.

You can learn more about home insurance here: moneysmart.gov.au/insurance/home-insurance.

> *Energy and persistence conquer all things.*
> Benjamin Franklin

CONTENTS INSURANCE

Home owners often take out home insurance and contents insurance as a bundle, but there's a difference between the two, and contents insurance is something that also applies if you're renting the home where you live.

Contents insurance covers you for loss or damage to your personal possessions. That means it covers the items that are within your home, regardless of whether you rent or own that property.

So what sort of things are covered? Well, everything from your white goods to jewellery, clothing and furniture. And it's surprising how quickly the value of these things can add up. Just imagine what it would cost you to replace everything that you currently own within your house.

When taking out contents insurance, list the replacement value of each item you own to come to an estimated total. If you're looking for a starting point, there's a great online calculator at Understand Insurance[119] that can assist: understandinsurance.com.au/calculator/contents-calculator.

Meanwhile, when comparing policies, you also need to know what type of events are covered. Some policies only cover you for specific events, like burglary or fire, while others cover you for any accident.

You also need to check whether your policy only covers the current value or your possessions or offers new-for-old replacement. The latter means any payout will provide enough funds to go out and buy new items to replace the ones you lost.

Again, the cost of contents insurance can vary. Things that impact your contents insurance cost include: where you live, the type of security you have in place at that residence, and the excess you choose.

An excess is the amount of money you're prepared to initially outlay in the event of any loss before coverage kicks in, say, $500 or $1,000.

The key takeaway . . .

While home insurance covers the cost of rebuilding or repairing a structure, contents insurance covers you for the loss of your personal possessions. Regardless of whether you rent or own the property where you live, you should have contents insurance.

Frightening facts . . .

A recent national study[120] found under 30s are the least likely people to have house and contents insurance, four per cent of Australians have no house and contents insurance, and a jaw dropping 67–74 per cent of renters do not have contents insurance.

You can learn more about contents insurance at: moneysmart.gov.au/insurance/home-insurance/contents-insurance.

LANDLORD INSURANCE

We mentioned this one earlier, but will recap quickly here. If you are the owner of a rental property, landlord insurance is a must.

Landlord insurance includes building insurance that covers the cost of rebuilding or repairing your property in the event of a disaster but often is not as extensive as building insurance. It can also protect you if your tenant causes damage to your property, and it might also extend to covering the cost of the rent you lose should your property become uninhabitable.

You can read more about landlord insurance in the property investing section, while additional information is also available at: moneysmart.gov.au/investing/property.

CAR INSURANCE

Again, this is a topic we've touched on already but will revisit briefly here. Your vehicle is likely to be among the most valuable assets you currently own, so insurance should be a priority.

When it comes to car insurance, there are four main types:

Compulsory third party (CTP) – This is compulsory insurance that you pay for when you register your vehicle. It covers you in the event someone else is injured or dies as a result of an accident you're involved in.

All cars driven on Australian roads are required to have CTP insurance. However, how it's applied can vary from state to state. In some states you can choose your insurer, in others the transport authority does that for you.

Compare the Market has a good guide to what happens in each state and territory: comparethemarket.com.au/ctp-insurance.

Remember, if your vehicle is not registered, you are not covered by CTP. Driving an unregistered vehicle simply isn't worth the risk.

Third party property – This type of insurance covers you in the event you damage someone else's car or property in an accident. It does not cover damage to your own vehicle. However, some insurers also offer 'uninsured motorist extension' as part of this policy. This covers your vehicle if another driver is responsible for an accident but they're not insured.

Third party property, fire and theft – In this instance, you are covered for damage to another person's vehicle, while your car is covered in the event of fire or theft.

Comprehensive – This is the most complete insurance you can have for your vehicle. It covers you for damage to another person's car or property as the result of an accident you are responsible for, and it also covers damage to your vehicle, along with fire and theft.

You can read more about car insurance here: moneysmart.gov.au/insurance/car-insurance.

WILLS AND TESTAMENTS

No one likes to ponder the prospect of what will happen when they die, but it's a very real part of life and important to consider at any age.

This planning becomes even more critical if you have a family. That's where wills come in. A will is a legal document that outlines what should happen to your money and your property in the event of your death.

A will protects your loved ones and allows the things you've worked hard for to be distributed to the people who matter most. If you have children who are younger than 18, it also allows you to nominate a guardian to care for them.

As Law Depot[121] explains, a will enables you to:

- *Choose who will get your property after your death*
- *Choose how your property will be divided among your various beneficiaries*
- *Give specific items of property to specific people (including charities)*
- *Appoint someone you trust to administer your estate*
- *Appoint a guardian for your minor children.*

If you die without a will, your assets will be distributed by a court-appointed administrator according to the laws of your jurisdiction. That usually means property and assets will be distributed among your immediate family, including your spouse and children, according to a predetermined formula.

If you have no immediate family (as in no family who are more closely related to you than cousins), your assets will go to the government.

HOW DO YOU MAKE A WILL?

Will kits are readily available to purchase online, but it's always a good idea to have your will looked over by a public trustee or solicitor, who will usually charge a fee. This ensures your will properly reflects your wishes and is legally binding.

To make a will, you need to be:

- Over 18. (There are exceptions to this, like if you are in the military, legally emancipated or married.)
- Of sound mind, which means you know you are making a will, you understand your relationship to the people within it, and know what property you own, or how much of it you own, and are fully aware of the items you are dispersing.

Your will must be in writing. It can be typed, handwritten or printed. It must also be signed by you and at least two other witnesses who are not named as beneficiaries within the will.

When you make your will, you should be mindful of exactly what property or items you want to go to whom, and bear in mind that this may change over the course of your life.

Even if you have a will you should review it periodically, especially when your circumstances change, and make revisions if required. Life events, like having children, getting married, living in a de facto relationship, getting divorced or the death of a spouse, as well as acquiring or selling assets, can significantly impact your will.

As part of making your will, you will also need to appoint an executor to administer your estate. This person is responsible for distributing your assets according to your directions. Their duties also include notifying all beneficiaries in the will, determining taxes and liabilities, preparing financial statements and more.

The Queensland Government Public Trustee[122] notes that choosing the executor of your will is almost as important as the will itself.

When selecting the right person, they suggest considering the following:

- Does your executor have the necessary skills, and are they willing and able to administer your estate? (And will they be there when needed?)
- If you appoint a family member or loved one as your executor, you may place an extra burden on them at a time of stress, grief and loss.

- Will your choice of executor cause conflict among your beneficiaries? (It may be wise to appoint an independent executor.)
- If something goes wrong with the administration of your estate (for example, if property is damaged and not adequately insured), your executor may be personally liable for it.

If you prefer, you can appoint an external executor, such as a state government public trustee or a private company.

Once you've made a will, you should secure it somewhere safe and tell a person you trust exactly where that is. After all there's no point in documenting your wishes if no one can find them should you die.

State trustee bodies often have will safes, while your solicitor can also look after a copy of your will for you in their safe custody.

Frightening fact . . .

About half of all Australians die without a will[123], passing away without their real wishes being known.

You can learn more about wills at: moneysmart.gov.au/life-events-and-you/over-55s/wills-and-power-of-attorney.

Or you can find out about public trustees and how the laws apply in your state at: australia.gov.au/information-and-services/family-and-community/wills-and-powers-of-attorney/wills.

POWERS OF ATTORNEY

While a will is a document that protects your wishes in the event of your death, you can also appoint people to act in your interests when it comes to finances and health while you're still alive.

Known as powers of attorney, this is a legally binding agreement that enables another person to make specific decisions on your behalf.

There are three main types of powers of attorney:

GENERAL POWER OF ATTORNEY

This allows you to appoint someone else to make financial or legal decisions on your behalf, usually for a specific period of time.

For example, if you were looking to buy a house and the auction was to occur while you were away, you could draw up a general power of attorney for someone you trust to bid on your behalf and sign any purchase contracts.

If you were going overseas on an extended trip, you might also consider drawing up a general power of attorney for someone to manage finances on your behalf, like paying bills.

ENDURING POWER OF ATTORNEY

An enduring power of attorney is a more permanent type of arrangement. It enables you to appoint someone to manage your financial and legal affairs should you no longer be in a position to manage them yourself due to illness or incapacity.

For example, your parents may give you power of attorney to handle their financial affairs and legal obligations if they are facing a terminal illness or have been diagnosed with Alzheimer's.

Conversely, you may have enduring power of attorney documents drawn up that are enacted in the instance you suffer an accident that sees you without the capacity to make financial or legal decisions for yourself.

It's important to note, enduring power of attorney must be designated before a person loses the capacity to make decisions on their own behalf. You can set a time when an enduring power of attorney takes effect. This can be a specific date or in the event you are no longer able to make decisions for yourself.

It's also important to understand the scope of an enduring power of attorney differs from state to state. In Queensland, for example, enduring power of attorney can also enable someone to make personal[124] decisions on your behalf, in addition to financial and legal ones. In South Australia, however, it's strictly limited to financial and legal decisions[125].

The person given enduring power of attorney has a number of obligations they must fulfil, including acting in your best interests.

MEDICAL POWER OF ATTORNEY

Also known as advance health directive, enduring guardianship, enduring power of attorney (medical) and medical consent, medical power of attorney differs from state to state.

In this case, the aim is to authorise someone to make medical and/or personal decisions, such as where you should live, on your behalf.

In the case of these personal decisions, they can only be made by the person you nominate should you no longer be capable of making decisions by yourself.

To understand exactly what forms need to be completed in which state and territory, you should consult your relevant state body.

More information is available at:

New South Wales

- Power of attorney: tag.nsw.gov.au/attorney-faqs.html
- Enduring guardianship: tag.nsw.gov.au/enduring-guardianship.html

Victoria

- Power of attorney: publicadvocate.vic.gov.au/power-of-attorney/enduring-power-of-attorney
- Advance care directive: publicadvocate.vic.gov.au/power-of-attorney/advance-care-directive

Queensland

- Power of attorney: qld.gov.au/law/legal-mediation-and-justice-of-the-peace/power-of-attorney-and-making-decisions-for-others/power-of-attorney
- Advance care directive: qld.gov.au/law/legal-mediation-and-justice-of-the-peace/power-of-attorney-and-making-decisions-for-others/advance-health-directive

South Australia

- **Power of attorney:** opa.sa.gov.au/planning_ahead/enduring_power_of_attorney
- **Advance care directive:** advancecaredirectives.sa.gov.au

Western Australia

- **Power of attorney:** publicadvocate.wa.gov.au/E/enduring_power_of_attorney.aspx
- **Advance care directive:** publicadvocate.wa.gov.au/A/advance_health_directives.aspx

Tasmania

- **Power of attorney:** publictrustee.tas.gov.au/enduring-power-of-attorney/?gclid=EAIaIQobChMIhv26wY6v5wIV0rWWCh0TEgj0EAAYASAAEgLvs_D_BwE
- **Enduring Guardianship:** publictrustee.tas.gov.au/enduring-guardianship.html

ACT

- **Power of attorney:** ptg.act.gov.au/powers-of-attorney
- **Health direction:** health.act.gov.au/services/advance-care-planning

NT

- **Power of attorney:** nt.gov.au/law/processes/power-of-attorney
- **Advance personal plan:** nt.gov.au/law/rights/advance-personal-plan

SUPERANNUATION AND BINDING DEATH NOMINATIONS

Not many people realise this, but in the event of your death, any funds in your superannuation account are not necessarily considered part of your estate. Instead, the trustee of the super fund will pay a death benefit under the governing rules of that fund and the law.

So what does that mean? Basically, your superannuation is not considered a part of the assets that your will covers. So it might not go to the beneficiaries of your will.

That's where something called a binding death nomination comes into play. As the Australian Taxation Office[126] explains, a binding death nomination allows you to "nominate one or more dependants and/or your legal personal representative to receive your super".

In other words, a binding death nomination allows you to advise your superannuation trustee specifically who will receive your superannuation benefit in the event of your death.

Not all superannuation funds allow for binding death nominations, but if they do, it's a good way of ensuring your super benefit goes to the people you believe it should.

RISKY BUSINESS

OK, enough tough love about the tough topic of death, but we haven't finished with risk mitigation quite yet.

In this section we'll cover a couple of common situations where it pays to be cautious with your finances. Not all the topics we're about to discuss necessarily have a bad outcome, but the bottom line is you should go into each with your eyes wide open, understanding your personal risk and your obligations.

GOING GUARANTOR OR CO-BORROWER

It may never happen, but what would you say if a friend or family member asked you to enter into a loan as a co-borrower or guarantor?

"Um . . . Let me think about it," is probably the best response.

If you're asked to guarantee or enter into a loan with someone, you should give the concept very serious thought, because either way it could have very real financial implications. So what's involved in each case, and what's your personal risk?

Co-borrower

Co-borrowing is when you enter into a loan with someone else – as in, you sign a loan document along with another party. Technically, all named parties are responsible for repaying that loan, but should the other parties be unable to pay, that responsibility may just fall on you. And, yes, your ability to borrow further is also affected.

Example

Ruth decides it's a great idea to buy an investment apartment. She can't quite afford the mortgage herself, so she puts the idea to her elder sister, Eve, who might go in as a co-borrower on the loan.

Two years later, Ruth's life has changed dramatically. She's jobless and a little lost. Despite Ruth's hard times, the mortgage repayments remain due each month, and at this point Eve (as co-borrower) is responsible for ensuring those payments are met.

In the interim, Eve would have liked to buy her own home, but she can't because the loan she co-borrowed counts as a significant liability with all lenders.

The takeaway?

As MoneySmart[127] says, "If the person you borrow the money with is unable to pay their share of the loan, you will be responsible for repaying the full amount outstanding."

Guarantor

If a bank or credit provider is unwilling to give a person a loan on their own, you might be asked to be their guarantor.

This means you guarantee they will be able to meet the loan conditions. The implications here can be quite serious. Basically, you're staking your financial position on the fact that someone else will meet their obligations.

When you sign as guarantor, you are saying you will pay back the entire loan if the other party cannot or will not – and that's along with any fees, charges or interest. Meanwhile, you don't have any right to the property or asset that the loan actually covers.

In the worst-case scenario, you might be forced to use your own assets and savings to repay a loan, and if you can't meet those repayments your credit report could be impacted.

In the interim, being a guarantor might also affect your ability to obtain credit. So, should you decide to take out a personal loan, credit card or mortgage, the fact you are a guarantor and potentially liable for someone else's debt may impact your ability to borrow.

There is an exception to this, however, when it comes to the family guarantee or security guarantee that we mentioned earlier in property and deposits.

Under a family guarantee or security guarantee, the guarantor obligations are slightly different. This usually limits the guarantor's exposure to a portion of the debt, and you are there for security purposes only. In many cases, as a security guarantor you aren't liable for the regular repayment of the loan, and this is not taken into account as a liability should you apply for a loan.

The bottom line? Only go guarantor if you can afford to do so without putting your own assets at risk. Be aware that you may be liable for another person's debt, and your credit report may be impacted by their actions.

Sebastian's grand guarantor plan

Sebastian has grand plans to buy a very expensive classic car, restore it and then sell it. But to do so he requires a personal loan. His employment history's not great, so he asks his brother Marcus to "go guarantor" on the $80,000 loan to nudge him across the line with his credit provider.

In a bid to get his brother out of a bind, Marcus says yes and uses his house as security. Six months later, Sebastian's interest has clearly waned, but that doesn't mean the loan repayments stop coming.

Poor Marcus isn't exactly doing so well either. He's lost his job. Now he finds himself responsible for Sebastian's loan in addition to his own mortgage, but the worst thing is Marcus's house is collateral.

That may see the bank repossess it in order to recoup the money they lent to his brother for that abandoned classic car restoration plan.

LENDING MONEY TO FRIENDS AND FAMILY

This one's really tricky, and many people grapple with it over the course of their life – should you lend money to family and friends, and if you do, when and how should you ask it to be repaid?

In truth, there's no easy answer to this as it depends on your relationship with the borrower, their reliability and your own financial position.

As a rule of thumb, only lend the amount of money that you are prepared to lose or can afford to write off. Do not stake your own financial future on lending to another person. Understand that the loan may impact your relationship, and if you expect the loan to be repaid, outline the terms and conditions from the outset.

For more information on finances, family and friends look here: moneysmart. gov.au/borrowing-and-credit/borrowing-basics/loans-involving-family-and-friends.

LOVE AND MONEY

Just as family, friends and finances can present a challenging mix, so too can love and money.

Many people enter a new relationship with their hearts wide open and their financial defences down, and that can have ramifications in a host of different ways in both the short and long term.

While all might be rosy at the outset of a relationship, things can quickly turn sour. And if you have entered into a loan with your partner or even just a legal agreement like a lease with them, that can quickly put you in jeopardy.

So how can you protect yourself in matters of love and money, and what should you do if things don't pan out as planned?

JOINT BANK ACCOUNTS

If you're in a committed relationship, you might be considering a joint bank account, which has both pros and cons.

A shared account allows you both to access money from the same pool of funds. It streamlines the payment of general household expenses, like utilities, rent and groceries, and can see you attract higher compound interest in a savings account because you have the ability to channel two people's savings into one sum.

Legally, a joint account can also protect you if something happens to one member of the couple, as the other can still access the money in the account.

Meanwhile, joint bank accounts can also offer a sense of security and equality. They reflect the fact that even though you may not earn the same amount, you are equal in value when it comes to financial matters.

On the flipside, finances can really test a relationship, and your partner may not share the same financial goals, values and spending habits as you do.

For example, how would you feel if your partner was accessing your joint funds for slabs of beer and expensive car parts while you were hoping to set money aside for a holiday?

Or how would you feel if your partner came home with a swanky set of very expensive heels when you were hoping to pay off your credit card in full by the due date?

Without getting too deep into the ins and outs of relationships (because that's a whole other book), the best advice would be to enter into joint accounts cautiously.

Before you go signing up for joint access to joint funds, be sure you know your partner well enough to understand their financial priorities and spending habits. You'll probably need to have some tough conversations here about the future, goals and any concerning approaches to money. But a word to the wise: they're worth having sooner rather than later.

A Finder[128] survey found 52 per cent of couples argue about money, while a further survey by Relationships Australia noted:[129]

- 43 per cent of Australians had not discussed how their individual incomes would be shared before they made a commitment to their current or most recent partner.
- 56 per cent reported they had not discussed how they would manage their couple finances if one of them no longer had an income. (A further 14 per cent had only discussed their couple finances 'a little'.)
- Meanwhile, 74 per cent of women and 69 per cent of men reported that they had not discussed how they would divide their finances if their relationship ended prior to committing to their current or most recent partner.

Even legendary US investor Warren Buffet has touched on the topic of love and money, noting who you marry is the biggest financial decision you will ever make.

JOINT LOANS

We covered this a little earlier in terms of joint loans with friends and family, but in relationships the same caution should apply.

If you're considering entering into a joint loan with your partner, be very clear from the outset how both of you intend to pay that loan off.

Ask yourselves:

- How much will each of you contribute?
- How will those repayments be made?
- When do you both plan to pay it off by?
- What would you do if one person no longer has an income or if the relationship ends?

If the relationship subsequently breaks down, remember you may be liable for repaying that debt (not just your share, but the whole debt). You can't get out of loan contracts you made in the past, but you can take steps to protect yourself.

If a relationship breaks down and you have a joint loan, MoneySmart[130] suggests the following:

- If possible, discuss with your ex-partner who will take responsibility for paying each debt.
- Make sure you receive copies of account statements (or monitor the accounts online or by phone) to check that debts are being paid as agreed.
- Make sure all jointly accessed savings accounts are changed to two to sign.
- Make sure all redraw facilities and loan offset accounts are frozen and cannot be accessed without your consent and signature.
- If your ex-partner won't continue to repay joint debts (or their share), seek legal advice. If you're struggling to meet the debt, contact your credit provider to ask for a hardship variation.

You can find further information on joint loans and relationship breakdowns here: moneysmart.gov.au/media/283220/love-and-loans.pdf.

JOINT LEASES

At the beginning of a relationship, one of the major financial commitments you are first likely to incur might be signing a lease together. Again, this is a legal and financial agreement you should enter into with your eyes wide open.

How will you as a couple pay rent? How much will each of you pay? What will you do if the relationship ends and your partner moves out?

Remember, failing to honour the terms of a lease can result in you being blacklisted as a tenant. It can also result in you owing money to your landlord.

But should the worst occur, there are steps you can take. Options include:

Breaking the lease – In this case you need to notify the property manager, and you might be responsible for rent until the property is re-letted, advertising costs and the re-letting fee.

Jake and Julia

Loved up Jake and Julia sign a six-month lease on a three-bedroom house together. They're comfortably sharing the rental cost of $400 a week. Four months in, the relationship ends and Julia leaves.

Jake tries to get a friend in to rent one of the extra rooms, but he struggles to find one willing. He's also struggling to pay the full rent and is now three weeks in arrears.

Jake opts to end the lease. He and Julia are both liable for the arrears since they were both named on the lease. If they don't pay the arrears they could potentially be blacklisted. They are also required to pay rent until a new tenant can be found, along with an advertising and re-letting fee. (These charges vary from state to state.)

Getting someone else in – You could seek out another tenant to share the property with you to cover extra costs. You will need to have this person approved by the property manager and included on the lease.

Foot the bill yourself – You might be in a financial position to continue letting the property on your own.

More information on breaking a lease is available here: choice.com.au/money/property/renting/articles/breaking-a-rental-lease.

HAVING CHILDREN

This might seem a strange topic to list under love and money, but the following statistics will help put why this needs to be mentioned into context.

In 2018, the Australian Institute of Family Studies[131] put the cost of raising a child in a low-income family at $170 per week. Bear in mind, the likelihood is it could be significantly higher depending on schooling, child care and lifestyle.

Extrapolate that scenario out over a year and the minimum cost per child is $8,840 per annum. Multiply that by 17 years, and the cost is $150,280.

That means a lower income average Australian household with two children incurs costs of over $300,000 to raise their children to 17.

There are additional cost factors here, including the loss of income that comes from one member of the household potentially being out of the workforce.

In 2019, Finder[132] estimated that raising children could set a family back a further $300,000 in lost income.

That means raising two children to 17 could potentially cost a family well over $600,000.

The key takeaway here? Children are a financial investment, and where possible you should plan financially for their upbringing.

WHEN A RELATIONSHIP ENDS

If you've set about building a life together with a partner, you might have major assets like a property and major liabilities like a mortgage in both your names, along with everyday expenses like electricity, phone bills and credit cards.

It's fair to say that dividing these assets and this responsibility can be a tricky process.

MoneySmart[133] suggests the following:

Start with the practicalities

Sort out the practicalities first, like:

- Who will remain in the house
- How you will pay for bills, and whether you need to change the paperwork relating to them
- What to do with joint bank accounts
- How you will manage the financial and living arrangements for any children.

You might need legal assistance with this process, so talk to your lawyer or seek legal aid to see where you stand.

Gather documents

Then, gather your documents to know exactly where the two of you stand individually and as a couple. You will need documents that encompass all your financial activities, including mortgage certificates, bank statements and utility accounts.

Alter your accounts

Chances are you will need to update your accounts to reflect your changed relationship status. Some things will be easy to alter, like your electricity and phone accounts. Other things might require a bit of paperwork and you might need to divide things, like savings accounts.

Consider opening an account in your name only and have your pay go into this account. Look at closing joint accounts and credit cards, along with updating insurance information.

Know your position

You will need to put together a list of everything you own and owe together. This sets out your overall financial position and allows for the division of assets. This list will likely be lengthy, including things like furniture, cars, property, shares, superannuation and perhaps even business interests.

Some of these assets (such as property) might ultimately be sold, with proceeds divided between you.

Set out in writing how you intend to handle debt. What contribution will each party make, when and how often? Can you clear that debt by selling something you both agree on?

As an aside, when it comes to assets that are divided as part of a relationship breakdown, you may be eligible to roll them over rather than exchanging an asset that could incur capital gains tax.

As the ATO[134] explains, when an asset is transferred between parties a capital gains tax event usually occurs, however a 'rollover' means the transferor spouse disregards the capital gain or loss that would otherwise arise.

"In effect, the person who receives the asset (the transferee spouse) will make the capital gain or loss when they subsequently dispose of the asset. The cost base of the asset is also transferred to the transferee spouse."

You can read more about that here: ato.gov.au/general/capital-gains-tax/relationship-breakdown.

Get legal advice

A family lawyer is a great place to start when it comes to dividing the items you have accumulated in a relationship. They can help guide you through the process and avoid going to court.

Budget for your new financial position

The end of a relationship may mean you are in a very different financial position to what you were previously. You need to recognise and budget for this to ensure you live within your means and make the most of the resources you have.

Meanwhile, the Family Court of Australia[135] provides a helpful summary on property and finances after separation.

Importantly, it covers things like:

How does a court decide how to divide assets and debts?

There is no formula used to divide your property. No one can tell you exactly what orders a judicial officer will make. The decision is made after all the evidence is heard and the judicial officer decides what is just and equitable based on the unique facts of your case.

That said, the Family Law Act 1975[136] sets out the general principles the court considers when deciding financial disputes after the breakdown of a marriage.

These are based on:

- Working out what you've got and what you owe (your assets and debts and what they are worth)
- Looking at the direct financial contributions by each party to the marriage or de facto relationship, such as wage and salary earnings
- Looking at indirect financial contributions by each party, such as gifts and inheritances from families
- Looking at the non-financial contributions to the marriage or de facto relationship, such as caring for children and homemaking
- Future requirements – a court will take into account things like age, health, financial resources, care of children and ability to earn.

The way your assets and debts will be shared between you will depend on the individual circumstances of your family. Your settlement will probably be different from others you may have heard about.

Is there a time limit for applications for property adjustment?

If you were married, applications for property adjustment must be made within 12 months of your divorce becoming final.

If you were in a de facto relationship, applications for property adjustment must be made within two years of the breakdown of your de facto relationship.

If you do not apply within these time limits, you will need special permission of a court. This is not always granted.

You can learn more about finances and how they're affected by the breakdown of a relationship at:

- moneysmart.gov.au/getting-divorced-or-separating
- familycourt.gov.au/wps/wcm/connect/fcoaweb/family-law-matters/property-and-finance/property-and-money-after-separation/property-and-finances-after-separation
- ato.gov.au/Forms/Guide-to-capital-gains-tax-2019/?page=80
- ato.gov.au/Individuals/Super/In-detail/Withdrawing-and-using-your-super/Super-and-relationship-breakdowns
- ato.gov.au/Business/Private-company-benefits---Division-7A-dividends/In-detail/Division-7A---Marriage-or-relationship-breakdown.

Julie Hodge, family lawyer and author of *Moving On: What you need to know about separation & divorce* also provides some words of advice:

If you and your former partner (same sex or opposite) were in a de facto relationship under the the Family Law Act 1975 ("the Act") which may be the case after living together for two years or where there is a child from the relationship (and in other circumstances set out in the Act), then either party may apply to the Family Law Courts for property orders.

However, in most cases where a de facto relationship exists and there are grounds for a property settlement order to be made, parties agree on the property division which lawyers help them "make legal" under the Act.

Property settlements or orders result in the assets, liabilities, superannuation (in most states and territories of Australia) and financial resources of each of you at the time of settlement being divided between you. There is a process under the Act as to how the property pool of the parties is to be divided. The same process applies when a marriage breaks down.

It is important to be aware that the breakdown of significant relationships such as de facto relationships and marriages can take a toll on your finances. If you are concerned about a possible separation or wish to find out what steps can be taken to try to protect against the financial consequences of a relationship breakdown you should consult an experienced family lawyer.

(Please note, this is information only and is not legal advice and should not be relied upon in place of legal advice for your particular circumstances.)

9 FINANCIAL HARDSHIP

Despite the best laid plans, sometimes the cards of life simply do not stack up in your favour. You might lose a job, struggle in business or have something unforeseen occur that impacts your ability to earn money.

As a result, you could find yourself in financial hardship, and it's a tough place to be. Financial hardship can impact your lifestyle, your relationships and your mental wellbeing.

Pennies that should drop in Chapter 9 . . .

Chances are you may never need this chapter, but if you do, we hope it provides a clear path forward and the realisation you are far from the first to read it, and will not be the last.

This is a chapter devoted to when the going gets tough. And it can – no matter where you come from and how successful you are.

In the coming pages, we are all about action – looking at proactive strategies you can embrace to manage and then get yourself out of financial trouble, including:

- Debt consolidation
- Steps to take, who to speak with and how to avoid further issues
- Government aid
- Tools and tricks to minimise outgoings
- Bankruptcy – what it means, how it works and how you can avoid it
- A little perspective.

By the end of this chapter, we hope you have the tools to navigate any financial setbacks you may encounter, while keeping them in perspective, then have the knowledge to move back into a more positive direction.

After all, if you find yourself struggling with money, it's important to remember that it doesn't define who you are and what you're worth as a person. Some of the most successful business people and most renowned identities have faced financial hardship and stared it right on down.

It's what you do to address your financial hardship and what you learn from the experience that inevitably matters most.

If navigating your financial situation is proving tough, here's a step-by-step guide to handling financial hardship and why it's not a situation where you can afford to bury your head in the sand.

CREDIT AND LOANS STRESS

Whether you're struggling to repay a loan or simply can't make ends meet, financial hardship can feel like an insurmountable obstacle.

It is not insurmountable, but it does require a proactive approach. If you're having trouble meeting loan repayments on things like your credit card, personal loan or mortgage, the first thing you need to do is talk directly to your credit provider.

By law, credit providers, including the banks who handle your mortgage, have an obligation to work with you before they pursue you, and each organisation has an area dedicated to financial difficulty.

Speak with them about reducing your repayments to a more manageable level, or perhaps consolidating your credit cards and personal loans into one single loan with a lower interest rate and longer repayment term.

DEBT CONSOLIDATION

If you begin to encounter problems repaying numerous loans, you might want to consider the option of consolidating all your loans into one. This can help you reduce the payments you have going out each month, but it also comes with a risk that includes additional debt in the long run.

If you are considering debt consolidation or refinancing, always do your homework to ensure you are really going to get a better deal – not just now but also in the long term.

OK, so what do we mean? Well let's look at two very different scenarios . . .

Dave's debt drama

Dave has two credit cards ($10,000 and $5,000) and what was an interest-free purchase ($5,000). That's a total of $20,000 debt.

The interest on Dave's credit cards is 13.74 per cent, while his interest-free loan is currently 22.74 per cent. That means each month Dave pays a minimum amount of $300 on his credit cards and $100 on his other loan. That's a total of $400.

Dave looks to consolidate his loan and opts for an unsecured personal loan with a rate of 14 per cent.

Now he needs to pay $466 each month, as the personal loan is over five years. This will see Dave pay a total of $27,960 over the five-year term, including $7,960 in interest.

That's not really an ideal outcome.

Delia's debt dream

Delia has the same debts but when she consolidates, she does her interest rate homework. She opts for an unsecured personal loan with an interest rate of just nine per cent.

She has to pay $416 a month over the same five-year term. This equates to $24,910 or $4,910 in interest, a savings over Dave of $3,050.

ZERO-BALANCE TRANSFERS

When it comes to credit cards, chances are you have heard of zero-balance transfers. This is an offer by a credit card company to transfer your outstanding credit card balance and then pay zero interest for a short period of time. That can be 12 months, 16 months, 24 months, 26 or longer.

In the process you pay no interest on the balance outstanding, and it can work to your advantage – but only if you're smart.

Zane's zero-balance transfer

Zane racked up a pretty impressive credit card bill when he travelled overseas last year. At present he has a $3,000 debt at an interest rate of 19.99 per cent. Each month, Zane pays above and beyond the minimum amount, contributing a total of $250 towards his card. But still at the outset, $50 of that is going just to interest.

At this rate it will take him more than 13 months to clear that card.

Instead, Zane opts for a zero-balance transfer, and he still commits to paying $250 per month. Now all his money is going directly to the debt, not the interest, and within 12 months he's credit card free.

There are a couple of catches Zane should be mindful of here, however. Often zero-balance transfers revert to very high interest rates if you do not pay off the amount outstanding within the zero-interest period.

That means if there is any debt remaining it could come with a very high interest rate that may then take further time to pay down.

The bottom line is . . . only opt for a zero-balance transfer if you really commit to repaying the outstanding balance within the zero-interest period.

GENERAL LIVING EXPENSES

If your financial situation is so dire that you are having trouble handling everyday expenses, there are services available to assist.

But first, let's start with some of those monthly bills. Like your credit provider, utilities companies, including phone and electricity providers, will work with you to an extent if you indicate you are in financial trouble, but first you need to tell them.

Get on the phone and talk to your provider about securing additional time to pay, reducing your plan or whether there are additional discounts you may be eligible for. If you're not comfortable doing this by yourself, a free counsellor from the National Debt Helpline[137] may be able to assist.

Similarly, if you're having trouble paying your rent, talk to your real estate agent. They may be able to assist you with some interim leniency to get you back on track. And don't forget, if you receive some Centrelink allowances you might also be eligible for rent assistance[138].

Charities may also be able to help you out with everyday items, including food vouchers and parcels, clothing and furniture, and the part payment of utility bills.

If you receive a Centrelink allowance you may also be eligible for an advance payment[139]. This type of payment sees you advanced a sum, which you then repay out of your standard fortnightly allowance.

GOVERNMENT AID

Australia boasts a pretty comprehensive social security system known as Centrelink, which is designed to ensure residents are supported through hard times.

Under some circumstances, you may be eligible to access Centrelink[140] payments, including:

- Jobseeker payments like the Newstart allowance and youth allowance
- The age pension
- Family payments, such as family tax benefit, parental leave pay, parenting payment and single income family supplement
- Payments for people with disabilities, such as mobility allowance, sickness allowance, essential medical equipment, disability support pension
- Carers payments, like carer payment and carer allowance.

You can see which payments you may be eligible for depending on your circumstances at: humanservices.gov.au. Scroll down the home page and click the link to Payment and Services Finder.

DEBT COLLECTORS

If you fall behind on your loans or utilities bills, you may get a call from a debt collector. These agencies are hired by your lender or utilities company to collect unpaid money on their behalf. As MoneySmart[141] explains, debt collecting is legal, but what they cannot do is harass or bully you.

They further note debt collectors can contact you to:

- Ask for payment
- Offer to settle or make a payment plan
- Ask why you haven't met an agreed payment plan
- Review a payment plan after an agreed period
- Advise what will happen if you don't pay
- Repossess goods you owe money on, as long as they've been through the correct process.

If you are contacted by a debt collector for an outstanding debt you owe, it's in your interests to work with them to resolve the issue. If you don't, they can pursue legal action, and if a judgement is made against you in court, that will end up on your credit rating and impact your ability to borrow in the future.

So how can you work with them?

- Be upfront about your financial situation and why you have not repaid the debt or amount outstanding.
- If you are struggling to pay, advise them you are experiencing financial hardship.
- Work out a suitable payment plan to repay the funds. (Be realistic when entering into a payment plan, factoring all other financial obligations you need to meet.)
- Meet the terms of your repayment plan. (If you can't, let them know in advance.)
- Reply to any letters or phone calls within a reasonable time frame.
- Advise them if your contact details change.

In your own interests, you should keep good records of all correspondence you have had with a debt collector. This includes records of the payments you have made, dates of contact, payment plan details and notes of who said what.

If you are experiencing genuine financial hardship, MoneySmart notes a debt collector may:

- Let you pay back smaller amounts over a longer time
- Close the debt if you pay part of the debt in a lump sum
- Waive the debt, if you're on a low income, have no major assets and your situation is unlikely to change.

The critical thing to remember here is that you cannot simply ignore correspondence from a debt collector. One way or another, you must act to avoid legal proceedings, further expense and a negative impact on your credit rating.

MoneySmart has a whole section dedicated to dealing with debt collectors, including advice on what to do if you dispute the debt, if you feel you are being harassed or if you're threatened with legal action.

You can find that advice here: moneysmart.gov.au/managing-debt/dealing-with-debt-collectors.

BANKRUPTCY

If you're really struggling to repay your debts, you might be pondering the option of bankruptcy, but this is not a decision you should enter into lightly.

Bankruptcy is basically a formal process that legally recognises you cannot pay your debts. As a result, most of the debts you have will be written off.

That's the upside, but the downside is significant. Declaring bankruptcy will significantly and irreversibly affect your chances of borrowing money in the future for a lengthy period of time.

If you declare bankruptcy, MoneySmart[142] explains:

- You stay bankrupt for three years.
- Your bankruptcy stays on your credit report for five years.

- Your name is on the National Personal Insolvency Index permanently.
- A trustee looks after your affairs.
- You must ask your trustee for permission to travel overseas.
- You can't be a director of a company without court permission.
- You may not be able to work in certain trades or professions. (See AFSA's employment restrictions.)

That means bankruptcy should be avoided wherever possible.

Instead, consider:

- Making a payment plan with your creditors
- Offering to make a smaller payment on your debt
- Contacting your credit provider to enact financial hardship arrangements
- Speaking with a financial counsellor
- Calling the free National Debt Helpline on 1800 007 007 to explore other options.

DEBT AGREEMENTS

A debt agreement may sound harmless, but like bankruptcy, it is something that goes on your credit record, it will affect your ability to borrow, and it will result in a permanent listing on the National Personal Insolvency Index.

So what exactly does it involve?

A debt agreement (or Part IX debt agreement) is an arrangement you come to with a creditor or creditors where you agree to pay what you can on any outstanding loan/s.

For example, you might have a credit card with an outstanding balance of $10,000, and a personal loan of $10,000, but as you recently lost your job, you can no longer afford repayments on either or to pay back those loans in full.

Instead, you come to a debt arrangement with your creditors where you pay back just $5,000 on each loan to wipe the slate clean.

Once that sum has been paid off, the debt is considered paid. However, the long-term repercussions are far more wide reaching.

MoneySmart[143] explains, once you've signed a debt agreement:

- It's listed on your credit report for five years or more.
- You must tell new credit providers about it if you owe more than the credit limit.
- Your name is on the National Personal Insolvency Index for five years or more.
- You may not be able to work in certain professions.

Again, you would be much better served if you had contacted your credit providers when you first found yourself in trouble and negotiated a payment plan to get you out of debt.

You should also speak with a financial counsellor or contact the National Debt Helpline (1800 007 007) to fully understand the repercussions and explore other options available.

More information about debt agreements is available here: moneysmart.gov.au/managing-debt/bankruptcy-and-debt-agreements.

RECOUPING LOST MONEY

So what if the shoe's on the other foot and you're struggling because someone owes you money? What should you do then? Well, it's a bit of a process, but it works like this . . .

Proof of debt

The first hurdle is to prove someone does actually owe you money. That means you should always get things in writing when it comes to any loans you give people, work you do for a fee or items you expect payment for.

This written 'agreement' would ideally be in the form of a contract that's signed by both parties. It could also be an invoice or perhaps even less formal – a text message or email exchange. The key components of this correspondence are that the parties can be identified and the agreement is evidenced.

Polite reminders

If someone's failed to pay you money that's owed to you in the time frame expected, step one is to politely remind them in writing. Be sure you clearly state the amount involved, what it was for, the original due date or conditions and the exact date of when you now expect that sum to be paid.

Giving notice

If you've issued a reminder and politely attempted to recoup money owed, it's time to get a little more serious in your correspondence. This involves contacting the person in writing with a letter of demand.

A letter of demand should set out the details of the debt, the agreement that was in place between the parties, how the agreement has been breached and what you require to happen, within what time frame, to resolve the matter.

If appropriate, you can finish off by stating that should the matter not be resolved within the time frame stated, you reserve your right to take necessary legal action to recover the debt.

By issuing this notice, you give the other party the opportunity to respond and hopefully resolve the dispute before any formal legal action is taken. Depending on the size of the debt and the circumstances surrounding it, you might prefer to have this letter drafted by a lawyer.

You can contact your local Legal Aid or community legal centre for free assistance if you qualify. Otherwise, you will need to engage and pay for a private practice lawyer.

Things get legal

If the letter of demand fails to result in payment, it's time to consider legal action, where you apply to your relevant civil court to have the matter resolved.

Each state operates independently when it comes to civil proceedings, but they are remarkably similar. You may want to engage a lawyer, or if you feel confident, you might represent yourself in court.

Alternatively, you can reach out to your local community legal centres and Legal Aid agencies to see if you qualify for free legal advice to assist. You can also find lots of relevant information and forms on your local court's website.

The Australian Competition and Consumer Commission has the full list of relevant links for small claims here: accc.gov.au/contact-us/other-helpful-agencies/small-claims-tribunals.

FINANCIAL HARDSHIP RECAP

THINGS TO BE WARY OF

Relying on credit cards – If you're already short of cash, the last thing you want to do is dig yourself further into debt by falling back on credit. Credit cards incur a high rate of interest and will require regular repayments, so using them only acts as a short-term solution.

Instead of falling back on credit, talk to your lending institution and a financial counsellor.

You may be able to manage your existing debt by consolidating any outstanding loans into a lower interest loan or by a temporary hardship variation.

Payday loans – These days it's not unusual to see payday loan companies spruiking their offerings on the internet and TV. These loans attract a higher interest rate than other types of credit, and their charges and fees can also soon add up. Again, talk to a financial counsellor before opting to go down this path.

Debt solution companies – Like payday loans, debt solution companies seem to be all over the media at the moment, and they may sound like the perfect answer to your money woes. In fact, some of these services can actually make your financial position worse by charging high fees at a time when you can't afford them.

Your first port of call should be your current lender to work out the best course of action, along with a free financial counsellor who can set you on the right path.

TOP TIPS

Work out what you owe – If you're having trouble making ends meet, take a good hard look at your incomings, outgoings and debt. Work out exactly where your money is going each month and the types of debts you have outstanding.

Eliminate extraneous expenses – Eliminate extraneous expenses that you can do without, including digital subscriptions, dining out, etc. You won't have to go without these forever; you might just need to do without them now.

Talk to your lender – If you are struggling to make repayments on a credit card, personal loan or mortgage, talk directly with your financial institution (sooner rather than later).

They may be able to offer you a temporary hardship variation on your loan repayments while you get the situation under control.

Alternatively, they may be able to switch you to a loan with a lower interest rate that will help you direct your savings where you need to.

Seek advice – There are a range of free services available to assist people in managing their debt, including free confidential counselling. These counsellors can also help you negotiate with your creditors. You can find them on the National Debt Helpline (1800 007 007) or at ndh.org.au.

MoneySmart also has a host of great resources to assist you when it comes to navigating money problems and debt. A great place to start is here: static. moneysmart.gov.au/files/publications/do-you-need-urgent-help-with-money.pdf.

A NOTE ON FINANCIAL HARDSHIP

Financial hardship can happen, even to people with previous wealth and relative security. It is a situation that you can recover from if you take the right steps. If you're struggling, acknowledge it. Find the right tools and services to assist you and work your way back out from debt.

In the interim, your bank balance does not define the type of person you are or the one you wish to be, and you are worth far more than the cash that's in your wallet.

If you do find yourself correlating your happiness to the amount of money you earn, you might be interested to learn that a large analysis published in the journal *Nature Human Behavior* using data from the Gallup World Poll, a survey of more than 1.7 million people from 164 countries, put a price on optimal emotional well-being at between $60,000 and $75,000 a year (for an individual).

The researchers found that a higher figure – $95,000 – is ideal for "life evaluation", which takes into account long-term goals, peer comparisons and other macro-level metrics. The researchers also found that it may be possible to make too much money, as far as happiness is concerned. They observed declines in emotional well-being and life satisfaction after the $95,000 mark, perhaps because being wealthy – past the point required for daily comfort and purchasing power, at least – can lead to unhealthy social comparisons and unfulfilling material pursuits.

These findings don't mean that getting a huge pay rise won't lead to individual satisfaction, it simply suggests that a group of people making $200,000 a year is likely no happier than a group of people making $95,000.

Source: https://money.com/ideal-income-study

10

FLY – BELIEVE IN YOURSELF

We've talked a lot about the cold hard figures of cash management, investing and finance in a bid to arm you with the information you need to succeed.

But the reality is this: understanding finance isn't just about money. Ultimately, a firm grasp on financial decision-making allows you to set goals, dream big and live life on your own terms.

It enables you to have the things you want, enjoy the lifestyle you imagine and make informed choices along the way.

It's also important to understand that thinking about and planning your financial future is a process and a mindset.

Pennies that should drop in Chapter 10 . . .

In this chapter we're stepping back from money and talking about life, dreams and the ability to shoot for the stars. After all, money should be your servant, not your master, nor your only ideal. The pages ahead are a teeny weeny bit of cold hard facts and a lot about what each of us has the potential to achieve.

We're hoping it helps you understand that now is the opportunity to seize the moment, today is the chance to take action, and you are the person in control of your destiny.

In Chapter 10, we're talking:

- Goal setting
- Mindset
- Practical tips gleaned from personal experience
- The value of asking questions
- The importance of believing in yourself.

At the end of Chapter 10, we hope you are equipped with the knowledge, the strength and the opportunity to spread your wings and fly!

> *Don't ask what the world needs. Ask what makes you come alive, and then go do that, because what the world needs is people who have come alive.*
>
> Howard Thurman

YOURS, FOR THE TAKING

At age 15, 17 or even 25, it's hard to imagine where you'll be in five or 10 years' time. It's tempting not to chart a course and instead sit back and see where life takes you.

But the question is this: in years to come, will you be the person who life says you are or the one you decided to be?

And that's where you have the ability to make a real change to your own future by considering what you want and how you plan to achieve it.

LIFELONG GOAL SETTING

"Start where you are, use what you have, do what you can." – Arthur Ashe

Dreams are only limited by your imagination, but achieving them comes from setting clear goals. So, ask yourself, what is it you want in life financially now and in the future?

Is it a car in two years' time, a house by 25 or a secure retirement in your 60s? Is it financial security for when you start a family, to pay down your home loan faster or to travel extensively overseas?

The world is your oyster and opportunity is there for the taking, but clearly setting out what you want allows you to plan the steps you need to take to get to the destination you desire.

So, let's talk about some tried and tested tips on goal setting and how it's a lifelong practice that can serve you incredibly well.

Figure 12 – 10 tips to FLY

☑ **TIP 1** Care about the future you	☑ **TIP 6** Know your worth
☑ **TIP 2** Write it down	☑ **TIP 7** Know where your money goes
☑ **TIP 3** Find your supportive tribe	☑ **TIP 8** Leverage
☑ **TIP 4** Embrace fear	☑ **TIP 9** Spread risk
☑ **TIP 5** If you don't know, ask	☑ **TIP 10** Be patient, be opportunistic

TIP 1 – CARE ABOUT THE FUTURE YOU

"That's a problem for future Homer. Man, I don't envy that guy."
– Homer Simpson

The future can be hard to imagine. In fact, in many ways your future self can feel like a foreign person. After all, this person is separated from you by time and life events, and who can tell exactly where the future you will be?

Well, you can. You can be a major influencer on the life, health and happiness of that person if you just care about them a little bit more. You have the power to plan and act on behalf of your future self.

Hmm, sound a bit wishy-washy? Consider this: as people we tend to be masters of deferring things until later. As Raiz Invest[144] reflects in a great blog on this topic, that's exactly why 13 per cent of Australians still continue to smoke and 40 per cent have no idea how much money they've got stashed in superannuation. After all, the repercussions of either of those are something the future you can sort out later, right?

Umm, no. As we mentioned earlier, borrowing from the eternal wisdom of Albert Einstein, *"A clever person solves a problem, a wise person avoids it."*

So as you set off into life, consider the future you as a best friend whose interests you should fiercely protect. How would you like that person to be looked after? What things in life do they deserve?

When you make decisions, run them by your future self too. Would they think that wise or a wasted opportunity?

By considering your future self, you can gain real clarity, and with clarity comes the ability to act.

TIP 2 – WRITE IT DOWN

"Where your mind goes, energy flows." – Penny Reilly

Once you've thought about your future self and their wellbeing, write the ideal scenario down as a goal. In fact, write down *all* your goals – even the ones you have for the immediate short term – then put them somewhere you can see them to remind you.

Your goals may change, but if you put them in writing you begin to make yourself accountable for achieving them.

It's a bit like subliminal advertising – you see it, you imagine it, you envisage what it's like, and you begin to take the necessary steps to make that goal a reality.

In short, writing goals down and keeping them in view allows them to remain front of mind. And in the sage words of author Bob Proctor, *"Thoughts become things. If you see it in your mind, you will hold it in your hand."*

Crystallising your goals doesn't just have to be in writing either. They can be visual cues or even digital. That's where things like vision boards come into play. Used in professions like interior design, vision boards or even perhaps a Pinterest board or Instagram account allows you to collect and collate things that inspire and influence the person you want to be or the things you wish to have.

TIP 3 – FIND YOUR SUPPORTIVE TRIBE

"The choices you make now, the people you surround yourself with, they all have the potential to affect your life, even who you are, forever." – Sarah Dessen

There's a great saying that you are the people you surround yourself with, so choose wisely when it comes to those who inspire you and influence your behaviours. Find the tribe who helps you succeed, who relishes in that success and lifts you higher in life.

In terms of goals and finances, seek out mentors and positive influences who will support you emotionally and intellectually towards your goals and will help you in the areas where you may not be strong.

Be clear on who your support network is at any given time – these people will change over time as your needs and knowledge change. Value and respect them as they will propel you forward.

> ## *Winners are losers who got up and gave it one more try.*
> Dennis DeYoung

TIP 4 – EMBRACE FEAR

"Fear is an idea-crippling, experience-crushing, success-stalling inhibitor inflicted only by yourself." – Stephanie Melish

It doesn't matter who you are or what stage of life you're at, fear is familiar to us all. It's the loud voice in the background recounting countless reasons why we should or shouldn't act.

Spoiler alert: fear doesn't necessarily get any easier to quieten, but it does become more rational to deal with.

In fact, fear can be your worst enemy, but it can also be your best friend because it often indicates you're about to step beyond the comfort zone.

So perhaps consider this . . .

F.E.A.R. has two meanings:
Forget Everything And Run
OR
Face Everything And Rise

The choice is yours. Once you are driven by a vision instead of fear, anything is possible.

If you're ever feeling crippled by adversity, take a read of *Three Feet from Gold: Turn Your Obstacles into Opportunities* by Greg S. Reid and Sharon Lechter, which features countless examples of where success was just on the other side of adversity or failure.

TIP 5 – IF YOU DON'T KNOW, ASK

"The only dumb question is the question you don't ask." – Paul MacCready

It's tempting to believe everyone else has all the answers. They don't. Some might just have more insight into an area where your knowledge is temporarily lacking.

The only way to address this is by recognising what you don't know and seeking knowledge when you need to by asking the right people the right questions at the right time.

If you're looking to make life decisions and you don't know the answer to something, seek out an expert's opinion, and don't be afraid to ask why they've come to the conclusion that they have.

TIP 6 – KNOW YOUR WORTH

"Know your worth. Know the difference between what you're getting and what you deserve." – Unknown

When it comes to finances, it's easy to sit back and let things tick on as they always have. If financial push comes to debt shove, it's also tempting to bury your head in the sand.

You can't. You cannot simply sit back and bury your head in the sand. Quite frankly, you owe it to yourself not to. That's why you should always know your net worth at any point in time. When you understand your financial position, you have the power to improve it.

Keep a balance sheet. Know your assets and liabilities. Know how that impacts what you're seeking to achieve.

TIP 7 – KNOW WHERE YOUR MONEY GOES

"Don't tell me what your priorities are. Show me where you spend your money and I'll know what they are." – James W. Frick

Life's busy, we get it. But not too busy to understand where you spend your hard-earned money and how you could better employ it. Keep a tally of where your money goes, have a budget for where it needs to be directed, save for the unexpected, identify additional savings, and put extra money to work for your goals.

There are plenty of apps, spreadsheets and budgeting aides to help you do this, with many of them outlined in Chapter 2.

TIP 8 – LEVERAGE

"It is much easier to put existing resources to better use than to develop resources where they do not exist." – George Soros

Debt can be a dirty word, but when used wisely it allows you to leverage your current financial position and take it to the next realm.

If you have equity or savings, use them effectively to increase your wealth through investing in areas like property or shares.

When employing leverage, understand both the risks and the rewards involved. Know where you stand now, where you potentially could be, the best possible outcome and the worst that could occur.

Weigh the risk, understand the fear, only embrace the liability you are comfortable with, and be prepared to ask the questions you need to in a bid to ensure you get the outcome you want.

TIP 9 – SPREAD RISK

"Why not go out on a limb? Isn't that where the fruit is?" – Frank Scully

The word risk comes with connotations of reckless behaviour and throwing caution to the wind. But it needn't be reckless, and it shouldn't be undertaken without the right information.

In financial terms, when you're seeking to achieve goals, risk should be calculated. It should also be spread wisely to minimise negative outcomes.

When it comes to spreading your financial risk:

- Diversify your investments (don't put all your eggs in one basket)
- Protect the assets you own (insurance)
- Have sufficient emergency funds (expect the unexpected)
- Minimise debts where you can (set a goal and work to pay down loans)
- Always read the fineprint (know what you're taking on; ask questions if you don't understand).

TIP 10 – BE PATIENT, BE OPPORTUNISTIC

"Great works are performed not by strength but by perseverance."
– Samuel Johnson

Be patient, have a plan and seize opportunity when it arises. In life, success rarely happens overnight; it takes goals, work and perseverance.

Harness financial tools available to you like smart investments, diversification and the power of compound interest. Then build your financial masterpiece, piece by piece, and watch it grow.

SPREAD YOUR WINGS AND FLY

"Don't be afraid to try and soar, your wings already exist. All you need to do is fly." – Unknown

Remember, you are the sum of infinite possibilities and the ultimate creator of your destiny.

Know yourself, trust your instincts, love and respect who you are, and have faith that all will guide you in the direction of your dreams. There might be stumbles, there might be mistakes, but these too will be invaluable, offering the opportunity to learn and take a different path next time.

Consider where you are, where you want to be, and plot the course to a future that excites and deserves you.

The wind is at your back, the horizon in your view, your world lies before you. Now take that step towards your future, spread your wings and FLY.

ABOUT THE AUTHORS

JAI AND MARLIES HOBBS

Jai and Marlies are a husband and wife team, originally from Cairns and now based in Noosa. Jai is a mortgage broker with over 15 years' experience, and Marlies is a former property development lawyer with a passion for education and creative projects. They have two sons, Troy and Zac, a cavoodle, Ruby, and horses, Zoe and Twisty.

Together they have built more than 10 properties, started, owned and operated several businesses, including a mortgage brokerage, retail shop and cafes, a franchise company, online shop, ready-made meal business and property developments.

Along the way they've celebrated some amazing successes, bounced back from some major setbacks and learned some tough lessons.

Some of their successes include doing the biggest deal on *Shark Tank* (Season 2) for their national food franchise business Paleo Cafe. That deal later fell through in due diligence, but it taught them a valuable lesson.

In 2015, Marlies won Franchise Council of Australia National Franchise Woman of the Year, and the team won Best New QSR in 2014. She was named emerging AusMumpreneur of the Year in 2014, as well as other accolades for Paleo Cafe and Healthy Everyday.

In 2014, Marlies released her first publication *The Paleo Café Lifestyle & Cookbook*, which quickly became a national bestseller.

Meanwhile, Jai placed second in the world for the Next-Gen in Franchising Awards in Texas in 2015 and is a multi-award-winning mortgage broker, having helped thousands of people achieve their financial and property goals over the past 15 years.

It's fair to say that Jai and Marlies have experienced some extremely challenging times as well. They feel grateful to have not only survived those lessons but to have come through the other side stronger, both personally and as a couple, and definitely much wiser!

Having journeyed through the highs and lows, with backgrounds in law, finance, business, health, property and, most proudly of all, parenthood, they gained a passion to help educate and inspire future generations to soar into life after school.

They wanted to equip young people with a comprehensive reference book that they could keep with them and refer to the relevant sections as and when they needed them.

Jai and Marlies hope this handbook will help guide young people to make informed financial decisions and protect them, where possible, from learning things the hard way and enduring unnecessary financial pain.

CASSANDRA CHARLESWORTH

Cassandra Charlesworth is a journalist with over 20 years' experience in newspapers, television news and feature writing.

Having started her career at Channel 10, Sydney, she is an award-winning former regional newspaper editor who now specialises in real estate as a freelance writer for publications including *Elite Agent Magazine*, *The Courier Mail* and realestate.com.au.

Cass shares Jai and Marlies's passion for empowering young people with the knowledge that they need to make better financial decisions.

Looking back, a book like *FLY* was just the tool she would have benefitted from in her teens, 20s and beyond. It's just the book she'll also be passing to her children as they ready to spread their wings.

GOOD READS FOR MINDSET AND MONEY

- *The Winner's Bible* – Dr Kerry Spackman
- *Think and Grow Rich* – Napoleon Hill
- The Barefoot Investor books – Scott Pape
- *Join the Rich Club* – Peter Switzer
- *A Surfer's Guide to Property Investing* – Paul Glossip
- *Get Rich, Lucky Bitch* – Denise Duffield-Thomas (for the ladies)
- *Rich Dad, Poor Dad* – Robert Kiyosaki
- Noel Whittaker's books

LINKS AND RESOURCES

- https://www.gooduniversitiesguide.com.au/study-information/funding-your-education/degree-costs-and-loans
- https://www.ato.gov.au/individuals/tax-file-number/apply-for-a-tfn/australian-residents---tfn-application
- https://www.ato.gov.au/Rates/Individual-income-tax-rates
- https://www.superguide.com.au/comparing-super-funds/super-funds-returns-financial-year
- https://www.superguide.com.au/boost-your-superannuation/employer-join-super-fund-they-use
- https://www.sbs.com.au/language/english/how-do-i-pay-for-my-studies-in-australia_2
- https://www.studyassist.gov.au/help-loans/hecs-help
- https://www.fairwork.gov.au/employee-entitlements/types-of-employees
- https://www.fairwork.gov.au/find-help-for/young-workers-and-students/what-age-can-i-start-work
- https://www.moneysmart.gov.au/borrowing-and-credit/car-loans
- https://www.nab.com.au/personal/personal-loans?cid=sem:p50461713019&psk=nab%2520personal%2520loans&psm=e&psn=g&psd=c&psa=1t1&&gclid=EAIaIQobChMI3vzU5dqx5wIVyA0rCh03bwIXEAAYASAAEgLa4_D_BwE&gclsrc=aw.ds
- https://www.canstar.com.au/car-insurance/7-ways-can-void-car-insurance
- https://www.qld.gov.au/transport/buying/unregistered/uvp

- https://www.canstar.com.au/car-insurance/car-insurance-under-25s
- https://www.budgetdirect.com.au/car-insurance/research/car-accident-statistics.html
- https://www.finder.com.au/car-insurance-exclusions
- https://www.fairtrading.nsw.gov.au/housing-and-property/renting/starting-a-tenancy/tenancy-databases
- https://www.abs.gov.au/ausstats/abs@.nsf/Lookup/by%20Subject/4130.0~2015-16~Main%20Features~Recent%20Home%20Buyers~7
- https://www.finder.com.au/home-loans/first-home-owners-grant
- https://www.commbank.com.au/guidance/property/negative-gearing-and-tax-201605.htmlhttps://www.realestate.com.au/home-loans/what-is-stamp-duty
- https://www.realestate.com.au/advice/how-conveyancing-works
- https://www.fool.com/investing/how-to-short-a-stock.aspx
- https://www.commsec.com.au/support/frequently-asked-questions/1401.html
- https://www.marketwatch.com/story/why-you-should-never-short-sell-stocks-2015-11-19
- https://www.marketindex.com.au/short-selling
- https://www.asx.com.au/education/investor-update-newsletter/201705-short-selling-explained.htm
- https://www.moneysmart.gov.au/investing/investment-warnings/virtual-currencies
- https://www.dummies.com/personal-finance/investing/what-is-a-blockchain-and-how-does-it-work
- https://www.investopedia.com/news/how-do-i-buy-ethereum
- https://finance.yahoo.com/quote/ETH-USD/history
- https://www.moneysmart.gov.au/investing/financial-advice/working-with-a-financial-adviser
- https://www.moneysmart.gov.au/investing/financial-advice/financial-advisers-register
- https://business.nab.com.au/millennials-generation-entrepreneurs-25435
- https://www.smh.com.au/business/workplace/australian-gen-zs-keener-to-own-homes-and-have-families-than-millennials-20190517-p51oja.html

- https://www.abr.gov.au/business-super-funds-charities/applying-abn
- https://www.ato.gov.au/business/registration/work-out-which-registrations-you-need/business-or-company-registrations
- https://www.ato.gov.au/rates/key-superannuation-rates-and-thresholds/?page=11
- https://www.ato.gov.au/Business/GST
- https://www.hrblock.com.au/tax-tips/beginners-guide-to-gst
- https://www.ato.gov.au/Business/GST/Tax-invoices
- https://www.finder.com.au/loans-for-startups
- https://www.business.gov.au/people/pay-and-conditions/employees-pay-leave-and-entitlements
- https://www.fairwork.gov.au/awards-and-agreements/awards
- https://www.employment.gov.au/self-employment-new-business-assistance-neis
- https://www.business.gov.au/Finance/Seeking-finance/How-to-crowdfund-your-business
- https://journals.sagepub.com/doi/full/10.1177/0042098017736257
- http://www.floodcommission.qld.gov.au/__data/assets/pdf_file/0016/11716/QFCI-Final-Report-Chapter-12-Performance-of-private-insurers.pdf
- https://www.news.com.au/national/insurance-companies-definition-of-flood-leaves-queensland-flood-families-in-limbo/news-story/e748ea661ad43fbb361a4df2ebe5d08d?sv=4fcb4a7373cb3dd9c95fb031e0aefdc
- http://understandinsurance.com.au/calculator/contents-calculator
- https://www.moneysmart.gov.au/insurance/car-insurance
- https://www.comparethemarket.com.au/ctp-insurance
- https://www.qld.gov.au/law/births-deaths-marriages-and-divorces/deaths-wills-and-probate/estates/being-an-executor-of-an-estate
- https://www.tag.nsw.gov.au/wills-faqs.html
- https://www.sfg.com.au/education_tools/education_guides/education_flyers/superannuation_flyers/what_is_a_binding_death_benefit_nomination
- https://www.andersons.com.au/lawtalk/2015/june/superannuation-in-my-will
- https://www.ato.gov.au/Individuals/Super/Withdrawing-and-using-your-super/Death-benefits

- https://moneysmart.gov.au/managing-debt/bankruptcy-and-debt-agreements
- https://moneysmart.gov.au/managing-debt/debt-consolidation-and-refinancing
- https://static.moneysmart.gov.au/files/publications/do-you-need-urgent-help-with-money.pdf
- https://moneysmart.gov.au/managing-debt/dealing-with-debt-collectors
- https://ndh.org.au/about-national-debt-helpline
- https://www.fool.com/knowledge-center/how-much-of-your-income-should-go-toward-living-ex.aspx

ENDNOTES

1   "(HILDA) Survey – Melbourne Institute – University of Melbourne" https://melbourneinstitute.unimelb.edu.au/__data/
    assets/pdf_file/0009/2874177/HILDA-report_Low-Res_10.10.18.pdf. Accessed 8 Feb. 2020.

2   "Financial Stability Snapshot | RBA – Reserve Bank of Australia." https://www.rba.gov.au/snapshots/fin-stability-
    snapshot/. Accessed 8 Feb. 2020.

3   "Generation MillZ: what Australian millennials and Gen Z are . . ." 20 May. 2019, https://www2.deloitte.com/au/en/
    pages/media-releases/articles/generation-millz-australian-millennials-gen-z-thinking-200519.html. Accessed 8 Feb.
    2020.

4   "Corelogic December 2019 Home Value Index: A Strong Finish . . ." 2 Jan. 2020, https://www.corelogic.com.au/news/
    corelogic-december-2019-home-value-index-strong-finish-housing-values-2019-corelogic-national. Accessed 8 Feb.
    2020.

5   "House price bounce leaves first home buyers behind – ABC . . ." 12 Jan. 2020, https://www.abc.net.au/news/2020-01-
    13/property-price-bounce-leaves-first-home-buyers-behind/11854662. Accessed 8 Feb. 2020.

6   "Australia Youth Unemployment Rate – Trading Economics." https://tradingeconomics.com/australia/youth-
    unemployment-rate. Accessed 8 Feb. 2020.

7   "Deloitte Global Millennial Survey 2019 | Deloitte | Social . . ." https://www2.deloitte.com/global/en/pages/about-
    deloitte/articles/millennialsurvey.html. Accessed 8 Feb. 2020.

8   "What you need to know about contactless payments – Finder." 20 Jan. 2020, https://www.finder.com.au/contactless-
    payment. Accessed 6 Feb. 2020.

9   "Personal loan interest rates – Fixed and variable rates – NAB." https://www.nab.com.au/personal/personal-loans/
    interest-rates. Accessed 7 Feb. 2020.

10 "Credit Card Comparison Tool – Compare Credit Cards – NAB." https://www.nab.com.au/personal/credit-cards/
    calculators-and-tools/compare. Accessed 7 Feb. 2020.

11 "Interest rates for NAB home loans – NAB." https://www.nab.com.au/personal/interest-rates-fees-and-charges/home-
    loan-interest-rates. Accessed 7 Feb. 2020.

12 "Credit cards – Moneysmart.gov.au." https://moneysmart.gov.au/credit-cards. Accessed 7 Feb. 2020.

13 "Credit card calculator – Moneysmart.gov.au." https://moneysmart.gov.au/credit-cards/credit-card-calculator.
    Accessed 7 Feb. 2020.

14 "Compound interest – Moneysmart.gov.au." https://moneysmart.gov.au/saving/compound-interest. Accessed 6 Feb.
    2020.

15 "Help for young workers and students – Fair . . ." http://www.fairwork.gov.au/find-help-for/young-workers-and-
    students. Accessed 6 Feb. 2020.

16 "Help for young workers and students – Fair . . ." http://www.fairwork.gov.au/find-help-for/young-workers-and-
    students. Accessed 6 Feb. 2020.

17 "Journalists Published Media Award [MA000067] Pay Guide." 27 Jun. 2019, https://www.fairwork.gov.au/
    ArticleDocuments/872/journalists-published-media-award-ma000067-pay-guide.pdf.aspx. Accessed 10 Feb. 2020.

18 "Fair Work Commission | Australia's national workplace . . ." https://www.fwc.gov.au/. Accessed 6 Feb. 2020.

19 "Journalists Published Media Award [MA000067] Pay Guide." 27 Jun. 2019, https://www.fairwork.gov.au/
    ArticleDocuments/872/journalists-published-media-award-ma000067-pay-guide.pdf.aspx. Accessed 10 Feb. 2020.

20 "Journalists Published Media Award [MA000067] Pay Guide." 27 Jun. 2019, https://www.fairwork.gov.au/
    ArticleDocuments/872/journalists-published-media-award-ma000067-pay-guide.pdf.aspx. Accessed 10 Feb. 2020.

21 "Pay Guide – Hospitality Industry (General) Award 2010 . . ." 23 Jan. 2020, https://www.fairwork.gov.au/
    ArticleDocuments/872/hospitality-industry-general-award-ma000009-pay-guide.pdf.aspx. Accessed 10 Feb. 2020.

22 "Individual income tax rates | Australian Taxation Office – ATO." 15 Oct. 2020, https://www.ato.gov.au/Rates/Individual-
    income-tax-rates/. Accessed 30 Oct. 2020.

23 "Individual income tax rates | Australian Taxation Office – ATO." 27 Jun. 2019, https://www.ato.gov.au/Rates/Individual-
    income-tax-rates/. Accessed 6 Feb. 2020.

24　"What Does Car Insurance Cost in Australia? | Canstar." 29 Aug. 2019, https://www.canstar.com.au/car-insurance/what-does-car-insurance-cost/. Accessed 3 Feb. 2020.

25　"50/30/20." http://fiftythirtytwenty.com/. Accessed 27 Feb. 2020.

26　"Budget planner – Moneysmart.gov.au." https://moneysmart.gov.au/budgeting/budget-planner. Accessed 7 Feb. 2020.

27　"Australians' record debt is making us work longer, spend less . . ." 17 Oct. 2019, https://www.abc.net.au/news/2019-10-18/household-debt-leaves-australians-working-longer-spending-less/11608016. Accessed 7 Feb. 2020.

28　"2019 Australian Household Credit Card Debt Statistics | finder . . ." 19 Dec. 2019, https://www.finder.com.au/credit-cards/credit-card-statistics. Accessed 7 Feb. 2020.

29　"Australia Talks can help you understand how you . . . – ABC." 5 Oct. 2019, https://www.abc.net.au/news/2019-10-06/australia-talks-explained/11570332. Accessed 7 Feb. 2020.

30　"The Barefoot Investor – Scott Pape." https://barefootinvestor.com/. Accessed 7 Feb. 2020.

31　"Savings goals calculator – Moneysmart.gov.au." https://moneysmart.gov.au/saving/savings-goals-calculator. Accessed 7 Feb. 2020.

32　"How do I pay for my studies in Australia? – SBS." 1 Nov. 2017, https://www.sbs.com.au/language/english/how-do-i-pay-for-my-studies-in-australia_2. Accessed 10 Feb. 2020.

33　"How do I pay for my studies in Australia? – SBS." 1 Nov. 2017, https://www.sbs.com.au/language/english/how-do-i-pay-for-my-studies-in-australia_2. Accessed 10 Feb. 2020.

34　"Degree costs and loans | The Good Universities Guide." https://www.gooduniversitiesguide.com.au/study-information/funding-your-education/degree-costs-and-loans. Accessed 10 Feb. 2020.

35　"Youth Allowance for students and Australian . . . – Centrelink." 9 Jan. 2020, https://www.servicesaustralia.gov.au/individuals/services/centrelink/youth-allowance-students-and-australian-apprentices/how-much-you-can-get. Accessed 10 Feb. 2020.

36　Youth Allowance for students and Australian . . . – Centrelink." 9 Jan. 2020, https://www.servicesaustralia.gov.au/individuals/services/centrelink/youth-allowance-students-and-australian-apprentices/how-much-you-can-get. Accessed 10 Feb. 2020.

37　"Repayment history and defaults — OAIC." https://www.oaic.gov.au/privacy/credit-reporting/repayment-history-and-defaults/. Accessed 10 Feb. 2020.

38　"A checklist for buying your first car – CommBank." https://www.commbank.com.au/guidance/consumer-finance/checklist-for-buying-your-first-car-201711.html. Accessed 2 Feb. 2020.

39　"Term Deposit Calculator – ING." https://www.ing.com.au/savings/calculators/term-deposit.html. Accessed 2 Feb. 2020.

40　"Car loans | ASIC's MoneySmart." https://www.moneysmart.gov.au/borrowing-and-credit/car-loans. Accessed 2 Feb. 2020.

41　"Registration costs – Roads and Maritime Services." 20 Dec. 2019, https://www.rms.nsw.gov.au/roads/registration/fees/registration-costs.html. Accessed 2 Feb. 2020.

42　"Home (Department of Transport and Main Roads)." https://www.tmr.qld.gov.au/. Accessed 2 Feb. 2020.

43　"7 Things That Might Void Your Car Insurance | Canstar." 2 Mar. 2017, https://www.canstar.com.au/car-insurance/7-ways-can-void-car-insurance/. Accessed 2 Feb. 2020.

44　"What won't car insurance cover? 13 exclusion traps to . . . – Finder." https://www.finder.com.au/car-insurance-exclusions. Accessed 2 Feb. 2020.

45　"Young Drivers – TAC – Transport Accident Commission." https://www.tac.vic.gov.au/road-safety/tac-campaigns/young-drivers. Accessed 2 Feb. 2020.

46　"Car Accident Statistics 2019 – Budget Direct." https://www.budgetdirect.com.au/car-insurance/research/car-accident-statistics.html. Accessed 2 Feb. 2020.

47　"Car Accident Statistics 2019 – Budget Direct." https://www.budgetdirect.com.au/car-insurance/research/car-accident-statistics.html. Accessed 2 Feb. 2020.

48　"Car Insurance For Under 25 year Olds: What Are . . . – Canstar." 20 Oct. 2017, https://www.canstar.com.au/car-insurance/car-insurance-under-25s/. Accessed 2 Feb. 2020.

49　"Car Insurance For Under 25 year Olds: What Are . . . – Canstar." 20 Oct. 2017, https://www.canstar.com.au/car-insurance/car-insurance-under-25s/. Accessed 2 Feb. 2020.

50   "Car Accident Statistics 2019 – Budget Direct." https://www.budgetdirect.com.au/car-insurance/research/car-accident-statistics.html. Accessed 2 Feb. 2020.

51   "2012 Volkswagen Golf 77TSI VI Auto MY12.5 – Used Car . . .." https://www.redbook.com.au/cars/details/2012-volkswagen-golf-77tsi-vi-auto-my125/SPOT-ITM-301720/. Accessed 2 Feb. 2020.

52   "Transfer & motor vehicle duty fees : VicRoads." 23 Sep. 2019, https://www.vicroads.vic.gov.au/registration/registration-fees/transfer-and-motor-vehicle-duty-fees. Accessed 2 Feb. 2020.

53   "Transfer & motor vehicle duty fees : VicRoads." 23 Sep. 2019, https://www.vicroads.vic.gov.au/registration/registration-fees/transfer-and-motor-vehicle-duty-fees. Accessed 2 Feb. 2020.

54   "What Does Car Insurance Cost in Australia? | Canstar." 29 Aug. 2019, https://www.canstar.com.au/car-insurance/what-does-car-insurance-cost/. Accessed 3 Feb. 2020.

55   "Vehicle registration & TAC fees – VicRoads." 10 Sep. 2019, https://www.vicroads.vic.gov.au/registration/registration-fees/vehicle-registration-fees. Accessed 3 Feb. 2020.

56   "Car Running Costs Statistics 2019 | Car Research & Statistics . . ." https://www.budgetdirect.com.au/car-insurance/research/car-owner-cost-statistics.html. Accessed 3 Feb. 2020.

57   "Emergency Roadside Assistance – Roadside Care . . . – RACV." https://www.racv.com.au/on-the-road/roadside-assistance/roadside-care.html. Accessed 3 Feb. 2020.

58   "Telstra." https://www.telstra.com.au/. Accessed 4 Feb. 2020.

59   "What are Early Termination Charges – Support – Telstra." https://www.telstra.com.au/support/category/account-billing/understand-bill/what-are-early-termination-charges. Accessed 4 Feb. 2020.

60   https://www.tica.com.au/

61   "TICA – Australia's Largest Tenancy Database." https://www.tica.com.au/. Accessed 10 Feb. 2020.

62   "National Tenancy Database: Tenancy Checks for Property . . ." https://www.tenancydatabase.com.au/. Accessed 10 Feb. 2020.

63   "TRA – TRADING REFERENCE AUSTRALIA." https://tradingreference.com/. Accessed 10 Feb. 2020.

64   "NRAS Tenants – NRAS Australia." http://www.nrasaustralia.com.au/national-rental-affordability-scheme-nras-tenants. Accessed 27 Feb. 2020.

65   "NRAS Tenants | Department of Social Services, Australian . . ." 23 Aug. 2018, https://www.dss.gov.au/housing-support/programs-services/housing/national-rental-affordability-scheme/nras-tenants. Accessed 27 Feb. 2020.

66   "4130.0 – Housing Occupancy and Costs, 2015-16." 16 Jul. 2019, https://www.abs.gov.au/ausstats/abs@.nsf/Lookup/by%20Subject/4130.0~2015-16~Main%20Features~Recent%20Home%20Buyers~7. Accessed 10 Feb. 2020.

67   "First Home Loan Deposit Scheme | NHFIC." https://www.nhfic.gov.au/what-we-do/fhlds/. Accessed 10 Feb. 2020.

68   "Helping Australians Buy Their First Home | Liberal Party of . . ." 12 May. 2019, https://www.liberal.org.au/latest-news/2019/05/12/helping-australians-buy-their-first-home. Accessed 10 Feb. 2020.

69   "Property price thresholds – NHFIC." https://www.nhfic.gov.au/what-we-do/fhlds/property-price-thresholds/. Accessed 10 Feb. 2020.

70   "First Home Super Saver Scheme | Australian Taxation . . . – ATO." 8 Jan. 2020, https://www.ato.gov.au/Individuals/Super/Withdrawing-and-using-your-super/First-Home-Super-Saver-Scheme/. Accessed 10 Feb. 2020.

71   "Cash Rate | RBA – Reserve Bank of Australia." https://www.rba.gov.au/statistics/cash-rate/. Accessed 10 Feb. 2020.

72   "Transfer duty rates | Homes and housing | Queensland . . ." 26 Feb. 2019, https://www.qld.gov.au/housing/buying-owning-home/advice-buying-home/transfer-duty/how-much-you-will-pay/calculating-transfer-duty/transfer-duty-rates. Accessed 10 Feb. 2020.

73   "What is Conveyancing and How it Works – realestate.com.au." 28 Dec. 2018, https://www.realestate.com.au/advice/how-conveyancing-works/. Accessed 16 Dec. 2019.

74   "What is negative gearing? – CommBank." https://www.commbank.com.au/guidance/property/negative-gearing-and-tax-201605.html. Accessed 15 Dec. 2019.

75   "Working out your net capital gain or loss | Australian Taxation . . ." 7 Nov. 2018, https://www.ato.gov.au/General/Capital-gains-tax/Working-out-your-capital-gain-or-loss/Working-out-your-net-capital-gain-or-loss/. Accessed 16 Dec. 2019.

76   "Transfer duty estimator | Homes and housing | Queensland . . ." 30 Oct. 2019, https://www.qld.gov.au/housing/
      buying-owning-home/advice-buying-home/transfer-duty/how-much-you-will-pay/calculating-transfer-duty/estimate-
      transfer-duty. Accessed 11 Feb. 2020.

77   "Property investment | ASIC's MoneySmart." 15 Oct. 2018, https://www.moneysmart.gov.au/investing/property.
      Accessed 15 Dec. 2019.

78   "Using equity to buy an investment property – NAB." https://www.nab.com.au/personal/life-moments/home-property/
      invest-property/equity-to-invest. Accessed 16 Dec. 2019.

79   "Landlord Responsibilities And Obligations | Tenancy Check." https://www.tenancycheck.com.au/landlord-information/
      obligations/landlord-responsibilities-and-obligations/. Accessed 15 Dec. 2019.

80   "Property Management Fees – Which Real Estate Agent." 4 Jun. 2019, https://whichrealestateagent.com.au/property-
      management/fees/. Accessed 16 Dec. 2019.

81   "The very best in property management fees – Rent.com.au." https://www.rent.com.au/agents/blog/best-property-
      management-fees/. Accessed 16 Dec. 2019.

82   "Rentvesting: The strategy for first-home buyers that's 'creating . . ." 11 Feb. 2017, https://www.domain.com.au/news/
      rentvesting-the-strategy-for-firsthome-buyers-thats-creating-a-city-of-landlords-20170209-gu7skx/. Accessed 22 Dec.
      2019.

83   "Real Estate Agent Fees & Commissions in 2018 – Agent Select." https://www.agentselect.com.au/selling-tips/real-
      estate-agent-fees-commissions. Accessed 16 Dec. 2019.

84   "ASX Sectors (GICS) – Market Index." https://www.marketindex.com.au/asx-sectors. Accessed 12 Jan. 2020.

85   "CBA – Share Dividends." https://www.sharedividends.com.au/cba-dividend-history/. Accessed 22 Dec. 2019.

86   "What Are Franking Credits? – Investopedia." 29 Aug. 2019, https://www.investopedia.com/terms/f/frankingcredit.asp.
      Accessed 22 Dec. 2019.

87   "Margin Call Definition – Investopedia." 1 Jul. 2019, https://www.investopedia.com/terms/m/margincall.asp. Accessed
      4 Jan. 2020.

88   "What is margin lending? – CommBank." 3 Nov. 2017, https://www.commbank.com.au/guidance/investing/what-is-
      margin-lending--201711.html. Accessed 4 Jan. 2020.

89   "How do I invest in index funds in Australia? A . . . – Finder." https://www.finder.com.au/how-to-invest-in-index-funds-
      in-australia. Accessed 12 Feb. 2020.

90   "Explainer: What are REITs? (Real Estate Investment . . . – Canstar." 3 Jun. 2019, https://www.canstar.com.au/investor-
      hub/explainer-reits/. Accessed 18 Jan. 2020.

91   "Cryptocurrencies | ASIC's MoneySmart." 24 Oct. 2018, https://www.moneysmart.gov.au/investing/investment-
      warnings/virtual-currencies. Accessed 18 Jan. 2020.

92   "Cryptocurrencies | ASIC's MoneySmart." 24 Oct. 2018, https://www.moneysmart.gov.au/investing/investment-
      warnings/virtual-currencies. Accessed 18 Jan. 2020.

93   "Self-managed super fund (SMSF) | ASIC's MoneySmart." 14 Feb. 2019, https://www.moneysmart.gov.au/
      superannuation-and-retirement/self-managed-super-fund-smsf. Accessed 6 Jan. 2020.

94   "How to bundle investments with a wrap or master trust – CHOICE." 9 Mar. 2017, https://www.choice.com.au/money/
      financial-planning-and-investing/managed-funds-and-trusts/buying-guides/wraps-and-master-trusts. Accessed 11 Feb.
      2020.

95   "2019 Small Business Counts – ASBFEO." 1 Jul. 2019, https://www.asbfeo.gov.au/sites/default/files/documents/
      ASBFEO-small-business-counts2019.pdf. Accessed 19 Jan. 2020.

96   "Millennials a generation of entrepreneurs | Business . . ." 1 Aug. 2017, https://business.nab.com.au/millennials-
      generation-entrepreneurs-25435/. Accessed 19 Jan. 2020.

97   "Australian Gen Zs keener to own homes and have families . . ." 21 May. 2019, https://www.smh.com.au/business/
      workplace/australian-gen-zs-keener-to-own-homes-and-have-families-than-millennials-20190517-p51oja.html.
      Accessed 19 Jan. 2020.

98   "Report REP 558 Insolvency statistics: External . . . – ASIC." 12 Dec. 2017, https://download.asic.gov.au/
      media/4570724/rep558-published-12-december-2017.pdf. Accessed 19 Jan. 2020.

99   "Business structures | business.gov.au." 2 Dec. 2019, https://www.business.gov.au/Planning/Business-structures-and-
      types/Business-structures. Accessed 19 Jan. 2020.

100 "Sole trader | Australian Taxation Office – ATO." 10 Nov. 2016, https://www.ato.gov.au/Business/Starting-your-own-business/Before-you-get-started/Choosing-your-business-structure/Sole-trader/. Accessed 19 Jan. 2020.

101 "Business structures | business.gov.au." 2 Dec. 2019, https://www.business.gov.au/Planning/Business-structures-and-types/Business-structures. Accessed 19 Jan. 2020.

102 "Company | Australian Taxation Office – ATO." 27 Sep. 2018, https://www.ato.gov.au/Business/Starting-your-own-business/Before-you-get-started/Choosing-your-business-structure/Company/. Accessed 19 Jan. 2020.

103 "Business structures | business.gov.au." 2 Dec. 2019, https://www.business.gov.au/Planning/Business-structures-and-types/Business-structures. Accessed 19 Jan. 2020.

104 "Register for an Australian business number (ABN) | business . . ." 9 Oct. 2019, https://www.business.gov.au/Registrations/Register-for-an-Australian-business-number-ABN. Accessed 19 Jan. 2020.

105 "Register for goods and services tax (GST) | business.gov.au." 19 Nov. 2019, https://www.business.gov.au/Registrations/Register-for-taxes/Register-for-goods-and-services-tax-GST. Accessed 19 Jan. 2020.

106 "Registering for GST | Australian Taxation Office – ATO." https://www.ato.gov.au/Business/GST/Registering-for-GST/. Accessed 19 Jan. 2020.

107 "Tax invoices | Australian Taxation Office – ATO." 4 Apr. 2019, https://www.ato.gov.au/Business/GST/Tax-invoices/. Accessed 25 Jan. 2020.

108 "Work health and safety | business.gov.au." 9 Jan. 2020, https://www.business.gov.au/Risk-management/Health-and-safety/Work-health-and-safety. Accessed 25 Jan. 2020.

109 "Medicare: a quick guide – Parliament of Australia." 12 Jul. 2016, https://www.aph.gov.au/About_Parliament/Parliamentary_Departments/Parliamentary_Library/pubs/rp/rp1617/Quick_Guides/Medicare. Accessed 26 Jan. 2020.

110 "Medicare: a quick guide – Parliament of Australia." 12 Jul. 2016, https://www.aph.gov.au/About_Parliament/Parliamentary_Departments/Parliamentary_Library/pubs/rp/rp1617/Quick_Guides/Medicare. Accessed 26 Jan. 2020.

111 "MBS Online." 22 Nov. 2019, http://www.mbsonline.gov.au/. Accessed 26 Jan. 2020.

112 "What is covered by Medicare? – PrivateHealth.gov.au." https://www.privatehealth.gov.au/health_insurance/what_is_covered/medicare.htm. Accessed 26 Jan. 2020.

113 "Income protection | ASIC's MoneySmart." 29 Mar. 2019, https://www.moneysmart.gov.au/insurance/life-insurance/income-protection. Accessed 26 Jan. 2020.

114 "Life cover | ASIC's MoneySmart." 29 Mar. 2019, https://www.moneysmart.gov.au/insurance/life-insurance/life-cover. Accessed 26 Jan. 2020.

115 "Total & permanent disability cover | ASIC's MoneySmart." 29 Mar. 2019, https://www.moneysmart.gov.au/insurance/life-insurance/total-and-permanent-disability-cover. Accessed 26 Jan. 2020.

116 "Home insurance | ASIC's MoneySmart." 19 Dec. 2018, https://www.moneysmart.gov.au/insurance/home-insurance. Accessed 1 Feb. 2020.

117 "12 12 Performance of private insurers – Queensland Floods . . ." 30 Mar. 2012, http://www.floodcommission.qld.gov.au/__data/assets/pdf_file/0016/11716/QFCI-Final-Report-Chapter-12-Performance-of-private-insurers.pdf. Accessed 1 Feb. 2020.

118 "Insurance companies' definition of flood leaves Queensland . . ." 8 Feb. 2011, https://www.news.com.au/national/insurance-companies-definition-of-flood-leaves-queensland-flood-families-in-limbo/story-e6frfkvr-1226001854330?sv=4fcb4a7373cb3dd9c95fb031e0aefdc. Accessed 1 Feb. 2020.

119 "Contents calculator – Understand Insurance." http://understandinsurance.com.au/calculator/contents-calculator. Accessed 1 Feb. 2020.

120 Booth, K., & Tranter, B. (2018). When disaster strikes: Under-insurance in Australian households. Urban Studies, 55(14), 3135–3150. https://doi.org/10.1177/0042098017736257

121 "Last Will and Testament FAQ – Australia – LawDepot." https://www.lawdepot.com/law-library/faq/last-will-and-testament-faq-australia/. Accessed 1 Feb. 2020.

122 "About executor services – The Public Trustee of Queensland." 8 Jan. 2020, https://www.pt.qld.gov.au/executor-services/about-executor-services/. Accessed 1 Feb. 2020.

123 "Wills FAQs | The NSW Trustee and Guardian." https://www.tag.nsw.gov.au/wills-faqs.html. Accessed 1 Feb. 2020.

124 "Power of attorney | Your rights, crime and the law . . ." 20 Nov. 2017, https://www.qld.gov.au/law/legal-mediation-and-justice-of-the-peace/power-of-attorney-and-making-decisions-for-others/power-of-attorney. Accessed 1 Feb. 2020.

125 "Enduring Power of Attorney | Office of the Public Advocate." http://www.opa.sa.gov.au/planning_ahead/enduring_ power_of_attorney. Accessed 1 Feb. 2020.

126 "Death benefits | Australian Taxation Office – ATO." 28 Nov. 2018, https://www.ato.gov.au/Individuals/Super/ Withdrawing-and-using-your-super/Death-benefits/. Accessed 1 Feb. 2020.

127 "Tax & super | ASIC's MoneySmart." 4 Feb. 2019, https://www.moneysmart.gov.au/superannuation-and-retirement/ how-super-works/tax-and-super. Accessed 1 Feb. 2020.

128 "1 in 2 Aussie couples argue about finances | finder.com.au." https://www.finder.com.au/press-release-jul-2017- heated-conversations-1-in-2-aussie-couples-argue-about-finances. Accessed 9 Feb. 2020.

129 "January 2019: Finances and Relationships — Relationships . . ." https://www.relationships.org.au/what-we-do/ research/online-survey/january-2019-finances-and-relationships. Accessed 9 Feb. 2020.

130 "Credit Factsheet – Love and Loans – ASIC's MoneySmart." https://www.moneysmart.gov.au/media/283220/love-and- loans.pdf. Accessed 9 Feb. 2020.

131 "New estimates of the costs of raising children in Australia . . ." https://aifs.gov.au/media-releases/new-estimates- costs-raising-children-australia. Accessed 11 Feb. 2020.

132 "How much does it cost to raise children in Australia? | finder . . ." 25 Nov. 2019, https://www.finder.com.au/life- insurance-and-the-cost-of-raising-children. Accessed 11 Feb. 2020.

133 "Getting divorced or separating – Moneysmart.gov.au." https://moneysmart.gov.au/getting-divorced-or-separating. Accessed 9 Feb. 2020.

134 "Relationship breakdown | Australian Taxation Office – ATO." 28 Jun. 2019, https://www.ato.gov.au/general/capital- gains-tax/relationship-breakdown/. Accessed 11 Feb. 2020.

135 "Property and finances after separation – Family Court of Australia." http://www.familycourt.gov.au/wps/wcm/ connect/fcoaweb/family-law-matters/property-and-finance/property-and-money-after-separation/property-and- finances-after-separation. Accessed 9 Feb. 2020.

136 http://www8.austlii.edu.au/cgi-bin/viewdb/au/legis/cth/consol_act/fla1975114/

137 "National Debt Helpline – Free financial counselling." https://ndh.org.au/. Accessed 5 Feb. 2020.

138 "Rent Assistance – Services Australia – Centrelink." 4 Nov. 2019, https://www.servicesaustralia.gov.au/individuals/ services/centrelink/rent-assistance. Accessed 5 Feb. 2020.

139 "Advance payment – Services Australia – Centrelink." 11 Dec. 2019, https://www.servicesaustralia.gov.au/individuals/ topics/advance-payment/30201. Accessed 5 Feb. 2020.

140 "Centrelink online accounts – What payments you can claim . . ." 2 Dec. 2019, https://www.servicesaustralia.gov.au/ individuals/services/centrelink/centrelink-online-accounts/what-payments-you-can-claim-online. Accessed 5 Feb. 2020.

141 "Dealing with debt collectors | ASIC's MoneySmart." 24 May. 2018, https://www.moneysmart.gov.au/managing-your- money/managing-debts/dealing-with-debt-collectors. Accessed 5 Feb. 2020.

142 "Bankruptcy and debt agreements – Moneysmart.gov.au." https://moneysmart.gov.au/managing-debt/bankruptcy- and-debt-agreements. Accessed 5 Feb. 2020.

143 "Bankruptcy and debt agreements – Moneysmart.gov.au." https://moneysmart.gov.au/managing-debt/bankruptcy- and-debt-agreements. Accessed 5 Feb. 2020.

144 "Why you don't care about Future you – Raiz Invest." https://raizinvest.com.au/blog/why-you-dont-care-about-future- you/. Accessed 8 Feb. 2020.

INDEX

C